The Tobacco
State League

ALSO BY CHRIS HOLADAY

*Professional Baseball in North Carolina:
An Illustrated City-by-City History, 1901–1996*
(1998; paperback 2006)

by Chris Holaday *and* Marshall Adesman
*The 25 Greatest Baseball Teams
of the 20th Century Ranked* (McFarland, 2000)

Edited by Chris Holaday
*Baseball in the Carolinas:
25 Essays on the States' Hardball Heritage*
(McFarland, 2002)

The Tobacco State League

A North Carolina Baseball History, 1946–1950

CHRIS HOLADAY

Foreword by CHARLIE DANIELS

McFarland & Company, Inc., Publishers
Jefferson, North Carolina

LIBRARY OF CONGRESS CATALOGUING-IN-PUBLICATION DATA

Names: Holaday, J. Chris, 1966– author.
Title: The Tobacco State League : a North Carolina baseball history, 1946–1950 / Chris Holaday ; foreword by Charlie Daniels.
Description: Jefferson, North Carolina : McFarland & Company, 2017 | Includes bibliographical references and index.
Identifiers: LCCN 2016047647 | ISBN 9781476666709 (softcover : acid free paper) ∞
Subjects: LCSH: Tobacco State League—History. | Minor league baseball—North Carolina—History.
Classification: LCC GV875.T59 H65 2016 | DDC 796.357/6409756
LC record available at https://lccn.loc.gov/2016047647

BRITISH LIBRARY CATALOGUING DATA ARE AVAILABLE

ISBN (print) 978-1-4766-6670-9
ISBN (ebook) 978-1-4766-2603-1

© 2017 Chris Holaday. All rights reserved

No part of this book may be reproduced or transmitted in any form or by any means, electronic or mechanical, including photocopying or recording, or by any information storage and retrieval system, without permission in writing from the publisher.

On the cover: Members of the Smithfield-Selma Leafs gather for a group photograph before a home game in 1946 (author's collection)

Printed in the United States of America

McFarland & Company, Inc., Publishers
Box 611, Jefferson, North Carolina 28640
www.mcfarlandpub.com

Table of Contents

Foreword by Charlie Daniels — 1
Preface — 3
Introduction — 4

Part I

1. Beginnings — 7
2. 1946: True Professionals — 15
3. 1947: Expansion and Big League Farm Clubs — 28
4. 1948: Sanford's Spinners on a Roll — 39
5. 1949: A Pair of .400 Hitters and a Dunn-Erwin Pennant — 48
6. 1950: Newcomers and Attendance Struggles — 62
7. Requiem for a League — 84

Part II

8. Managers — 89
9. All-Star Selections — 110
10. Umpires — 117
11. League and Team Information — 120

Part III

12. Player Register — 136

Bibliography — 283
Index — 285

Foreword
by Charlie Daniels

My memories of the old Tobacco State League involve sitting in the stands at Legion Stadium and watching the Wilmington Pirates take the field under the lights, with the hope that Johnie Edens would have his fastball working and that some of the guys could get on so Hoggy Davis could clear the bases with one of his towering home runs.

When we couldn't be there in person we listened to the games on the radio, and I'll never forget what the announcer would say when the Pirates got a couple of runners on: "And the Pirates have begun to move!"—exciting words to avid young fans who for one reason or another couldn't make it to the ballpark that night.

I remembered becoming a member of the Knothole Club, a group of kids who got in free for performing small tasks like chasing down foul balls, which in those days were not given away but returned to the team to be used again.

One night I had scoreboard duty. The scoreboard stood in center field and was manually operated by hanging the appropriate number of runs for each team in the correct square on its front. The Pirates scored a run and I hung the score on the opponent's side of the board.

My Daddy took a walk out to center field to inform me of my mistake and that I was being roundly cussed in the stands.

I don't know if any of my Pirate heroes ever made it from the Tobacco State League to the big show, but they played a part in my young life and I'm sure thankful for the memories.

Foreword by Charlie Daniels

The league brought the great game of baseball to small town America and inspired many a young man to play and enjoy America's pastime.

Grammy Award–winning musician and Grand Ole Opry member Charlie Daniels was born in Wilmington, North Carolina, in 1936. He was inducted into the Country Music Hall of Fame in 2016.

Preface

This book was a long time in the making. The project began as an offshoot of *Professional Baseball in North Carolina*, the book I wrote for McFarland nearly 20 years ago. I realized at that time the memories of these professional leagues—ones that once played such an important cultural role in small towns—were fading fast. I wanted to write a league history and, since I have always had an affinity for the small towns of Eastern North Carolina, I chose the Tobacco State League. Finally, after getting sidetracked several times, I have brought the story of the league to press.

The most important resources for this project were the players I was fortunate enough to meet. Most have passed on now, but without them taking the time to share their memories and open their scrapbooks I could never have attempted this project. Thanks go to Howard Auman, Pete Howard, Otis Stephens, Gaither Riley, George Erath, Crash Davis, Ducky Detweiler, Duncan Futrelle, Buddy Frazier, Ford Jordan and Cecil Tyson. This book is for you.

For image resources, I would like to thank Kim Cumber of the North Carolina Department of Archives and History and Peggy Neal of the Raleigh *News and Observer*. I would also like to thank fellow collectors Bart Swarr and Frank Dennison as well as author Webster Lupton for his input. Thanks also to Mike Lento for his imaging expertise. Special thanks to Charlie Daniels for sharing his memories, and Paula Szeigis, his publicist, for putting me in touch.

And thanks most of all to my wife, Sue, who kept encouraging me to finish this project.

Introduction

North Carolina has always been a baseball hotbed, and the years immediately before World War II were no exception. The state had dozens of medium-sized towns and cities, and minor league baseball had really begun to flourish in them by the 1930s. In 1940, 31 towns fielded teams that were truly professional, meaning players were paid set salaries and the teams and leagues abided by the rules of the National Association, the governing body of minor league baseball.

The minor leagues were organized in a hierarchical structure and classified by letters. Before World War II, the highest level, essentially one step below the major leagues, was designated AA. That included the International League (in which the Durham and Charlotte teams play today) and the Pacific Coast League. Two levels below that, Class B, included the Piedmont League, in which most of North Carolina's larger cities of the day played. At one time or another it included Charlotte, Asheville, Durham, Winston-Salem, Raleigh and Greensboro. Class D was the bottom rung of the ladder, though leagues at that level were also the most common. In eastern North Carolina, the Class D Coastal Plain League (teams in the larger towns of the region including Goldsboro, Wilson, Rocky Mount, New Bern and Kinston) played the only professional baseball in the late 1930s.

The popularity that the minor leagues were beginning to enjoy came to a screeching halt, however, with the United States' entry into World War II. Lack of players and wartime travel restrictions made it unfeasible for most teams to operate, particularly those at the lower levels where finances were always tight even in the best of times. By 1944 not a single minor league team was playing in North Carolina.

Introduction

A common sight in eastern North Carolina: Farmers inspect their tobacco crop. As part of a Farm Security Administration project, this photo was taken in 1939 by Dorothea Lange as she traveled through rural North Carolina and documented farm life (Library of Congress).

When the end of the war seemed in sight, professional baseball began to return to the small towns. In North Carolina, the 1945 season saw the resumption of play in the North Carolina State League, a Class D circuit that included clubs in the western part of the Piedmont such as Lexington, Salisbury, Concord, and Mooresville. That season also saw the founding of the Carolina League, which included many of the state's prominent cities such as Greensboro, Durham and Raleigh. In 1946, the Coastal Plain League announced it would resume play after a four-year hiatus. Americans, eager to put the war behind them, returned to the national pastime.

The period immediately following World War II became the golden age for minor league baseball. In small towns from coast to coast, professional baseball teams were popping up. It became a matter of civic pride for each town's residents and groups of businessmen got together to fund teams. After all, if the neighboring town had a team, then why shouldn't they?

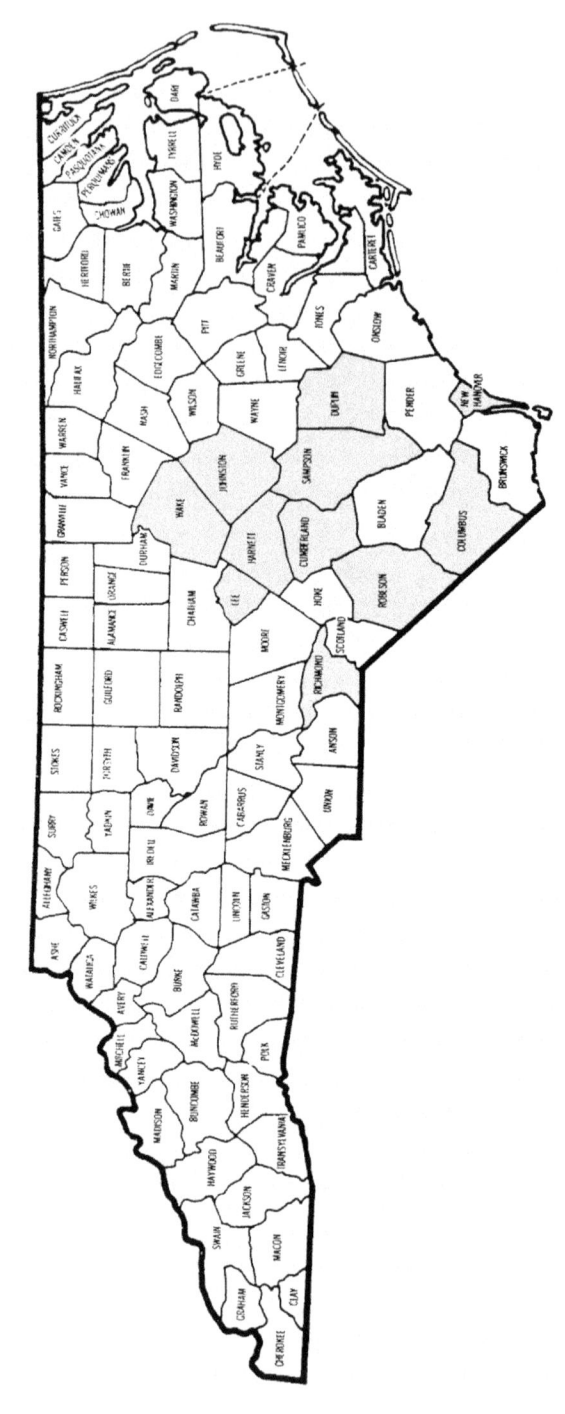

North Carolina with the highlighted counties that hosted, at one time or another, a Tobacco State League franchise (Library of Congress, edited by the author).

PART I

• 1 •

Beginnings

In the 1930s, baseball ruled the American sports scene. It truly was the national pastime and nowhere as that more apparent than in the small towns of North Carolina. Come early spring, from the workers laboring in the textile mills to the farmers readying their tobacco fields, the sport was always the subject of many passionate discussions. College football and basketball were merely minor distractions to occupy the months when there was no baseball. Heaven forbid anyone discuss things like hockey or soccer. Baseball was king.

In 1902, a plan was put into place to organize and classify all professional baseball below the level of the major leagues and the National Association of Professional Baseball Leagues was established. With a hierarchy that essentially had the larger cities at the top and smaller ones at the bottom, leagues were given such classifications as A, B, C and D. Each level had guidelines member clubs had to follow for salaries, roster size, rules on the field of play, etc. Players were required to sign binding professional contracts. Though it has evolved greatly (the current AAA, AA, A, Rookie classifications were implemented in 1963), this is still essentially the same system in place today.

Semi-pro baseball has always operated outside the National Association. It does have its guidelines and money is involved but the rules have often been—to say the least—flexible. If a businessman or mill owner wanted to put up the money to fund a team then so be it. Just like true professional baseball, owners charged admission and ran the business hoping to make a profit—though more often than not, running a team was a labor of love and owners only hoped to break even. Some semi-pro teams, particularly in the years before World War II, operated as traveling exhibition teams that put on games in various towns for a

Part I

share of the gate proceeds. If a team owner was lucky, he could convince other like-minded men in the area with similar resources to start teams and thereby form an actual league.

Semi-pro teams often attracted college players. These players could get paid a decent wage to play their sport without jeopardizing their college careers since they didn't officially sign professional contracts. Semi-pro players could pull in $20 per week, not bad considering the average mill hand made $10 and had to put in many more hours. Some players could make even more thanks to gifts from appreciative local business owners or maybe a hat being passed in recognition of an outstanding performance on the field. A summer spent playing semi-pro baseball could be quite lucrative for a young college student.

Teams at the semi-pro level also relied heavily on local talent. Everyone from the star high school shortstop to the 40-year-old ex-pro who taught at the local high school might join the team. Filling out rosters were often veteran players who were essentially baseball mercenaries. They came and went, always in search of a paycheck playing the sport. Sometimes they would stay a season, sometimes a week; there was never a shortage of willing arms or bats.

Thanks to the organizing efforts of Herbert "Doc" Smith, the first semi-pro incarnation of the Tobacco State League was formed in 1935. Smith, a native of the Harnett County town of Angier and a longtime minor league catcher who had played in the Texas League and the Southern Association, sought out willing businessmen to fund teams in other towns and join his Angier club in a league. He found them in the Lee County town of Sanford, Erwin in Harnett County, and in Johnston County, where a team was formed to represent the neighboring towns of Smithfield and Selma. The name of the new league was chosen to reflect primary crop in that part of the state. Erwin took the title that first season with a 34–20 record, then defeated Smithfield-Selma in a championship series, four games to two.

In the spring of 1936, efforts to renew the league failed, primarily due to lack of finances. Sanford, however, did manage to continue on in an organized semi-pro circuit as they joined the new Peach Belt League, which included towns such as Aberdeen in Moore County. The other three former Tobacco State League members did field teams that summer but were limited to occasional exhibition games.

1. Beginnings

A new league was formed in 1937. Angier again entered a team, as did Erwin. Clayton, in Johnston County, also signed on along with a combined team called Wakelon, which represented the Wake County communities of Wakefield and Zebulon. The schedule called for four games per week and it was agreed that teams would not have a salary limit. Player pay essentially came down to what teams could afford. The only restriction as far as players went was that teams could not use players who had previously been under a professional contract in that same season.

As in 1935, Erwin claimed the regular season crown in 1937. They then faced Angier in a play-off series that went the full seven games before prevailing. Some games in that series reportedly drew close to 3,000 fans to Erwin's ballpark.

In 1938, the league consisted of Angier, Erwin, Sanford, Zebulon, Laurinburg, as well as Fayetteville, whose entry represented the city's Faytex mill. Chick Doak, head baseball coach at NC State College, was tapped to be league president. Angier claimed both the regular season pennant and—after a seven-game series against Sanford—the playoff title.

It was back to a four-team circuit in 1939 as only four members could be rounded up: Angier, Erwin, Sanford and Zebulon. Sanford dominated the league and easily claimed the pennant with a 37–16 record. The Spinners then went on to cruise to the playoff title as well.

The following season the league lineup was Sanford, Raleigh, Erwin and the Moore County town of Hemp (renamed Robbins in 1943). Though Raleigh already had a long history of minor league baseball it—surprisingly—had not fielded a professional team since 1932. In was in Raleigh, however, that the league soon had trouble. American Tobacco, sponsor of the team, decided to drop out in late June. A new team was hastily assembled with a new sponsor, Seaboard Air Line Railroad, but league woes continued. In July, Sanford played in and won the state semi-pro baseball tournament for the second consecutive year. The win entitled the Spinners to play in the national tournament in Wichita, Kansas. They had declined in 1939 but stated in 1940 they planned to go, which would essentially mean abandoning the Tobacco State League. In the end the league decided to throw in the towel on

Part I

July 24. Sanford's Spinners did go on to Wichita where they finished a very respectable fourth.

In 1941, Sanford made the leap to professional baseball and joined the Class D Bi-State League. Organized in 1934, that league was comprised of teams from Virginia and North Carolina, including Burlington, 50 miles to the north of Sanford. The move threw the Tobacco State League into disarray. The loss of its most prominent team, combined with growing competition for players from true professional baseball as well as the countless semi-pro leagues that were always popping up, left the Tobacco State League unable to organize for 1941.

Those early semi-pro days of the Tobacco State League featured a colorful array of characters. Often-controversial ex-major leaguer Rube Benton, a native of Clinton, came out of retirement to pitch a game for Erwin on June 27, 1937, his 47th birthday. Benton, who won 150 games over 15 seasons with the Cincinnati Reds and New York Giants, also picked up the win in his Tobacco State League cameo appearance.

Angier pitcher (and later manager) Mickey O'Quinn claimed to be a veteran of the Spanish-American War. No one was really sure if this was true, but if so, he would have been at least in his late 50s.

Angier's manager in 1935 was pitcher DeWitt Perry. A veteran who had played for Durham, Wilmington and Raleigh in the Class B Piedmont League, he had risen as high as Hollywood in the Pacific Coast League before returning to his native North Carolina.

Erwin was led for a couple of seasons by player/manager Edwin "Babe" Bost. The son of the general manager of Erwin Mills, Bost had played basketball and baseball at Duke University.

Bill Holland, a student at East Carolina Teacher's College, played for Angier in 1937. The following season he signed a pro contract and worked his way up to the Washington Senators, where he pitched a few innings at the end of the 1939 season.

Connie Ryan from Louisiana State University played second base for Angier in 1938. Ryan went on to spend much of twelve seasons as a big league infielder. He later turned to coaching and managed both the Atlanta Braves and Texas Rangers in the 1970s. Over a decade after he played in Angier, Ryan had another connection to the Tobacco State

1. Beginnings

League. His younger brother, Terry, spent most of the 1949 season as a backstop for the Clinton-Sampson Blues.

Another Louisiana native, pitcher Al Jurisich, spent half of the 1938 season with Angier. He later worked his way up through the Cardinals' farm system and eventually made it to St. Louis for two seasons after serving in the military. Jurusich also pitched two seasons with the Philadelphia Phillies as well as several more for the San Diego Padres in the Pacific Coast League. The league's Louisiana connection also included Al Bodney and Bob Dexheimer. Both were Tulane University football players.

Lefthander Woody Upchurch came and went with Angier clubs for several seasons. A native of Buies Creek, he had attended Campbell College and played for the Durham Bulls in the Piedmont League for parts of two seasons. Back in semi-pro ball in 1933 he pitched for Angier before moving on to Ayden in the Coastal Plain League the following season. In 1935, Upchurch caught the eye of Philadelphia Athletics owner Connie Mack

A star lefty for Wake Forest College, Tommy Byrne was signed by Yankees regional scout Gene McCann in July of 1940. He went on to pitch in 13 big league seasons and appear in four World Series with the New York Yankees, winning two. After his baseball career, Byrne returned to the town of Wake Forest, where he eventually served as mayor for 14 years (courtesy Frank Dennison).

Part I

and he was signed to a major league contract. He made his big league debut that September and appeared in three games before the season ended. He was still with the club the following spring and pitched in seven games before being released in late May. Upchurch then returned to North Carolina and signed on with Angier, where he pitched and even managed the club in 1937. Unfortunately, an injury to Upchurch's pitching arm in an auto accident cut short his mound career.

The Angier mound corps in 1939 featured Tommy Byrne from Wake Forest College. Byrne went on to have a long major league career and won two World Series with the New York Yankees. A native of Baltimore, he returned to North Carolina after his baseball career and eventually spent more than a decade as mayor of Wake Forest.

University of Richmond pitcher Porter Vaughan, who took the

Porter Vaughan (left) and Ray Scarborough and were two players from the semi-pro years of the Tobacco State League who went on to appear in the big leagues. Vaughan pitched for Sanford during summer break from the University of Richmond. He went on to appear in three seasons for the Philadelphia Athletics. Scarborough, who graduated from Wake Forest, had a much longer career in the majors and won 80 games over ten seasons for five teams (courtesy Frank Dennison).

1. Beginnings

Star infielder Lawrence "Crash" Davis went straight from Duke University to the major leagues when signed by the Philadelphia Athletics in 1940. He spent three seasons with the A's before answering the call of military service. In 1948, Davis returned to his home state and signed with the Durham Bulls of the Carolina League. He would go on to spend the next five seasons in the league, also playing for Raleigh (seen here) and Reidsville. In 1986 his name was immortalized in baseball lore when chosen as that of the lead character of the movie *Bull Durham* (courtesy Crash Davis).

mound for Sanford in 1939, made it up to the Philadelphia Athletics for parts of three seasons. He is one of the few players to have gone directly from college baseball to the major leagues, a feat he accomplished in 1940.

Years later, Lawrence "Crash" Davis, a Duke University star who made it to the big leagues, recalled those days of the semi-pro Tobacco State League in an interview with the author:

> In '39 I played in the Tobacco State League, another semi-pro league. I played for Sanford, North Carolina, and made $140 per month. That league included teams from towns like Zebulon and Angier and we played about five or six games

Part I

a week. They also had the state semi-pro tournament in High Point and we went up and won that, too. We really had a good ball club. Tommy Byrne and Ray Scarborough, who both went to the big leagues, they played for Wake Forest. Angier went and got them to play and they tried to beat us but they couldn't. We didn't lose many ball games. We had three guys from Duke: myself, first baseman Eddie Shokes—he played with Cincinnati for a while—and Glenn Price. We also had Porter Vaughan pitching for us down there. Porter played with me when I was at Philadelphia.

We drew good crowds down there. But oh, those lights. People can't imagine what it was like playing under those lights. One night I stuck a ball in my hip pocket and I told Hoover, the shortstop, to watch what happens if a ball is ever hit to my left. It was so dark out in the outfield when a ball did go past me to my left I just took the ball out of my pocket and threw to first. They called him out! Of course a big argument resulted from that.

Lewis Isenhour owned that team. He owned a brick company and he loved baseball. He treated us well and boy we had fun down there. That was a great summer.

◆ 2 ◆

1946: True Professionals

With new teams and leagues springing up across the country, civic leaders in the medium sized towns of southeastern North Carolina began to believe that their communities could likewise support the game at a professional level. Led primarily by the efforts of Raleigh sports promoter Sam Allen, plans were made to form a new Class D league in southeastern North Carolina.

Class D teams, at the lowest level of professional baseball, were composed primarily of young, inexperienced players. Unlike the lowest level of pro ball in today's system, Rookie League, Class D teams did include a few season veterans, sometimes with major league experience. Though the current system of minor league "farm teams" was really beginning to grow after the war, many clubs at this level operated as independents. Without a major league affiliate, they made money by selling players to higher-level teams. These clubs would try to find and sign talented young players, and if the player performed well, they might be able to sell his contract for a profit.

Allen made efforts to organize teams in many of the area towns and on February 6, he announced that Wilmington would join the new league. He then held a meeting for other interested groups in Clinton on February 7. In the end, only six teams became charter members; Sanford, Clinton, and Wilmington were each granted their own franchises while the other three spots went to teams representing more than one town. Smithfield and Selma, in Johnston County, received a joint franchise, as did the Harnett County towns of Dunn and Erwin. A team from Angier and the nearby Wake County town of Fuquay Springs rounded out the league. The lineup meant that the greatest distance a team would have to travel was 125 miles between Sanford

Part I

Baseball Schedule

FOR ALL HOME
GAMES OF

The Sampson Blues

AT CLINTON BALL PARK

1946 Season

	MAY	JUNE	JULY	AUG.	SEPT.
Sanford	9 13 30	8 18 29	9 20 21 31	10 29	1
Angier	12 22	1 11 21	1 13 23	2 12 22	2
Dunn	16 26	5 15 25	6 17 27	2 15 26	
S'field	8 18 27	7 17 26	8 19 29	8 18 28	
Wilm'ton	14 24	2 13 23	3 4 14 25	3 4 14	

A schedule for Clinton's 1946 season (author's collection).

and Wilmington. The distances were much less between some towns; only 18 miles separated Dunn and Angier and it was around 22 miles between Dunn and Smithfield.

Though distances between most league members were short, the towns—and their reasons for existence—were very different from each other.

Wilmington, on the Cape Fear River, was an important port city with a history dating back to the 1730s. It prospered during the colonial period and later played an important role as a main port and railroad terminus for the Confederacy during the Civil War. During World War II, shipbuilding was a huge industry in Wilmington and North Carolina Shipbuilding Company launched over 200 ships for the war effort.

Sanford was founded at a railroad intersection in 1874 and quickly became a transportation hub. It was soon discovered that local clay was perfect for bricks and by the late 1950s it was claimed that 10 percent of all bricks used in the United States were produced in Sanford.

The city of Dunn, a logging town and turpentine distilling center, was incorporated in 1887. Industry in neighboring Erwin, however, was built around the Erwin Cotton Mill, which was completed in 1904.

2. 1946: True Professionals

The mill, which closed in 2000, produced vast quantities of raw denim and earned Erwin the moniker of "Denim Capital of the World."

Clinton, incorporated in 1852 and surrounded by rural farmland, developed as a large agricultural marketing center. Clinton's claims to fame included being the birthplace William R. King, a U.S. senator who served all of six weeks as vice president in 1853, and Theophilus Holmes, a U.S. Army officer who served with distinction during the Mexican-American War but was a rather ineffective Confederate general during the Civil War. Both were born on plantations in the area.

Smithfield grew around an 18th century tavern and ferry crossing on the Neuse River, both owned by a Mr. Smith. It eventually became the seat of Johnston County but in the late 1940s it may have been most famous for being the birthplace of actress Ava Gardner, whose star was rapidly rising in Hollywood. Smithfield's slightly smaller next-door neighbor to the northeast, Selma, sprung up in the years just after the Civil War when a new railroad station was established.

The new league's final entry represented the towns of Angier, in Harnett County, and nearby Fuquay Springs, in Wake County. These towns were important centers for agriculture and the growth of tobacco played a large role in local commerce.

The largest city in the league, Wilmington also had the longest history of professional baseball. Off and on since 1901, the city had fielded teams at the professional level, the most recent time being 1935 in the Class B Piedmont League. Quite a few players on those early teams went on to make appearances in the major league, several of them quite notably. The 1933 and '34 squads included former University of North Carolina star Johnny Peacock in the outfield. Converted to a catcher, the Wayne County native went on to have a solid big league career, primarily with the Boston Red Sox. The last Wilmington team, in 1935, featured 18-year-old shortstop Eddie Miller. He went on to be named a seven-time National League All-Star during his 14-year big league career with the Reds, Braves, Phillies and Cardinals.

When baseball supporters in Wilmington decided to organize a new professional franchise they sought admission to several leagues during the latter part of 1945. First unsuccessfully trying the Piedmont League, they next tried to gain entry into the Coastal Plain League when it was reorganizing after the war hiatus. They lost out to Fayetteville, however,

Part I

and then bid for a place in the Class B Tri-State League. When that fell through, they had to settle for the Tobacco State League, becoming the new league's sixth franchise.

Besides Wilmington, Sanford was the only other town in the new league to have previously had professional baseball. Well-known for its successful semi-pro baseball teams, the town finally entered the sport on a professional level in 1941 when they joined the Class D Bi-State League. A circuit made up of teams from Virginia and North Carolina, it lasted through the 1942 season before folding due to the war.

With the teams lined up for the new league in early 1946, a name had to be selected. It was decided that the new professional circuit would retain the name of the earlier semi-pro league in which several of the town had participated. The next order of business for the Class D Tobacco State League was to select a president. That honor went to Wilmington's J. E. L. "Jimmy" Wade. A real estate developer and city council member, Wade had served as the city's Commissioner of Public Works, a member of the NC General Assembly, and would later be elected mayor of Wilmington.

James E. L. Wade (shown in 1956) served as the Tobacco State League's first president. A political figure in Wilmington for half a century, he served as mayor and city councilman (courtesy Special Collections Department, New Hanover County Public Library).

By March, all of the teams had hired managers. At Dunn-Erwin, 29-year-old veteran Jimmy Guinn was hired as the team's skipper. Smithfield-Selma secured the services of

2. 1946: True Professionals

Sanford manager Gaither Riley (left) and star slugger Hank Nesselrode (courtesy Gaither Riley).

Part I

veteran Mickey Balla, who had managed at Hagerstown in the Class B Interstate League in 1945. Sanford signed on Gaither Riley, a veteran of the Coastal Plain League, while former University of North Carolina star Paul Dunlap was set to guide Angier-Fuquay. Well-traveled Mickey Katkaveck, who had spent several seasons in the St. Louis Cardinals' farm system, was hired by Wilmington. Probably the most well-known manager in the league was at Clinton, where Willie Duke took the helm. A collegiate star at NC State, he began playing professional baseball in 1934 and had risen as high as Minneapolis in the American Association. After three years of service in the U.S. Navy, Duke was returning to baseball as the age of 36.

Class D rules allowed each club to hire up to four "veterans," players who had more than three years of experience at a professional level. Of course veteran players had to be paid more, which is why every team combined one of those roster spots with that of manager. The rest of the 15-man lineup was filled out with "class men," younger players who had less than three years of experience, and rookies, who were often local. Some were fresh out of high school while others had semi-pro or industrial league experience. Payrolls were set at $1500 per month, not including managers.

The league also had to hire umpires to oversee all contests in the 120-game schedule. Umpires were paid $250 per month with a $100 per month expense account to cover travel costs. Like the players, professional umpires began at the lower levels of professional baseball and hoped to work their way up.

As Opening Day approached, the teams struggled to make all of the necessary preparations. Several clubs scrambled to find uniforms and in all of the towns ballparks were painted and spruced up. At Angier, the existing ballpark was totally renovated with new bleachers, grandstand and fence, and lights were installed for the first time. At Lumberton's Armory Field, dugouts, a press box and public address system were added. Finally, on May 7, the 126-game season got under way.

The Sanford Spinners soon proved to be the most talented team in the new league. Outfielder Hank Nesselrode, who had played in Sanford before the war, returned to the team after four years of military service and batted .354, leading the league in home runs (30) and RBIs (150).

2. 1946: True Professionals

The 1946 Sanford Spinners, powered by the mighty bat of Hank Nesselrode (back row, far left) and the right arm of Howard Auman (back row, middle), battled Clinton's Sampson Blues for the regular season title right down to the final game of the season (courtesy Howard Auman).

Shortstop Joe Nessing, the league's best fielder at that position, also had a good season, hitting .314. Catcher Paul Crawford, who would play in the minor leagues through the 1955 season with teams including the Durham Bulls and the Norfolk Tars, hit .285. Howard Auman (22–8) and Bill Stone (16–8) anchored the Spinner's strong pitching staff. Despite a managerial change–Sanford native and former Elon College star Zeb Harrington took over in midseason–the team had a great regular season and took home the league pennant with a 71–48 record.

The Clinton Sampson Blues (the name refers to a famed local variety of huckleberries) also had a great season despite a bad beginning. In mid–May, a fire broke in the team's locker room and soon spread to the grandstand and the adjoining gymnasium at Clinton High School. Fortunately, the team was on the road at the time but much of their equipment was destroyed and damage to the ballpark and gym was estimated at $30,000. The Blues, as they were called for short, managed to recover from the setback and finished the season only half a game behind Sanford with a 70–48 record. Outfielder Willie Duke

Part I

(27 HR, 109 RBIs), who managed the at the beginning of the season before giving way to former big leaguer Van Lingle Mungo, won the batting title with a .393 average while third-baseman Lonnie Smith (.304, 21 HRs) led the league in runs with 117. Early in the season, the star of the strong pitching staff was Lee Peterson. After going 6–1, he caught the attention of the St. Louis Cardinals and was sold to that organization (and assigned to Winston-Salem, where he won 16 game). Even with Peterson's departure, the Blue's pitching staff was deep; Bob Keane (23–4) and Earl Mossor (21–8), a rookie from Tennessee, were two of the best in the league. Manager Mungo, who had 130 big league wins to his credit, took a turn on the mound five times and had a 1–1 record.

A notable player who made a brief appearance in a Clinton uniform was pitcher John Burrows. A veteran lefthander who had made his professional debut in 1933, Burrows worked his way up to the major leagues and pitched for the Philadelphia Athletics and Chicago Cubs during the war. Despite 19 wins for Atlanta in 1945, he was without a team the following season. Possibly attempting to recover from an injury, the 32-year-old pitched briefly (a total of 11 games) for three lower level clubs in 1946. With Clinton, Burrows was 0–1 in two games.

The Smithfield-Selma Leafs finished that first season with a record of 58–62, putting them in third place. Outfielders Dick Woodard (.336, 98 RBIs) and Leo Niezgoda (.333) were the team's best hitters while Hearn Robinson (14–9) and Alton Bird (12–8) led the pitching staff. Woodard, a rookie, would play for the Leafs all five seasons the team existed and finish as one of the Tobacco State League's all-time best hitters. Second baseman Mickey Balla, the league's only manager to survive the whole season without being fired, was named to the post-season All-Star team.

An interesting member of the Leafs' 1946 pitching staff was lefty Fred Gay. A veteran who had made his pro debut in 1935 as a New York Yankees farmhand, Gay had pitched for several high-level teams including the Kansas City Blues of the American Association and the Hollywood Stars of the Pacific Coast League. After missing three seasons due to military service, Gay attempted a comeback with the Leafs. In four games, however, he posted an 0–2 record and gave up 13 runs. He had short stints with three other teams that season before officially retiring.

2. 1946: True Professionals

Pitcher Joe Eonta (left) and shortstop Pete Howard of the 1946 Smithfield-Selma Leafs (courtesy Pete Howard).

Part I

The Angier-Fuquay Springs Bulls finished the regular season with a record of 57–62, 14 games back and in fourth place. Qualifying for the final playoff spot, the team featured a talented offense including first baseman Marvin Lorenz (.338, 86 RBIs, 87 runs) and third baseman Joe Mills (.306). Outfielder-manager Paul Dunlap (.361, 81 RBIs) and outfielder Otis Stephens (.324), who joined the team in mid-season after being released from the military, also hit well and produced runs. Overall, the Bulls led the league with a .295 team batting average. The pitching staff, which featured Ray Bomar (11–8), was not as strong but still had some solid performers. On July 12, Ray Hardee turned in one of the season's most impressive performances as he pitched a no-hitter against Clinton and won 12–0.

1946 Angier-Fuquay Springs Bulls. From left to right (front row) are Ray Hardee, unidentified, Harry Fortune, Sam Sellers, Paul Hunt, Ken Jackson and Gus Rogers; (back row) Andy Scrobola, Ray Bomar, Otis Stephens, Roscoe Gentry, Jim House, Marvin Lorenz, Joe Mills and Bill Ratteree (courtesy Otis Stephens).

2. 1946: True Professionals

Given the same name as many of that city's earlier teams, Wilmington's Pirates finished fifth in the league with a record of 52–66. When the team failed to win games early in the season, manager Mickey Katkaveck was replaced by thirty-six-year-old Gus Brittain. A Wilmington native, Brittain had played for his hometown team in the Piedmont League in the early '30s and made it up to the Cincinnati Reds as a catcher for a few games in 1937. He led the Pirates in batting with a .318 average in 61 games, playing almost every position on the team including pitcher. The only other offensive star on the team was All-Star shortstop Andy Cullen (.283), who scored 95 runs and led the league with 30 stolen bases. The Pirates pitching staff featured Nate Andrews (9–2), who had spent parts of eight seasons in the big leagues and was a National League All-Star in 1944. He began that season with the Cincinnati Reds, was released and then signed by the New York Giants. He won one game for the Giants (over the Reds) before deciding to retire to his native North Carolina. Andrews, raised in Robeson County, made a home for his family near Wilmington and agreed to help out the local Pirates in early July. He lost his first two games but went on to win nine in a row.

The Dunn-Erwin Twins brought up the rear in the league standings that first season. With a 48–70 record, they finished 22½ games behind first place Sanford and went through three managers; Jimmy Guinn was fired in early July and replaced by Alton Stephenson, who was in turn replaced by Dwight Wall. Despite the overall team struggles, the Twins did have a pair of star outfielders: Eddie Bass (.323, 19 HR, 110 RBIs) and Granville "Shamrock" Denning (.304, 80 RBIs). Bass, a native or Erwin, had a long minor league career but only spent one season in the Tobacco State League. His career included stops in towns as far ranging as Miami and even St. Hyacinthe in the Canadian province of Quebec. Pitcher James Turnage, also a native of Erwin, won six games after spending the first half of the season with Kinston. A former Marine, he was awarded a Purple Heart at the Battle of Iwo Jima in 1945.

On August 13, during a game at Wilmington, a fight over a disputed call broke out between Pirates skipper Gus Brittain and manager Van Mungo of the visiting Clinton Blues. Fans rushed the field and it nearly became a full riot before being brought under control by police.

Part I

The 1946 Dunn-Erwin Twins finished in the cellar despite featuring two of the top hitters in the league: Eddie Bass (back row, far left) and Shamrock Denning (front row, second from right) (author's collection).

As a result, two of the league's most recognizable names had to pay the price. Brittain was fined $50 by the league and $50 by the National Association and placed on organized baseball's ineligible list. The Wilmington team was fined $250 while Mungo was fined $50 and suspended for the remainder of the season. National Association President Judge Bramham called the incident "one of the worst displays of rowdyism in the minor leagues in 20 years."

In the post-season, pennant-winning Sanford was matched up with Angier-Fuquay Springs but was upset, four games to two. To add insult to injury, Bulls' pitcher Jim House (11–10) tossed a no-hitter against the Spinners in the deciding game. In the other semi-final, Clinton met Smithfield-Selma and came away with an easy four-games-to-one series victory. In the finals, the surprising Bulls beat the Blues in a hard-fought series that went a full seven games to take the championship.

2. 1946: True Professionals

William G. Bramham presided over the National Association of Professional Baseball Leagues, the governing body for the minor leagues, from 1933 until his retirement after the 1946 season. A judge and attorney based in Durham, he had served as president of the North Carolina State League (1916–17), the Piedmont League (1920–32), the South Atlantic League (1924–30), the Virginia League (1925–28), and the Eastern Carolina League (1928–1929) (minor league program, author's collection).

Final Standings

Club	W	L	T	Pct.	GB	Attend.
Sanford	71	48	1	.597	—	—
Clinton	70	48	0	.593	.5	—
Smithfield-Selma	58	62	2	.483	13.5	—
Angier-Fuquay	57	62	2	.479	14	—
Wilmington	52	66	1	.441	18.5	57,615
Dunn-Erwin	48	70	0	.407	22.5	47,174

• 3 •

1947: Expansion and Big League Farm Clubs

With the success of the 1946 campaign, the Tobacco State League decided to expand to eight teams in 1947. The two new franchises went to Lumberton and Red Springs, towns that had both been members of the semi-pro Twin State League in 1946. As the name would imply, Lumberton—and the Lumber River on which it is located—were named for the primary product of the area during Colonial times. Founded in 1786, Lumberton was the seat of Robeson County. Red Springs, named for 19th century spa famous for its iron-rich mineral water, was also located in Robeson County, a few miles northwest of Lumberton.

Both new clubs were members of major league farm systems; Lumberton was affiliated with the Chicago Cubs while Red Springs was owned and operated by the Philadelphia Athletics. Neither town had fielded a professional club before so considerable work had to be done on their respective ballparks to get ready for the season. Lights were added to Lumberton's Armory Field and the grandstand was remodeled to add restrooms, box seats and a concession stand. Similar preparations took place at Robbins Park in Red Springs; lights were installed and seating for 1000 more fans was added.

Among the original six teams the only change was that the Angier-Fuquay Springs team was moved to the town of Warsaw, a railroad depot town on the line to Wilmington. A group of businessmen from that town, calling themselves the Duplin Athletic Association, bought not only the team but the Angier ballpark's lights, stands, and fence as well. These were then moved and reassembled at the team's new home, located less than 15 miles from their nearest league neighbor, Clinton.

Season Opens April 29   Schedule of the Tobacco State League—1947   Season Closes September 1

	At Clinton	At Warsaw	At Sanford	At Red Springs	At Lumberton	At Wilmington	At Selma-Smithf'ld	At Dunn-Erwin
Clinton		Apr 29 May 13,27 Jun 10,24 Jul 7,23 Aug 6 Sep 1	May 12,26 Jun 8,22 Jul 6,20 Aug 5,19,21	May 10,24 Jun 7,21 Jul 10,17 Aug 2,17,31	May 6,20 Jun 2,16,30 Jul 14,29 Aug 12,26	May 7,21 Jun 4,18 Jul 2,15,31 Aug 14,28	May 4,18 Jun 1,15,29 Jul 11,27 Aug 10,24	May 2,16,30 Jun 12,26 Jul 4,26 Aug 9,23
Warsaw	Apr 30 May 14,28 Jun 11,25 Jul 8,24 Aug 7 Sep 1		May 1,15,29 Jun 12,26 Jul 9,25 Aug 8,22	May 8,22 Jun 5,19 Jul 3,16 Aug 1,15,29	May 12,26 Jun 9,23 Jul 5,19 Aug 5,19,20	May 3,17,31 Jun 14,28 Jul 12,28 Aug 11,25	May 9,23 Jun 6,20 Jul 4,18 Aug 3,17,31	May 6,20 Jun 3,17 Jul 1,14,30 Aug 13,27
Sanford	May 11,25 Jun 9,23 Jul 5,19 Aug 4,18,20	May 2,16,30 Jun 13,27 Jul 10,26 Aug 9,23		Apr 30 May 14,28 Jun 11,25 Jul 8,24 Aug 7 Sep 1	May 3,17,31 Jun 14,28 Jul 12,28 Aug 11,25	May 10,24 Jun 7,21 Jul 4,17 Aug 2,16,30	May 6,20 Jun 3,17 Jul 1,13,30 Aug 13,27	May 3,22 Jun 5,19 Jul 3,16 Aug 1,15,29
Red Springs	May 9,23 Jun 6,20 Jul 9,18 Aug 3,16,30	May 7,21 Jun 4,18 Jul 12,15,31 Aug 14,28	Apr 29 May 13,27 Jun 10,24 Jul 7,23 Aug 6 Sep 1		May 1,15,29 Jun 12,26 Jul 4,25 Aug 8,22	May 6,20 Jun 3,17 Jul 1,14,30 Aug 13,27	May 11,25 Jun 5,19 Aug 4,18,20	May 3,17,31 Jun 14,28 Jul 11,27 Aug 11,25
Lumberton	May 5,19 Jun 3,17 Jul 1,13,30 Aug 13,27	May 11,25 Jun 8,22 Jul 6,20 Aug 4,18,21	May 4,18 Jun 1,15,29 Jul 11,27 Aug 10,24	May 2,16,30 Jun 13,27 Jul 4,26 Aug 9,23		Apr 30 May 14,28 Jun 11,25 Jul 8,24 Aug 7 Sep 1	May 7,21 Jun 4,18 Jul 2,15,31 Aug 14,28	May 10,24 Jun 7,21 Jul 10,17 Aug 3,17,31
Wilmington	May 8,22 Jun 5,19 Jul 3,16 Aug 1,15,29	May 4,18 Jun 1,15,29 Jul 4,18 Aug 10,24	May 9,23 Jun 6,20 Jul 4,18 Aug 3,17,31	May 5,19 Jun 2,16,30 Jul 13,29 Aug 12,26	May 5,19 Jun 2,16,30 Jul 4,23 Aug 6 Sep 1		May 1,15,29 Jun 12,26 Jul 10,25 Aug 8,22	May 11,25 Jun 8,22 Jul 6,20 Aug 5,19,21
Smithfield-Selma	May 3,17,31 Jun 14,28 Jul 12,28 Aug 11,25	May 10,24 Jun 7,21 Jul 4,17 Aug 2,16,30	May 5,19 Jun 2,16,30 Jul 14,29 Aug 12,26	May 12,26 Jun 8,22 Jul 6,20 Aug 5,19,21	May 8,22 Jun 5,19 Jul 3,16 Aug 1,15,29	May 2,16,30 Jun 13,27 Jul 9,26 Aug 9,23		Apr 29 May 13,27 Jun 10,24 Jul 7,24 Aug 6 Sep 1
Dunn-Erwin	May 1,15,29 Jun 13,27 Jul 4,25 Aug 8,22	May 5,19 Jun 2,16,30 Jul 13,29 Aug 12,26	May 7,21 Jun 4,18 Jul 2,16,31 Aug 14,28	May 4,18 Jun 1,15,29 Jul 12,28 Aug 10,24	May 9,23 Jun 6,20 Jul 9,18 Aug 2,16,30	May 12,26 Jun 9,23 Jul 5,19 Aug 4,18,20	Apr 30 May 14,28 Jun 11,25 Jul 8,23 Aug 7 Sep 1	

Schedule for the Tobacco State League's 125-game season in 147 (author's collection).

Part I

Despite the loss of their team, baseball in Angier continued on and a new ball club was soon organized to play in the semi-pro Cape Fear League.

The other Tobacco State League changes for 1947 were a new league president, Fayetteville businessman Arthur Moore (it was decided the president should come from a town outside the league), and a schedule increase from 118 games to 126. Ticket prices were

Since Tobacco State League teams could carry no more than 15 players, this photo of the Sanford Spinners was probably taken during spring training in 1947. From right to left, are (first row) unidentified, Guthrie Watson, John McFadden, unidentified and Bob Pugh; (second row) Phalti Shoffner, Bruce Hedrick, Joe Nessing, Jimmy Wilson, Cecil Cotton and Jimmy Guinn, (third row) Hank Nesselrode, three unidentified, Hoyt Clegg and Jim House; (fourth row) unidentified, George Bortz, unidentified, Ned Butcher and manager Zeb Harrington (author's collection).

3. 1947: Expansion and Big League Farm Clubs

raised by five cents for adults to 65 cents, by-laws were added to establish what to do in case lights failed during a game, and it was decreed that umpires could no longer ride team buses. Placing a team in Lumberton did cause some difficulty for those creating the league schedule, as Sunday baseball was not allowed in the town. Opening Day for the loop was chosen as April 29.

Led by manager Zeb Harrington, a legendary local figure whose involvement in Sanford baseball dated back to the early '30s, the Sanford Spinners turned in an impressive performance in 1947. Finishing 12½ games ahead of second place Lumberton, the team posted a record of 86–39. In fact, the team was so far ahead of the competition that late in the season the regulars were given the day off to visit a local

The home plate wedding ceremony of Smithfield-Selma Leafs outfielder Joe Eonta in 1947. Eonta, a native of Pennsylvania, married local woman Ruth Wiggs and remained in Johnston County after his baseball career ended (courtesy Pete Howard).

Part I

swimming hole. Seven pitchers started that day's game, a shenanigan that resulted in a $125 fine by the league. The Spinners were powered by Hank Nesselrode (.352, 32 HRs, 166 RBIs), and his fellow outfielder Jimmy Wilson, who led the league in batting average (.385), runs (133) and hits (205). Second baseman Jimmy Guinn (.334, 42 SB, 131 runs) joined Nesselrode and Wilson on the All-Star team. Pitcher Bill Stone had another great season at 18–7 while John McFadden (15–5) was the league leader with an ERA of 2.44.

Guided by former big league pitcher Red Lucas, the expansion Lumberton Cubs won 71 games and lost 49, finishing their first Tobacco State League season in second place. First baseman Elzer Marx (.315, 100 RBIs, 122 runs), outfielder Charlie Jamin (.306, 117 RBIs) and rookie pitchers Bob Spicer (16–7) and Doug Lorman (16–6) were the team leaders. The pitching staff also included Charlie Osgood (2–3),

The 1947 Lumberton Cubs. From left to right are (front row) Bill Wood, Doug Lorman, Willard Ehrhardt, Bob Spicer, unidentified, Shelton Stanley and unidentified; (middle row) Jerry Cabaniss, Bill Kivett, two unidentified, Willie Crummie, Charlie Jamin, Bill Dalton and Andy Payonk; (back row) Ralph Dixon, unidentified, Wally Pearsall, Elzer Marx, John Zmijewski, Manuel Garcia, two unidentified and manager Red Lucas (courtesy Buddy Frazier).

3. 1947: Expansion and Big League Farm Clubs

who, at the age of 17, pitched three innings of one game for the 1944 Brooklyn Dodgers. Unfortunately he seemed to have lost the talent that won him a major league look and he was soon out of the game for good at age 20.

Farm clubs like Lumberton and Red Springs had a different makeup than other clubs, which were independent. Farm clubs were comprised of players from all over the country who were assigned to the team by the big league parent club. The independent clubs, on other hand, hired players from wherever they could find them—meaning players were often local. At Lumberton, to name a few, Spicer was from Virginia, Jamin's home was Jersey City, N.J., Marx was a Wisconsin native, Lorman was from Chicago, while popular centerfielder Wally Pearsall hailed from Brooklyn. Interestingly, both Lorman and Jamin made their permanent homes in Lumberton after their baseball careers were over.

The Wilmington Pirates took home third place in 1947 with a 68–57 record. Nate Andrews, now serving as manager, was 4–3 as a part-time pitcher. Outfielder Hargrove Davis hit .320 with 77 RBIs while his fellow outfielder William Benton hit .295 with 73 RBIs (along with 100 runs and 24 stolen bases). First baseman Harry Bridges also had a good season hitting .312 with 94 RBIs while speedy shortstop Fred Musumeci hit .267 and stole 38 bases.

Wilmington's pitching staff was bolstered that year by the signing of hometown boy Lewis Cheshire. The lefthander had been a star hurler for UNC and had pursued a professional baseball career after graduation in 1941. Like so many others, however, the war and military service interrupted those dreams. Able to resume playing in 1945, Cheshire signed with the Boston Red Sox and was sent to their Roanoke farm club in the Piedmont League. Eventually released in 1947, he returned home to join the Pirates where he became the Tobacco State League's top pitcher. Cheshire's 19–8 record and 2.83 ERA won him a spot on the All-Star team. Two of his fellow Pirates, righthanders Johnie Edens (15–11) and Roy Lamb (14–8, 2.53 ERA), also turned in fine seasons on the mound.

The 1947 Dunn-Erwin Twins, managed by second baseman Jack Bell and later by Bill Aurette, posted an even .500 record of 62–62 and finished 23½ games behind Sanford. Outfielder Carl McQuillan and

Part I

Pitcher Lewis Cheshire of the 1947 Wilmington Pirates. A native of Fayetteville, Cheshire was a standout lefty for the University of North Carolina. He signed his first professional contract in 1941 with the Red Sox organization and was sent to Danville, Virginia. The war soon interrupted his career and it wasn't until midway through the 1945 season he resumed pitching with the Roanoke Red Sox of the Piedmont League. In 1947 Cheshire signed with Wilmington and proceeded to lead the league with 19 wins and an ERA of 2.83. He won 19 more games for the Pirates in 1948 while also serving as business manager of the team. After his retirement from the pitching mound during the 1949 season, Cheshire remained with the Pirates' front office and served as a league director (*Raleigh News and Observer*/North Carolina State Archives).

outfielder/catcher Shamrock Denning both had outstanding seasons. Denning hit .333 with 101 runs scored, 25 stolen bases, and, 96 RBIs, an impressive total since he hit only five home runs, 96 RBIs. McQuillan, named to the league All-Star team, hit .331 with 19 home runs, 121 RBIs, and 103 runs scored. Despite the offensive power, the Twins' pitching staff was only average with John Komar leading the way with his 10–5 record and 1.86 ERA.

The Warsaw Red Sox, the league's relocated franchise, finished the season with a fifth place, 59–64 record. Rookie shortstop Ford Jordan (.333, 116 runs) was the team's leading hitter, followed by first baseman/manager Jim Milner (.316, 101 RBIs) and catcher Ted Jones (.315). Outfielders Otis Stephens (.299, 93 RBIs) and Andy Scrobola (.296) also made great contributions to the offense. Pitcher Jim Faircloth (17–6) was one of the league's best while Carl Johnson (13–10) was the league's strikeout king with 225.

In Clinton, the Blues went through three managers, beginning with Van Mungo (who batted .362 in 33 games at first base), and finished

3. 1947: Expansion and Big League Farm Clubs

Left: Jimmy "Punch" Milner learned his baseball skills in the textile mill villages of his native Alabama and in 1938 signed his first professional baseball contract with Mooresville in the Class D North Carolina State League. He quickly proved he could hit for average, if not power, and posted a .406 average in 59 games. He bounced around several teams over the next few seasons, always hitting well, until a stint in the army interrupted his career. He returned in 1945 and, though he had a good season and hit .291 with the Class B Richmond Colts, he was back with Mooresville the following season. In 1947 Milner was hired to manage Warsaw. Playing first base for the Red Sox, he hit .316 with 168 hits and 32 doubles but only two home runs. After that season Milner returned to the NC State league and signed with Lexington, the town he made his permanent home. He retired from baseball in 1951 after part of a season with the Concord Weavers of the NC State League. *Right:* Outfield Otis Stephens showed great promise as a rookie with Angier-Fuquay for half a season in 1946. He remained with the franchise when it relocated to Warsaw in 1947 and hit .299 with 93 RBIs and 103 runs scored (*Raleigh News and Observer*/North Carolina State Archives).

with a record of only 56–67, 29 games out of first. Shortstop Theron Evans was the Blues' offensive leader, batting .334 with 60 RBIs and though they had no real stars the team hit for a surprising .290 combined average. Suvern Wright was the leading pitcher on an otherwise weak staff at 14–9.

Unfortunately for Red Springs manager Manuel "Red" Norris, an area native from Whiteville, the Philadelphia Athletics didn't send him a particularly strong squad to work with. Norris, once a promising

Part I

SAMPSON COUNTY BASEBALL ASSOCIATION

Directors:
L. C. KERR
R. A. POOL
N. B. HILL
R. C. CARTER
G. E. RACKLEY
G. W. LOVE
B. B. BARWICK
C. C. TART, SR.
J. D. JOHNSON, JR.

OPERATING

"THE SAMPSON BLUES" BASEBALL CLUB

Tobacco State League Class D
CLINTON, N. C.

L. C. KERR,
President
R. A. POOL,
Vice-President
N. P. PARKER,
Secretary-Treasurer

September 15, 1947

Mr. G. M. Trautman, President
National Association of Professional Baseball Leagues
Columbus, Ohio

Dear Mr. Trautman:

We are today mailing assignment papers of player Robert F. Vorell's contract to Leaksville Club.

This is pursuant to your directive of September 11, 1947.

Very truly yours,

Clinton Baseball Club

L. C. Kerr, President

Copy: Leaksville Baseball Club
Leaksville, N. C.

Letter written by the Clinton ball club concerning the reassignment of player Robert Vorell. After hitting .297 in 92 games for the Blues, the first baseman's contract was sold to the Leaksville Triplets of the Class C Carolina League (courtesy Bart Swarr).

pitcher in the Brooklyn Dodgers organization in the late '30s before injuries took their toll, did the best he could with the talent available but the Robins (named for the prominent local Robbins textile mill that owned the ballpark as much for the a bird) finished in seventh place at 47–78. First baseman Joe Mangini and second baseman Gus Rogers, who both hit an even .300, were the team's best players. The speedy Mangini, a pro ball rookie at age 27 who had been a Marine Corps sergeant during World War II, also stole 38 bases and tallied an impressive 13 triples. The 21-year-old Rogers was a Robeson County native who had played part of the previous season with Angier-Fuquay.

The league cellar was occupied by the Smithfield-Selma Leafs in

3. 1947: Expansion and Big League Farm Clubs

1947. Forty games out of first, their record stood at 46–79. The solid offense included outfielders Dick Woodard (.381 in 69 games), Leonard Bernstein (.324), and Preston Carroll (.329). Unfortunately for the Leafs, Carroll was dealt to the Greensboro Patriots of the Carolina League in July. Shortstop Pete Howard hit .304, stole 59 bases and was the only member of the Leafs named to the league All-Star team. Catcher Sam Narron, who had appeared briefly in the big leagues, batted .385 in 27 games with the Leafs. The team's weakness was its pitching staff; Henry Koch (7–3) was the only pitcher on the team with a winning record.

In the semi-finals of the playoffs, Lumberton easily beat Dunn-Erwin four games to one while Sanford defeated Wilmington four games to three. In the finals, the Cubs, though leading the series three games to none, lost to the

Left: Left fielder Charlie Askew began the 1947 season with Wilson in the Coastal Plain League before joining Clinton. With the Blues he hit .333 in 56 games (author's collection). *Right:* Catcher Sam Narron, a native of eastern North Carolina, signed with the St. Louis Cardinals organization in 1934. He worked his way up the ladder and appeared in a handful of big league games before his career was interrupted by the war. Without a team and 33 years old in 1947, he returned home and signed with Smithfield-Selma. In 27 games he hit .385 with 7 HR (*Raleigh News and Observer*/North Carolina State Archives).

Part I

Spinners four games to three. All of the Cubs' playoff games that season that fell on a Sunday had to be played in Red Springs since Sunday baseball was not allowed in Lumberton.

Final Standings

Club	W	L	T	Pct.	GB	Attend.
Sanford	86	39	0	.688	—	37,517
Lumberton	71	49	2	.592	12.5	50,748
Wilmington	68	57	2	.544	18	63,219
Dunn-Erwin	62	62	4	.500	23.5	49,262
Warsaw	59	64	3	.480	26	36,865
Clinton	56	67	0	.455	29	36,778
Red Springs	47	78	0	.376	39	21,000
Smithfield-Selma	46	79	1	.368	40	28,847

• 4 •

1948: Sanford's Spinners on a Roll

The Tobacco State League's lineup remained unchanged for the 1948 season. The schedule, however, was upped from 126 games to 135 to take advantage of the good crowds most teams were drawing. Opening day was set for April 23 with the final game on Labor Day, September 6. Another change was in the number of players each team was allowed. For the first two seasons of the league's existence, the player limit had been set at 15 but for 1948 it was raised to 17. The monthly payroll was also increased to $2,600.

Before the season got underway, many local sportswriters picked Sanford as the favorite to take the pennant. The Spinners didn't disappoint as they once again dominated the Tobacco State League. Hank Nesselrode (.362, 27 HR, 159 RBIs) and Jimmy Wilson (.350, 145 runs, 212 hits) again led the team to the pennant, as they finished at 80–56. The Spinners strong pitching staff featured three of the league's best that season: John McFadden (20–9, 3.02 ERA), Hoyt Clegg (15–6) and Clarence Salter (17–7).

The power of Hank Nesselrode's bat was all the more apparent when his home run totals (30, 32 and 27 in his three seasons) are compared to others in the league. Only two other players in the Tobacco State League's five seasons managed to hit even 20 home runs in a single season: Clinton's Willie Duke (27) and Lonnie Smith (20) in 1946. This was partly due to the deep outfields of the league parks but at 6 feet 3 inches, Nesselrode definitely had more power than most. The West Virginia-born slugger, who turned 33 during the 1948 season, began his pro career in 1939 with South Boston, Virginia, in the Bi-State

Part I

League. He rose as high as Oklahoma City in the Texas League before four years of military service sidetracked his baseball career. Unfortunately, Nesselrode's feet were damaged by frostbite during the war, which robbed him speed as a runner and prevented him from regaining his status as a big league prospect. His bat, however, was not hindered and when he came to the plate for the Spinners he was as feared as Babe Ruth had been for the Yankees. After the 1948 season Nesselrode, a free agent, was drafted by the Quebec Braves of the Class C Canadian-American League but he decided to hang up his spikes instead.

Though there is no disputing the impact of Sanford's star players on the league that season, much of the Spinners' success can be attributed the very solid supporting cast. Rookie first baseman Culmer King hit .302 with 75 RBIs, shortstop Bobby Keane hit .303 and scored 98 runs while second baseman Jimmy Guinn hit .367 in 42 games. When Guinn went down with an injury, it opened up a roster spot for a veteran player so the Spinners signed Jim Poole. The son of a former major league player and longtime minor league manager by the same name, Poole hit .282 in 64 games. The dominant pitching staff didn't need much help but Richard Whitmire contribute nine wins and 42-year-old manager Zeb Harrington, who took an occasional turn on the mound, won four games.

Giving Sanford a run in the standings for much of the season, the Wilmington Pirates posted a 76–62 record and eventually finished in second place. Outfielder Hargrove Davis won the league batting title with a .366 average and drove in 92 runs. All-Star outfielder William Benton again had a great season, batting .351 with 123 RBIs and 120 runs. Pirate pitcher Lewis Cheshire (19–11) led the league in strikeouts (258) and ERA (2.35) and was again named to the league All-Star team.

Manager Red Norris turned Red Springs around in 1948, leading the team to a third place record of 75–62. Returning first baseman Joe Mangini, named to the league All-Star team, was the offensive leader batting .302 with 113 RBIs. He also hit an amazing 24 triples to go with his 38 doubles. Rookie second baseman Ernie Brockman, a Brink, New York, native, hit .314. The Robins had a strong pitching staff that season led by Harold Wood (17–9) and Al Burch (18–9). Burch, who also batted .354 playing part-time in the field, won 20 games the following season with Savannah. He advanced up the Athletics' ladder all the way

4. 1948: Sanford's Spinners on a Roll

Pitcher Bill Lloyd, seen with Wilson of the Coastal Plain League in 1947, signed with Smithfield in 1948. Though he posted only a 7–10 record he was fourth in the league with a 2.39 ERA. Lloyd returned to the Leafs in 1949 but was traded to the Fayetteville Scotties in midseason (author's collection).

to AAA but never received the call up to the big league club.

The Smithfield-Selma Leafs did substantially better than they had the previous season, finishing in fourth place with a record of 73–65. The Leafs began that year managed by Sam Narron (.317 in 49 games), but he was replaced by Virgil Payne (.301, 71 RBIs) on June 1. Payne was capable of playing most positions and was named to the All-Star team as a utility man. Dick Woodard (.399 in 36 games) was having another great season before being sold to Burlington of the Carolina League. Outfielders Preston Carroll (.323) and Joe Eonta (.301) turned in strong performances while pitcher Aaron Osofsky (24–5, 2.76 ERA) led the league in wins that season. Osofsky even tossed a 1–0 no-hitter against Lumberton on August 28.

Warsaw signed 30-year-old veteran Verne Blackwell as their skipper in 1948. A native of Kansas, Blackwell began his pro career in the late 1930s but missed four seasons while serving as a lieutenant in the Army Air Corps during the war. Returning to the diamond in 1946, he signed with Greenville

Part I

in the Coastal Plain League, where he hit .313 and drove in 144 runs. Blackwell split the 1947 season between Portsmouth in the Class B Piedmont League and Rocky Mount in Coastal Plain League and continued to wield a potent bat. With Warsaw he played first base and hit .313 in 41 games but in early summer parted ways with the team. Blackwell ended up 30 miles north, where he signed on with the Goldsboro Goldbugs of the Coastal Plain League.

Warsaw team officials replaced Blackwell with former major league pitcher Sam Gibson. The North Carolina native, who made his big league debut with Detroit in 1926, had two seasons of minor league managerial experience under his belt. He guided the Red Sox to a winning record of 71–67, but in fifth place they missed the playoffs.

Warsaw manager Sam Gibson gives a few pointers to pitcher Frank McVicker in 1948. The rookie righthander would win 15 games for Gibson's Red Sox that season (*Raleigh News and Observer*/North Carolina State Archives).

4. 1948: Sanford's Spinners on a Roll

Outfielders Andy Scrobola (.307, 84 runs) and Tom McGhee (.254, 17 HR, 72 RBIs) along with Second baseman Charlie Hutchins (.308, 86 RBIs), led the team's offense. Hutchins, who had been a rookie with Dunn-Erwin in 1947, was a member of the American Legion World Series Championship team from Shelby, North Carolina, in 1945. Lefthander John Dopkin (17–8) was the leading pitcher on the Red Sox's decent staff. Another player of note was third baseman Leo Katkaveck. A star basketball player at North Carolina State University, Katkaveck hit .324 in 19 games before being drafted by the NBA's Washington Capitols.

Warsaw outfielder Wally Schroeder, who joined the team late in the season from Goldsboro of the Coastal Plain League, hit .365 in 17 games. He was a prime example of the countless talented players who drifted around organized baseball in the late '40s. Schroeder played nine seasons and nearly 1100 game in the minor leagues, finishing his career with a batting average of .343. He took the field for seven different teams around the South but only spent part of one season at the A level with Augusta in the SALLY League. With only 16 major league teams and thousands of minor league players vying for a promotion, competition was fierce and being one step slow on the base paths or having only a mediocre throwing arm could be the difference between a career in the big leagues or a small rural town.

Pitcher Claude King won four games for Warsaw in 1948, the last of the Goldsboro native's three seasons in the minor leagues. His younger brother Clyde, however, spent well over half a century in the professional baseball as a player, manager, scout and front office executive. Clyde pitched for the Brooklyn Dodgers then eventually managed the San Francisco Giants, Atlanta Braves and New York Yankees.

The Clinton Blues, who signed a working agreement with the Detroit Tigers for the season, turned in another mediocre finish in 1948 with a record of 70–67. Guided by manager Marvin Lorenz (.333, 103 RBIs, 127 runs), who played first base and occasionally pitched, the team finished in sixth place. Outfielders Jim Williams (.378 in 83 games) and Don MacLean (.358, 115 RBIs) were also among the best hitters in the league. Though they had a strong offense, the Blues were hindered by an unreliable pitching staff. Rookie Charlie Corbett led all hurlers with 13 wins.

Part I

Hindered by injuries and a lack of consistent pitching, the Lumberton Cubs did not have a successful season in 1948 and finished the year in seventh place, 25 games out of first, with a 55–81 record. Veteran outfielder Charlie Jamin (.281), who managed the team, missed a considerable part of the season due to a dislocated ankle suffered while sliding into second base. A similar injury befell starting shortstop Shelton Stanley (.289), who was limited to only 55 games. First baseman Dean Padgett (.310, 16 HR, 115 RBIs, 105 runs) did his best to pick up the slack and carry the offense but the only pitcher with an ERA below 4.00 was rookie Boyce Bridgman. The eighteen-year old from South Carolina went 5–1 with a 1.58 ERA but, interestingly, never played professional baseball again.

Dean "Spec" Padgett, a native of Gastonia, NC, who had played for the University of South Carolina, was the rookie first baseman for Lumberton in 1948. Well-traveled during his solid minor league career, Padgett played for a number of teams in the Chicago Cubs farm system including Des Moines, Macon and Rock Hill. Padgett finished his career in 1957 with the Charlotte Hornets of the Class A South Atlantic League (*Raleigh News and Observer/ North Carolina State Archives*).

4. 1948: Sanford's Spinners on a Roll

The Cubs roster included two other rookies of note in 1948. Nineteen-year-old outfielder Pete Trabucco hit just .252 in 34 games. He went on to become a star slugger in the in the West Texas–New Mexico League where he spent several seasons with the Clovis Pioneers. Another 19-year-old, catcher Verlon Walker, also had a long minor league career. In 1948 he hit .256 in 60 games for Lumberton, the same season his older brother, Albert "Rube" Walker, was breaking into the big league Cubs' lineup as a catcher.

As an interesting side note, the polio epidemic that swept central North Carolina and other parts of the country in 1948 had an effect on Tobacco State League games that season. In mid–July, the Robeson County Health Department decreed that no children would be allowed at Cubs baseball games or other large gatherings due to the contagious nature of the disease.

Before the season, it had been reported that the Dunn-Erwin Twins had lost money in 1947 and were up for sale. The sale didn't take place, however, and J.E. Jackson and his investors found the funding to keep the team on the field.

Dunn-Erwin pitcher Emmett Williams poses behind the team bus in 1948. A native of Elm City, NC, Williams spent two seasons with the Twins and won eight games in 1947. He was used primarily as a reliever in 1948, appearing in 27 games (courtesy Tim Williams).

Part I

Unfortunately for the Twins, they found themselves back in the cellar with a lowly 48–89 record, this time 32 games behind perennial frontrunner Sanford. The team could just never find a winning combination and even went through three managers: Carl McQuillen, Babe Bost, and Gaither Riley (from June 21 on). McQuillen, whose older brother, Glenn, spent parts of several seasons in the big leagues with the St. Louis Browns, signed on with the Coastal Plain League's Greenville Greenies after departing the Twins. If there was a bright spot for the team it was yet another strong season at the plate by Shamrock Denning, who hit .323 with 105 runs and 92 RBIs. The Twins pitching staff was weak, however, with no one winning more than seven games. Attendance dropped considerably to 26,475, also last in the league.

Sanford easily handled Smithfield-Selma in the first round of the playoffs and came away with a four games to one victory. In the other semi-final match-up, Red Springs survived a tough series with Wilmington that went a full seven games. Surprisingly, the Red Robins had a much easier time with pennant-winning Sanford in the finals and took four games to the Spinners' one.

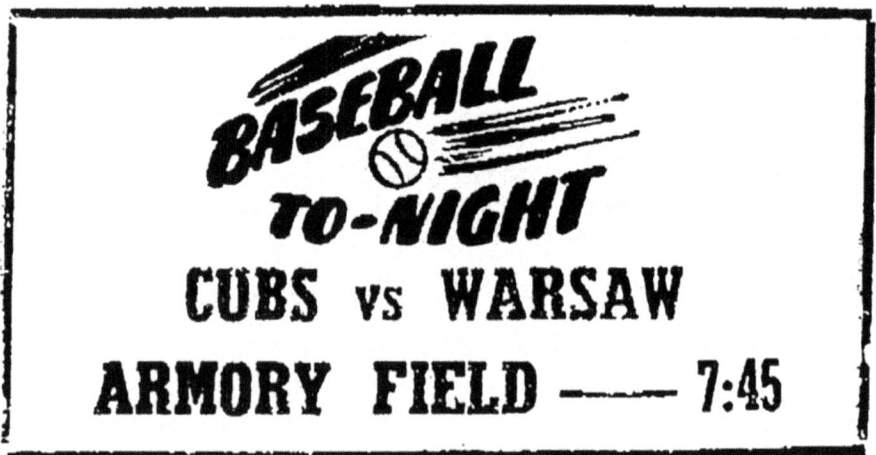

Sign promoting a game between Lumberton and Warsaw (author's collection).

4. 1948: Sanford's Spinners on a Roll

Final Standings

Club	W	L	T	Pct.	GB	Attend.
Sanford	80	56	5	.588	—	29,374
Wilmington	76	62	1	.551	5	77,842
Red Springs	75	62	2	.547	5.5	28,410
Smithfield-Selma	73	65	1	.529	8	36,552
Warsaw	71	67	0	.514	10	32,482
Clinton	70	67	2	.511	10.5	39,498
Lumberton	55	81	3	.404	25	38,772
Dunn-Erwin	49	89	2	.355	32	26,475

• 5 •

1949: A Pair of .400 Hitters and a Dunn-Erwin Pennant

Not long after the 1948 season wrapped up, team owners in Warsaw began to worry they couldn't compete in the league financially. Attendance figures had only been average in the town with the Red Sox drawing 36,865 in 1947 and 32,482 the following season. As was the team's performance on the field, this was only fifth-best both seasons. Though not a complete financial failure, the team owners felt they just couldn't afford to hire the kind of talent necessary to win. They decide to sell the franchise and soon found a buyer in businessman Mike Boosalis of Fayetteville. The Cumberland County city was booming thanks to its proximity to Ft. Bragg, one the U.S. Army's largest bases. A team representing Fayetteville had played in the Class B Tri-State League the previous two seasons and the Class D Coastal Plain League in 1946.

A much larger city than Warsaw, Fayetteville was welcomed into the league and chosen as host of the director's meeting to plan the 1949 season. On January 30 the league directors and President A.T. Moore assembled for a Cape Fear River cruise on the 100-foot yacht *Florida*, which belonged to Fayetteville businessman Oscar Breece. Afterwards, the directors and about 75 guests, including the field managers from most teams and members of the press, were entertained at Breece's Landing banquet hall, which overlooked the river. Jack Haley of radio station WWNF served as master of ceremonies for the festive event.

Decisions reached during the meeting included setting Wednesday, April 20, as opening day, lowering general admission ticket prices for adults from 65 to 60 cents, contributing $100 to the March of

5. *1949: A Pair of .400 Hitters and a Dunn-Erwin Pennant*

Dimes, and deciding one league umpire would be sent to each team's spring training camp. The league also proposed to the nearby Coastal Plain League that a post-season series between pennant winners be played but the idea was rejected.

In Wilmington, a contest was held in early March to decide if fans wanted to keep the name "Pirates." With options including "Sea Gulls," Azaleas" and "Coasters," 235 fans voted but in the end it came down to "Port City Pirates" or just "Pirates." The old name won, 92 votes to 80.

Though the name change didn't come about, others did in Wilmington. For one, the infield at Legion Stadium, which had been clay, was planted with grass for 1949. Secondly, the team hired Mike Conte as its new general manager. Conte, a Baltimore native, was the stepfather of Jack Dunn III, owner of the Baltimore Orioles of the International League. Some claimed the Orioles and the Pirates had an official working agreement, some claimed they didn't. Regardless there was definitely a connection between the teams and Dunn even visited the Pirates spring training camp.

To ready themselves for the season, most teams played a series of exhibition games against college teams, from other leagues that were training in the area or passing through. The Wilmington Pirates, for example, played their first exhibition on April 2 against Campbell College, then had games against Coastal Plain League members Kinston, Goldsboro, New Bern and Wilson, Owensboro of the Kitty League, Bluefield of the Appalachian League, and Albany and Hartford of the Class A Eastern League. (Actually training in Wilmington and sharing Legions Stadium with the Pirates was the Waterbury of the Class B Colonial League.)

The Pirates' schedule even included a contest against the barnstorming House of David team. Based in a religious commune in Michigan, the House of David team was famous for all of its members having long beards as well as their adeptness on the baseball diamond. They toured the country from the 1920s through the mid–1950s, splitting gate proceeds with any willing opponent.

Fayetteville and Lumberton both took on Wake Forest College in mid–April action. It might not have been the confidence builder the teams had hoped, however, as the college boys prevailed over the pros

BASEBALL
OPENING GAME
TOBACCO STATE LEAGUE
Fri. Night - April 28
RED SPRINGS ROBBINS
vs
LUMBERTON AUKS
ROBBINS PARK — 7:45
RED SPRINGS
Music By Combined Red Springs and Raeford High School Bands.

Sign promoting the opening day game for Red Springs. Interestingly, the team is referred to as the Robbins, the name of the local textile mill that owned the ballpark, rather than the Robins, as they were in official reports (author's collection).

in both contests. At Fayetteville, the Deacs won 2–0 while at Lumberton they handed the home team a 17–0 thrashing. In all fairness, Wake Forest was one of the top collegiate teams in the country that season. Led by All Americans Charlie Teague and Gene Hooks, they were runners-up at the 1949 College World Series.

5. 1949: A Pair of .400 Hitters and a Dunn-Erwin Pennant

The 1949 Lumberton Auctioneers team. With the exception of first baseman Cecil "Turkey" Tyson (back row, center) the players are unidentified (courtesy Cecil Tyson).

Soon after opening day it became apparent that the Dunn-Erwin Twins were the big surprise of the season. In one of those rare cases where a team went from last one season to first the next, they won the league pennant with a record of 81–54. The team, managed by former Wilmington catcher Jim Staton, had several stars. Among them were veteran Shamrock Denning (.354), the league leader in hits (185), runs (118) and RBIs (119), outfielder John Richards (.351, 105 RBIs, 107 runs) and pitcher Clancy Condit (20–9), who led the league in wins and strikeouts (264). Richards, Condit, and catcher Steve Marko (.326) were all named to the league's post season All-Star team. Having a winning team helped attendance, as it rose to 39,335.

Finishing five games behind Dunn-Erwin, Red Springs won 76 games and lost 59 to finish the regular season in second place. Outfielder Peanut Doak (.313), a star at N. C. State before the war, led the team in hitting but their real strength was the pitching staff. With Allen Pfeiffer (12–8, 2.38 ERA), Wallace Carpenter (10–5), and rookie Bill

Part I

Harrington (17–11), the Ronbins had a great staff. Unfortunately for the Robins, Philadelphia promoted Carpenter to their Carolina League club in Martinsville. They replaced his arm, however, with a strong bat when they sent over first baseman Tex Warfield from their Tarboro club in the Coastal Plain League. Essentially, the Athletics swapped Warfield with Ray Bauder, who had been playing first base for the Red Robins. It was a move that worked out well for Red Springs; in 36 games Warfield hit .348 and helped the club hold on to second place. Bauder,

Above: Fayetteville's first game in the league was against the mighty Sanford Spinners. Surprisingly, the Scotties defeated the defending pennant-winners, 14–2 (author's collection).*Opposite top:* During spring training in 1949, Red Springs pitchers (from left) Hugh Holder, Allen Pfeiffer and Jack Jordan confer with catcher Jim Vojcsik (*Raleigh News and Observer*/North Carolina State Archives). *Opposite bottom:* Dunn-Erwin's 1949 pitching staff included (from left) Duke Maas, Ed Smith and Ray Dietrich. Smith and Dietrich were out of professional baseball after the 1949 season but Maas would go on to win a World Series title with the New York Yankees in 1958 (*Raleigh News and Observer*/North Carolina State Archives).

5. 1949: A Pair of .400 Hitters and a Dunn-Erwin Pennant

Part I

on the other hand, had batted .266 at Red Springs but struggled at Tarboro and only managed a .171 average.

The Lumberton franchise was sold by the Chicago Cubs to a local group before the 1949 season but the team retained a working agreement with its former big league parent. Renamed the Auctioneers, the club played well and finished the season in third place. Attendance was first in the league, as the Auks (as they were called for short) drew 60,038 fans.

Imposing first baseman Cecil "Turkey" Tyson, who was listed at 6'5½" and 225 pounds, led the team with a .318 average while All-Star outfielder Bill Bohlender (.305, 88 RBIs, 101 runs) and third baseman Randy Dulworth (.280, 102 RBIs) were the leading run producers. Dulworth, who finished second in the league with 13 triples, recalled his season in Lumberton in an interview years later with the *Overton County News* in his hometown of Livingston, Tennessee. He remembered one evening in particular when–in appreciation of an outstanding play–a hat was passed through the crowd to take up a collection. The result was $27 in change, which was presented to him after the game.

The Lumberton pitching staff in 1949 featured lefty Gordon McDonald (15–6, 2.95 ERA) and righty Gus Viera (14–7, 3.49 ERA). Another pitcher of note was Mel Bosser. The veteran right hander had been a star prospect in the Washington minor league system with 23 wins in 1940 and 17 in '41. Like so many others, the war interrupted his promising career. He returned to baseball in 1946 after three years in the military and did make it into a few games with the Cincinnati Reds but was past his prime. At age 35, Bosser signed with Lumberton and pitched ten games, winning two, before moving to Burlington in the Carolina League.

Though they started the season off with a bang by destroying Fayetteville 18–0 on opening day, Sanford's Spinners proved to only be a fourth place team in 1949. The loss of Hank Nesselrode, who retired after the 1948 season, was felt as the team's offense lacked punch. Outfielder Ziggy Sklowdowski (.305), a former University of Florida running back, had speed and scored 77 runs but had no power. Another notable was outfielder Doc Greene, a veteran of the Pacific Coast and Texas Leagues. He played well in half a season before being dealt to

5. 1949: A Pair of .400 Hitters and a Dunn-Erwin Pennant

Fayetteville. The Spinners pitching staff, however, was excellent and featured Hoyt Clegg (19–9, 2.57 ERA), Sam Gibson (17–9) and Clayton Andrews (11–8, 2.68 ERA).

Much like they had previous season, the Smithfield-Selma Leafs played average ball and finished in fifth place with a record of 70–65. Virgil Payne began that season as manager but was replaced by veteran pitcher Buck Weaver, who in turn was replaced by catcher Paul Kluk on June 9. Kluk, a naval lieutenant who served on destroyers during the war, had played blocking back on the University of Georgia football team.

Amazingly, the Leaf's had three players hit .400 or better though outfielder Joe Parise (.416 in 101 ABs) and catcher/manager Paul Kluk (.412 in 148 ABs) both lacked enough at-bats to qualify for the batting title. Returning outfielder Dick Woodard (.400, 113 RBIs, 106 runs) played the full season, however, team and finished third in the league's batting race. Amby Foote (18–12, 3.24) and Carl Baham (12–5), who often did double-duty as an outfielder, were the Leaf's best pitchers.

The outfield for the 1949 Smithfield-Selma Leafs featured, from left, Mac Holland in left, Smokey Warren in center and Richard Woodard in right (*Raleigh News and Observer*/North Carolina State Archives).

Part I

Named the Fayetteville Scotties (a tribute to the many Scottish immigrants who settled the area), the league's relocated club won 61 games and lost 76, finishing sixth in the eight-team league. They began the season managed by long time minor league legend Cecil "Zip" Payne, an outfielder whose playing career had begun in 1929. Unfortunately, he was hit in the shin by a ball when it took a bad hop and the injury was severe enough to result in surgery. Payne then decided to retire from playing and leave the team since he was unable to fulfill the role of playing manager as he was hired to do. Outfielder Joe Roseberry, who had played under Payne for a couple of seasons with the Cardinals farm club in Winston-Salem, was appointed to take his place.

Games in Fayetteville were memorable that season for fans and players alike for a reason other than the action on the field: the new

FAYETTVILLE SCOTTIES

Fayetteville was only in the league for one season. The city fielded a team in the Class D Coastal Plain League in 1946, the Class B Tri-State League in 1947 and '48, and then moved to the Class B Carolina League in 1950 (author's collection).

5. 1949: A Pair of .400 Hitters and a Dunn-Erwin Pennant

mechanical scoreboard. If a half inning went scoreless, a large mechanical goose named Gertie would stick her head out from behind a giant baseball. She would then emerge to lay a "goose egg" in the appropriate place on the board. At other times a gosling would follow as Gertie made her run across the board.

Though he soon gave up managing, Roseberry remained with the team and had what is undoubtedly the most impressive season in league history. Not only did he win the batting title with an outstanding .408 average, but was one of the leading pitchers on the Scotties' weak staff and finished with a 7–7 record in 25 games. Surprisingly, it was an extremely close race for the batting title as Roseberry just edged out Wilmington's Hargrove Davis. The only real offensive help Roseberry had on the team came from first baseman Kit Kittrell who hit .285 with 82 RBIs. Cuban righthander Amado Diaz, who reportedly spoke no English, finished with a team-high 11 wins. One interesting player who was briefly a member of the Scotties' lineup was third baseman Kenny Reese. A former football star at the University of Alabama, Reese played halfback in the NFL for the Detroit Lions when he wasn't playing minor league baseball. He played fairly well for the Scotties but was released after only six games.

The 1949 Clinton Blues, again managed by Marvin Lorenz (.286, 89 RBIs), dropped another rung on the ladder as they finished in seventh place. Outfielder Andy Scrobola (.315, 100 runs), a native of Yonkers, NY, was the team's best hitter while pitcher Billy Price (12–5) dominated opposing hitters and had a league best ERA of 2.19. Other than these two players, the only other performance of note was by second baseman Nick Purchia (.277), who led the league with 118 runs scored.

The Wilmington Pirates dropped to last in the eight-team league, 33 games out of first. The Pirates began the season managed by former Baltimore Orioles infielder Ab Tiedemann. On May 17, however, the veteran infielder resigned from what was his first managerial position. Teidemann had hurt his shoulder in World War II and lacked the throwing ability he had once had. As the team slipped in standings he felt it was in the best interest of team to step down so team could Pirates could find a shortstop who could contribute as a player.

Before his departure, Tiedemann made a quote in *Wilmington*

Part I

5. 1949: A Pair of .400 Hitters and a Dunn-Erwin Pennant

Morning Star that showed just how rabid the fans of the Tobacco State League actually were. Said Tiedemann, it was "a league where the fans are the toughest. If a youngster gets past Class D ball, he has passed the worst of the storm. The spectators pay 60 cents and a majority of them want major league ball; $1.20 baseball. They can't expect it. I've seen twice as many boys ruined by the fans ragging them than by their own failure."

The Pirates also saw another key departure before mid-season; star pitcher Lewis Cheshire, who was also one of the owners of the team as well as the secretary-treasurer, actually released himself. Referred to in the local paper as a "chunky lefthander," Cheshire had won 19 games in each of the past two seasons but felt he was unable to get into proper playing shape and hung up his spikes.

Though Wilmington lacked in pitching, they did have a strong offense. Despite hitting for an impressive average of .4082 (with 106 RBIs), Hargrove Davis missed winning his second batting title by four one-thousandths of a point. Johnie Edens also turned in an amazing performance as he batted .362 with 70 RBIs while playing first, third and in the outfield. He was also the team's best pitcher with an 11–10 record. Pirate fans nearly missed out on Eden's performance that season: he had been purchased by the Raleigh Capitals of the Carolina League during the winter but the versatile star refused to leave his hometown.

First baseman Duncan Futrelle, playing half a season, hit .320 after coming over from the NC State League. Third baseman Ben Hester, fresh out of East Carolina College, showed promise with a .319 batting average but was only around for six weeks. Attendance in Wilmington, which had set the all-time league record in 1948 with 77,842, declined to 49,009, though this was still good enough for third in the league.

The first round of the 1949 playoffs paired Dunn-Erwin with Lumberton and Red Springs with Sanford. Pennant-winning Dunn-Erwin

Opposite top: The outfield for the 1949 Clinton Blues was patrolled, from left, by Andy Scrobola, Joe Stern and Harry Spain (*Raleigh News and Observer/ North Carolina State Archives*). *Opposite bottom:* The Wilmington Pirates got a new home when New Hanover Memorial Park opened in late May of 1949 (courtesy Special Collections Department, New Hanover County Public Library).

Part I

WILMINGTON PIRATES

5. 1949: A Pair of .400 Hitters and a Dunn-Erwin Pennant

had an easy time with Lumberton and won four games to one to advance to the championship while Red Springs beat Sanford, four games to two. The Red Robins then proceeded to upset the Twins, taking their second straight post-season championship, four games to two.

The 1949 season was the league's most successful. With the exception of Wilmington, attendance was up in every league city. In Lumberton it rose to over 60,000 from 38,772 in 1948. The Fayetteville franchise, which had not drawn particularly well in Warsaw, drew 57,000 in its new home. Probably due to its dismal, last-place season, Wilmington dropped from 77,842 in 1948 (a figure that would stand as the all-time league record) down to 49,000.

Final Standings

Club	W	L	Pct.	GB	Attend.
Dunn-Erwin	81	54	.600	—	39,335
Red Springs	76	59	.563	5	33,303
Lumberton	75	61	.551	6.5	60,038
Sanford	71	62	.530	9	36,046
Smithfield-Selma	70	65	.519	11	41,618
Fayetteville	61	76	.445	21	56,999
Clinton	60	78	.435	22.5	37,496
Wilmington	49	88	.358	33	49,009

Opposite top: The Wilmington Pirates as shown in the 1949 yearbook. The team went through four managers that season and finished in the league cellar (author's collection). *Opposite bottom:* The 1949 Dunn-Erwin outfield featured (from left) Jake Richards, Claude Haithcock and Shamrock Denning (*Raleigh News and Observer*/North Carolina State Archives).

• 6 •

1950: Newcomers and Attendance Struggles

In what would ultimately prove to be its final season of existence, the Tobacco State League went through several changes. Early in the winter, the owners of Fayetteville team decided to take advantage of an opening in the much more prestigious Class B Carolina League. They put their Tobacco State League franchise up for sale and after much speculating as to where it would end up, the destination emerged as the Richmond County town of Rockingham. Heath Penegar, owner of the Pontiac dealership in Rockingham, put together a group that also included Henry Smithey, manager of the town's Belk's department store, and Matt Gettings, manager of local radio station WAYN, who was to run the club. For road games, the club secured the use of a new bus loaned by the Rockingham Suburban Bus Lines. The bus, reported in the *Wilmington Star* to be "fully equipped with air foam cushions and a radio," was painted white with the club name on the sides as well as a large eagle on the sides and rear. The only negative to the addition of Rockingham, located 130 miles from Wilmington, was an increase in travel time and cost for some clubs.

In Lumberton, the club was again sold, this time to businessman Roy Dissinger. A former St. Louis Cardinals scout and general manager of the New Orleans Pelicans, Dissinger was a baseball entrepreneur of the highest level. The Pennsylvania native ran a baseball school in Melbourne, Fla., and began buying minor league clubs in the late 1940s. His first purchase was Anderson, SC of the Tri-State League. For the 1950 season, Dissinger's "farm system" consisted of five teams operating in various leagues, including Greenville (NC) of the Coastal Plain

6. 1950: Newcomers and Attendance Struggles

League. That gave him control of roughly 150 players, whom he hoped to sell to major league clubs.

On January 30, league directors met in Wilmington at Uncle Henry's Oyster Roast on Masonboro Sound to plan the upcoming season. The group, presided over by league president Arthur Moore, consisted of Hillary Caison, Dr. M.L. O'Brien and R.C. Carter of Clinton; Jim Francoline, E.J. Gleven and R.A. Hedgepeth of Lumberton; and Randy Bullard, H.E. Skipper, Red Norris, Dick Brown and Tom Cope from Red Springs; and Everett Mayton and Virgil Payne from Smithfield-Selma. Manager Zeb Harrington and retired slugger Hank Nesselrode represented Sanford while field manager Jim Staton was the lone emissary from Dunn-Erwin. In attendance from new member Rockingham was business manager Matt Gettings while the delegation from the host Wilmington Pirates consisted of former star player and now business manager Lewis Cheshire, along with team vice presidents Vic Stefano and M.A. Rooks.

On the agenda for the meeting was a wide range of topics including everything from determining fines for various offenses to selecting as the official league ball (the Goldsmith No. 97). April 28 was chosen as Opening Day and the 140-game season would wrap up on September 12. It was also decided no All-Star game would be held in 1950 but doubleheaders would take place on the Fourth of July and Labor Day.

The main issue on everyone's mind, however, was money. Teams were struggling for revenue and looking for new ways to fill the seats. The Red Springs club proposed playing some games in Laurinburg, located 18 miles west, in hopes that they would expose a new group of fans to the team. Similar plans were considered by Clinton, which discussed playing some games 13 miles to the east in former league town Warsaw.

The club that caused the most financial worry for the league over the winter was Smithfield-Selma. There were some rumors that the team might not be able to arrange its finances in time for the season but team leaders gave their assurances that they would be ready. The held to their word and the Leafs and the rest of the Tobacco State League clubs began play on Saturday, April 28.

Around the league, excitement ran high as Opening Day approached. The festivities for the games that evening featured high school bands,

Part I

Unidentified members of the 1950 Smithfield-Selma Leafs before a home game (*Raleigh News and Observer*/North Carolina State Archives).

color guards, and numerous promotions for both fans and players. In Lumberton, where the Auctioneers were taking on Red Springs, players had the opportunity to take advantage of prizes donated by local merchants. Lennon's Men's Store offered an Archdale dress shirt to the first Auk pitcher to strike out a man, a sport shirt to the first to hit a single, a Sheer Weight Van Husen sport shirt to the first to drive in a run, a Seersucker sport shirt to the first to scores a run, and a K-Venience Tie Rack to the first to hit a double. The first Lumberton player to hit a home run was guaranteed a pair of Riddell baseball shoes courtesy of Sellars Sporting Goods, which would also present a pair of Navigator sunglasses to the first to steal a base. McLeod Motors promised the Auk player who scored the third run a wash and grease job on his car. Various other merchants also offered prizes to players on the home team, including a sport shirt for the first to hit a triple, a Life

6. 1950: Newcomers and Attendance Struggles

Preserver Cushion for the first base on balls, a Woodbury Shave Kit for the first putout, and a box of Montag's Men's Stationery to the player who scored the second run.

Upon taking over the Lumberton club, Roy Dissinger hired Jim Francoline as business manager. A veteran of fifteen years in the minor leagues, Francoline had risen as high as Class A ball but retired from playing after the 1949 season. In May, Dissinger decided the younger players on the team could benefit from some more veteran leadership on the field so Francoline resigned his front office position and returned to the outfield. It proved to be a wise move as he hit .329 with 98 RBIs and was named to the league All-Star team.

Francoline wasn't the Lumberton Auctioneers' only outstanding player. Manager John Streza (.320, 111 RBIs) had been in pro ball since 1938. Once a promising prospect for the St. Louis Cardinals, the 6'3", 220 lb. first baseman hit .313 for Columbus in the SALLY League in 1941 before

MEET THE MANAGER

"BIG" JOHN STREZA

Big John started his baseball career in 1938. He signed a baseball contract with the St. Louis Cardinal organization, and was farmed out to Portsmouth, Ohio, of the Middle Atlantic League, and Union Springs, Ala., of the Alabama State League that summer. In '39 John was with Williamson, W. Va., of the Mountain State League. 1940 saw Big John with Houston of the Texas League and Mobile of the Southeastern League. The season of '41 John spent with Columbus, Ga. of the South Atlantic League and after a great year was sold to Rochester of the International League.

Jan. of 1942 John entered the service and was there until Jan. of 1946.

The '46, '47, '48 and '49 seasons played with Rochester of the International League, Shreveport of the Texas League, Durham of the Carolina League, Miami Beach of the Florida International League, and 2 years with Florence of the Tri-State League.

Big John has always been a heavy hitter with a .300 average and 100 RBI's.

A big likeable fellow who is hoping to give us a hustling ball club. We all wish you much success, Big Fellow.

The bio of Lumberton manager John Streza from the 1950 program (author's collection).

Part I

four years of military services interrupted his career. After the war Streza played for the Durham Bulls and the Miami Beach Flamingoes, amongst others, before being hired to skipper the Auctioneers.

Joining Streza in the infield was former New York Yankee Mike Milosevich. In pro baseball since 1935, Milosevich was a Yankees farmhand for his entire career before finally being called up to the big leagues during the war. He spent parts of 1944 and '45 with the Yankees, splitting time at shortstop with veteran Frankie Crosetti. Squeezed out of the majors in 1946 by the flood of players returning from the war, Milosevich spent the season at the AAA level with Kansas City and Newark. In 1947 he dropped another rung on the ladder to AA and split the season between Atlanta and New Orleans in the Southern Association. Roy Dissinger knew Milosevich from his time in New Orleans and hired him in 1949 to play for his Hazlehurst-Baxley club in the Class D Georgia State League. In 1950, Dissinger sent the 35-year-old Milosevich to Lumberton, partially to help build a strong team but also to help mentor his young players. The move paid off as Milosevich hit .314, led the league in both home runs (14) and RBIs (121) and was named as the league's All-Star shortstop.

The Lumberton team wasn't all seasoned veterans, however. Speedy nineteen-year-old second baseman Pete Ethier (.300, 43 SB, 135 BB), led the league in runs with 146 while rookie lefthander John Lagan (21–3) and righty Bill Bernier (18–5), in his second year of pro ball, were two of the best pitchers in the league. The Auks also got a boost in late July when they received several players, including rookie pitcher Bill Rothermel (8–2), from the Bristol (Conn.) Owls in the Class B Colonial League when that circuit folded.

In an interesting side note to the Lumberton season, famed baseball clown Max Patkin performed at the Auctioneers game on June 30. Patkin, a former minor league pitcher, discovered a knack for entertaining baseball crowds with comedy while playing in the military. After the war, he was hired as a "coach" by Cleveland Indians owner Bill Veeck, who was always looking for new ways to entertain fans. When Veeck sold the Indians in 1949, Patkin hit the road and took his comedy show from minor league town to minor league town. Before he retired over 50 years later, Patkin reportedly performed 4000 shows and even appeared as himself in the 1988 movie *Bull Durham*.

6. 1950: Newcomers and Attendance Struggles

The Sanford Spinners, skippered by Zeb Harrington for the fifth year, finished the season with a record of 90–44. The team's offense featured first baseman Herb May (.340, 93 RBIs) but the Spinners' real strength was the pitching staff. Hoyt Clegg, who stood only 5'8", dominated league hitters and posted a 24–5 record in his fourth season as a Spinner. 6'3" teenager Clayton Andrews' won 15 games and led the league with 2.63 ERA while lefty Rick Causey won 12 and struck out a league-best 148.

As discussed in January, the Red Springs club did agree to play 30 games in nearby Laurinburg. Officially given what is probably one of

Members of the 1950 Lumberton Auctioneers, as shown in that season's program (author's collection).

Part I

Above and opposite: Members of the 1950 Lumberton Auctioneers, as shown in that season's program (author's collection).

the longer names in the history of professional baseball, the team was renamed the Red Springs–Laurinburg Red Robins. The arrangement didn't last long, however, and the club announced in mid–June that all remaining home games would be played at Robbins Park in Red Springs.

Part I

The Philadelphia Athletics sent 31-year-old Bob "Ducky" Detweiler to Red Springs to manage their farm club. A once-promising prospect, Detweiler made it into a handful of big league games with the Boston Braves in 1942 but, like so many others, the war and military service cost him his prime playing years. Upon his discharge from the army, Detweiler resumed his playing career but failed to find his swing in the high minor leagues. He got it back, however, when he signed with Athletics' organization and joined their Federalsburg club in the Class D Eastern Shore League in 1947; in three seasons with the Federalsburg A's he never hit below .339. At Red Springs, Detweiler continued his torrid hitting pace and turned in a .342 average with 95 RBIs and a league-leading 19 triples while playing first base.

Detweiler turned to managing in 1949 and before retiring from the game after the 1952 season he had also skippered clubs in Cordele, Ga. and Lexington, NC, as well as Fayetteville, when that city fielded a team in the Class B Carolina League.

Nearly fifty years later Detweiler shared fond memories of his season in the Tobacco State League with the author:

> I remember a night in Smithfield, there was a fence that advertised Smithfield Hams in right center. Anyone hitting a ball over that sign would receive a ham. Well, I hit a home run over that sign and I was presented on the field with my ham: a live half-grown pig! I still laugh when I think of it. After the game a man offered me fifty dollars for the pig, and of course, I took it. Later in the year I hit a home run over a jeweler's sign in Laurinburg and I won a watch. I picked one out for my wife who was home in Maryland with our newborn baby girl.

Contests and promotions like the ones Detweiler recalled were common at Tobacco State League games. Outfielder Floyd Moser, who hit .271 with 58 RBIs for Red Springs that same season, possessed a strong and accurate arm. In a contest before a game in Rockingham, players had the chance to test their arms and win $10. They were given three throws from the outfield wall, 410 feet from home plate. "Two were six inches from the plate," Moser recalled years later in an interview with the *Moultrie* (SC) *Observer*. "One was on the plate. I won that 10 dollars."

Other than Detweiler and outfielder Al Parnell (.311, 80 RBIs), who was actually a native of Red Springs, the 1950 Red Robins team was only of average talent. One of the Tobacco State League's greatest

6. 1950: Newcomers and Attendance Struggles

Keith Miller, a native of Hamlet, NC, held down second base for the Rockingham Eagles. The 20-year-old, who was a student at Catawba College in the off-season, had been a star for the semi-pro Beaunit Travelers of the Twin State League for the previous two summers. Miller was an oddity in baseball: a right-handed infielder, he was also a hard-throwing left-handed pitcher (author's collection).

hitters, outfielder Hargrove Davis (.362), joined the ball club but was only around for 38 games. Despite their lack of star players, the Robins played well enough to take home third place with their 68–61 record.

The Rockingham Eagles took the field in 1950 for what would prove to be their only season. Veteran Jack Bell, who had spent the previous season as a player/manager with a semi-pro team in Lake City, SC, was hired as manager. He was replaced, however, in June by first baseman Cecil "Turkey" Tyson. Tyson (.315), who in 1944 had seen exactly one big league at-bat with the Phillies, teamed with Canadian outfielder and lead-off hitter Bill Duffy (.289, 99 runs) to provide much of the team's offense. Forty-one-year-old outfielder Willie Duke, finishing out a long distinguished minor league career, batted .348 in 38 games for the Eagles after coming over from the Carolina League. Outfield Bob Pugh (.253, 63 RBIs) was probably the team's most versatile player. He also won 11 games as a pitcher while filling in as both a starter and reliever. Pugh's skills weren't just limited to the baseball diamond: in the off-season he was a professional boxer who once faced the great Joe Louis in a four-round exhibition.

Part I

Two former major league pitchers made brief appearances for Rockingham in 1950, neither of whom appears in the official league stats since they played in less than 10 games. Jim Hopper took the mound on Opening Day for Eagles. A Charlotte native, Hopper had an outstanding season (15–9, 2.63 ERA) in 1943 with Toronto, the Pittsburgh Pirates' top farm club. Unfortunately military service called and he was out of pro baseball for two years. He returned in 1946 and made the Pirates' roster out of spring training. Hopper's stay proved to be short in Pittsburgh, however, and he appeared in two games. He spent the next two seasons being shuffled around the higher minor leagues, with stops in places including Seattle and Columbus,

Left: Tal Abernathy, a big left-handed pitcher from Chatham County, NC, pitched 20 innings for the Philadelphia Athletics between 1942 and 1944. His made his final professional mound appearances with Rockingham in 1950 at age 28 (courtesy Frank Dennison). *Right:* The résumé of pitcher Jim Hopper, seen here with Mooresville in 1948, included time in the high minor leagues with Toronto, Seattle and Columbus as well as two games with the Pittsburgh Pirates. He retired from baseball at age 30 after his brief stint with Rockingham (courtesy Norman Small).

Letter from Rockingham general manager Matt Gettings to field manager Jack Bell instructing him to give additional workouts to the players when they lose a game (author's collection).

Ohio. In 1948, Hopper returned to North Carolina and signed with Mooresville in the Class D NC State League. He won 12 games that season and was even better in 1949 with Landis in the same league, posting a 17–8 record. The official record indicates Hooper retired

Part I

after the 1949 season but somehow he became connected with the new Rockingham club. He signed on early and spent spring training with the club. With the Eagles, Hopper started three games, winning one, before deciding to retire from the game for good at age 30.

Tal Abernathy, a native of Bynum in Chatham County, was signed to replace Hopper. A former Elon College star, Abernathy appeared in seven big league games over three seasons for the Philadelphia Athletics during the war. He then spent several seasons with Memphis in the Southern Association before returning to North Carolina. There he played in the Class B Carolina League with Reidsville, Burlington and Greensboro. Like Hopper, the official record indicates Abernathy retired after the 1949 season but he pitched three games for the Rockingham Eagles in late May.

Enthusiasm for the Eagles remained high in Rockingham throughout the course of the season and the team ran several promotions to keep fans in the seats. On Knot Hole Night, all children under age 14 were admitted free and refreshments were sold to them at reduced prices. Ladies Night offered reduced ticket prices for women as well as special giveaways. Nylon hosiery from Belk's, a spring

Fifth Anniversary TROPHY

To Be Awarded
Penant Winner
1950

Donated By The
BYRON CO.
Publishers Of Dixie Annual

A local publisher in Clinton donated a trophy to be awarded to the 1950 league champion (author's collection).

6. 1950: Newcomers and Attendance Struggles

suit from Leder Brothers Store in the town and trips to a local beauty parlor were amongst the prizes offered only to female patrons. Before one game the local 4-H Club held a livestock auction with manager Turkey Tyson serving as the auctioneer, and at the June 9th game, one lucky fan was the recipient of a Bendix automatic washing machine courtesy of the team and Thrower Electric Company.

Overall, despite a lack of consistent pitching, the Eagles' offense kept them in the race the whole season. They even set a league record with 11 runs in one inning when they defeated Wilmington, 20–6, on August 3 (second baseman Jim Fister went 4–5 with two triples). The Eagles finished the regular season with a record of 63–69, 27½ games out of first. It was good enough, however, for fourth place and a spot in the playoffs.

A group of unidentified players from Clinton before a game at Smithfield (*Raleigh News and Observer*/North Carolina State Archives).

Part I

In 1950 the Clinton Blues' record was almost the same as the previous season as they finished in fifth place with a 61–72 record. Catcher Al Kluttz (.373 in 61 games), whose older brother Clyde was a big league backstop, began the season as manager and played well in half a season with the team. The Blues' offense lacked punch and other than Kluttz the only real standouts were All-Star second baseman Nick Purchia (.281, 89 RBIs) and speedy outfielder Bill Kay (.275, 131 runs), who led the league with 57 stolen bases and an amazing 180 bases on balls. Marvin Lorenz, who had managed the Blues the two previous seasons, began the year as the manager of the Smithfield-Selma Leafs but was rehired by the Blues (to become their fourth manager of the season) when the Leafs withdrew from the league on August 16.

The Wilmington Pirates, who had been fortunate enough to sign a working agreement with the Cincinnati Reds before the season, had some decent talent but it was not enough as they turned in a record of only 56–75 and finished in sixth place. Johnie Edens, named as the All-Star team's third baseman, returned and led the team with a .344 batting average. Once the team's star pitcher, he still took the mound occasionally and won five games with a 2.85 ERA. Despite a .349 career batting average and 48–39 pitching record, Edens retired from professional baseball at age 28 after the 1950 season.

First baseman Dwight "Red" Teague (.327, 94 RBIs) also had an outstanding season for the Pirates. An Alamance County, NC, native, Teague had spent the previous two seasons in the Cincinnati organization with the Lockport Reds in New York. Rookie outfielder Charlie Moir, who had played collegiate baseball at Appalachian State, contributed a .278 average and 73 RBIs. Another rookie in the outfield, 18-year-old Donald Roberts from Orange County, showed great promise with his .296 average and 75 RBIs. Unfortunately, a draft notice from the U.S. Army curtailed his professional career.

An uproar ensued when Wilmington fired manager Lowell "Bull" Hamons on May 20. The club reportedly claimed the change was at the request of the Cincinnati Reds, though the Reds denied this. In protest, the Pirates players threatened not to take the field for a game against Sanford. Knowing they risked suspension if they carried out the boycott, Hamons talked the players out if it. In the end, Red Teague was appointed temporary skipper until Steve Collins, who had managed

6. 1950: Newcomers and Attendance Struggles

Kinston in the Coastal Plain League for two seasons, was hired to take over.

Managerial troubles were not the only problem facing the Wilmington ball club in 1950. Despite playing in the league's largest town (by far) the Pirates were plagued by poor attendance and only 35,950 fans paid to see them that summer. There was talk of a possible move to Bennettsville, South Carolina in July but the team decided to stay put.

The Dunn-Erwin Twins returned in 1950 with Jim Staton as manager and Shamrock Denning as probably the best offensive player in the league. Poor attendance quickly became an issue, however. With only around 250 fans showing up per game, the team faced serious financial trouble and was on the verge of folding. Whiteville car dealer Paul Williamson stepped in and led a group that bought the team and moved it to that growing town of over 4000 residents in mid–June. The Red Comets of the semi-pro Border Belt League had been very popular in Whiteville and town leaders jumped at the chance to bring true professional baseball to town. Geographically, the move made sense as Whiteville was located roughly halfway between league members Lumberton and Wilmington. The town also fit well with the league's name; in 1950, Columbus County, of which Whiteville was the seat, had a reported 25,000 acres planted with tobacco.

Whiteville's Legion Memorial Field, built in 1947, became the new home of the ball club and the team name was changed to the Tobacconists. The new venue did pose a challenge to players: the outfield wall was nine feet high. It took two months of league play before a player (Pete Ethier of Lumberton) finally hit a ball over it.

The Tobs, as they were often called, began play in their new home on June 16. Taking the mound in that first game was something of a local celebrity. Whiteville native Charlie Ripple was a star lefthander for Wake Forest College before the war. He eventually worked his way up to the Philadelphia Phillies where he spent parts of three seasons. Out of contract in 1950, Ripple signed on with Whiteville when it was announced the town was getting a team. He struck out 12 Lumberton Auctioneers in his debut but took the loss, 4–5.

Whiteville's Shamrock Denning carried the league's most potent bat. He ended up winning the batting title with a .374 average and led

Part I

CLASS D

OFFICIAL NOTICE OF DISPOSITION OF PLAYER'S CONTRACT AND SERVICES

National Association of Professional Baseball Leagues

MAIL ONE NOTICE AT ONCE TO:
(1) President National Association.
(2) President of your League.
(3) Hand one to player. (If not possible, mail copy to player by registered mail.)
(4) Retain one copy for your files.

_____April 18th, 1950_____
(Date)

TO PLAYER___Clarence Condit, Jr._____. You are hereby officially notified of the following disposition of your contract:

Your contract has this date been conditionally assigned to the Durham Baseball Club of the Carolina League.

___Dunn-Erwin Baseball___ Club ___Tobacco State___ League

By ___[signature]___   ___Secty & Treas,___ (Title)

(CLUB WILL SELECT APPROPRIATE STATEMENT FROM LIST BELOW AND TYPE OR PRINT ENTIRE STATEMENT ABOVE)

DO NOT WRITE IN BOX

(a) You are released outright and unconditionally.
(b) Your contract has this date been assigned outright to the ___(Club Name)___ Club of the ___(League Name)___ League.
(c) Your contract has this date been conditionally assigned to the ___(Club Name)___ Club of the ___(League Name)___ League.
(d) Your contract has this date been optionally assigned to the ___(Club Name)___ Club of the ___(League Name)___ League.
(e) Your contract has this date been returned to the ___(Club Name)___ Club of the ___(League Name)___ League.
(f) Your contract has this date been assigned to the ___(Club Name)___ Club of the ___(League Name)___ League, subject to the option of ___(Club Name)___ Club of the ___(League Name)___ League.
(g) The right to recall your contract has this date been cancelled by the ___(Club Name)___ Club of the ___(League Name)___ League.
(h) Your contract has this date been recalled by the ___(Club Name)___ Club of the ___(League Name)___ League.

DO NOT WRITE IN BOX

RECEIPT

_____
(Date)

RECEIPT OF COPY OF THIS OFFICIAL NOTICE IS ACKNOWLEDGED

_____
(Player)

Place X in box if player is sent copy by REGISTERED mail.   [X] PLAYER SENT COPY OF THIS OFFICIAL NOTICE BY REGISTERED MAIL.

Form '06—11 49

Official Notice of Disposition of Player's Contract and Services dated April 18, 1950, conditionally assigning Clarence Condit, Jr., of the Dunn-Erwin Baseball Club to the Durham Baseball Club. After winning 20 games for the Dunn-Erwin Twins in 1949, Condit doubtless attracted the attention of many higher-level clubs. The move to the Durham Bulls in the Class B Carolina League was a big promotion but–perhaps due to injury–Condit posted only a 1–2 record. He was out of baseball after the 1950 season (courtesy Bart Swarr).

6. 1950: Newcomers and Attendance Struggles

in hits with 176. The rightfielder also drove in 95 runs, scored 87, and walked 98 times. Though never a power hitter, Denning was perhaps the league's best run-producer as well as one of the loop's biggest stars for all five seasons of its existence. He played two more seasons after the Tobacco State League folded, the first with Goldsboro in the Coastal Plain League, where he hit .341 in 1951. Signing with Fayetteville in 1952, Denning moved up to the Class B Carolina League. Despite the stiffer completion, he still hit .305 with 30 doubles.

Third baseman Hoggie Miller, who had been with the Dunn-Erwin team since 1946, also had a good season after the move to Whiteville. The he batted .321 with 80 RBIs, the highlight of his season, had to be accomplishing the rare feat of turning an unassisted triple play. One of the Tobacco State League's most consistent hitters, Miller played in

Unidentified members of the 1950 Sanford Spinners (*Raleigh News and Observer*/North Carolina State Archives).

Part I

The Lumberton

CLASS D TOBACCO STATE LEAGUE

Box 43
Lumberton, N. C.

April 27, 1950

Mr. George Trautman
Nat. Ass'n. Professional B.B. Leagues
720 E. Broad Street
Columbus 15, Ohio

Dear Sir:

   In reference to your letter of the 25th of April regarding George Somers.

   George Somers was issued a bus ticket to training headquarters at Melbourne, Florida. After being in camp a few days he developed a sore arm and left for home of his own free will.

   I have forwarded him $6.00 for meal money.

   Do you feel that we should reimburse him the difference between bus and train fare in view of the above circumstances.

           Yours truly,

           Russell B Filley
           Russell B. Filley
           Business Manager

Letter from the Lumberton Auctioneers to minor league president George Trautman regarding pitcher George Somers. After appearing in a few games for Lumberton at the end of the 1949 season, Somers gave up on his dream of a baseball career and went home from spring training in 1950 with a sore arm (courtesy Bart Swarr).

a total of 526 league games. In 1951 he signed with Shelby in the Western Carolina League, where he would finish in a tie for the league batting title. His .387 average was identical to that of teammate Oliver Bass, another Tobacco State League alumnus. In fact, Miller and Bass had been teammates previously at Dunn-Erwin in 1946.

  Despite the powerful bats, the Whiteville Tobs were hindered by a lack of reliable pitching and finished the season with a record of 39–92, leaving them in last place, 51 games out of first. Attendance did

6. 1950: Newcomers and Attendance Struggles

increase to 20,839 after the move to Whiteville, however, actually putting them ahead of second place Sanford, a much bigger town.

Attendance fell off dramatically in every league town in 1950 but the biggest problem was at Smithfield-Selma. In early July, team president Virgil Payne announced that if attendance didn't pick up the team would be moved to Jacksonville, Henderson or Bennettsville in South Carolina. Said Payne in an interview with the *Wilmington Morning Star*, "In my opinion we are not large enough to support it. For the past two or three weeks we have drawn only 500 to 600 persons per game. That is not quite enough to carry it since we depend entirely on the gate."

The threat of losing the team worked temporarily and attendance was up for a few games but it wasn't enough. On July 22, the Johnston County sheriff seized the assets of the Leafs including their uniforms, bats, batting cage and bus due to non-payment on a debt. The team was then forced to play their games wearing their opponents extra set of uniforms. Shortly thereafter, the team turned over its franchise to the league in hopes that a new owner could be found. The league hoped to find a local owner and a meeting was held at Smithfield's courthouse to gauge interest. Unfortunately, no deal could be worked out. Reports claimed the team might be relocated to Aberdeen in Moore County but that move that never happened.

While searching for a new ownership group, the league operated the club and designated it as "Orphan Annies" (a moniker given to teams without a home) and forced them to play all of their games on the road. When no one came forward to rescue the club they withdrew from the league for good after the August 16 game. At the time of their demise the Leafs had played 111 games and their record stood at 49–62. The team's star player was again outfielder Dick Woodard, who drove in 79 runs, drew 104 bases on balls and batted .351, third highest average in the league. He joined the Raleigh Caps of the Carolina League for the remainder of the season while manager and first baseman Marvin Lorenz (.301, 91 RBIs), named to the league All-Star team, signed on to guide Clinton for the final three weeks.

The demise of the Smithfield club left the league with an odd number of teams for the final weeks of the season, meaning every game day, one club was idle. In an attempt to make up for lost revenue, some

STATEMENT OF CLUB OWNERSHIP AND AFFILIATIONS

The **Lumberton Baseball** Club, of the **Tobacco State** League, in compliance with Major-Minor Rule 20 (2), hereby certifies:

1. This Club and its officials, employes, stockholders and owners are NOT in any manner or to any extent interested, directly or indirectly, in the ownership or operations of any other Major or Minor League clubs, except as follows:

(A) *Ownerships*: (For example: "This Club (or **Roy Dissinger**, president of this Club) owns **50** shares of **100** total shares of the **Greenville Baseball Club**, of **Coastal Plain** League.) (*If no ownership, so state*)

(B) *Other interests*: (For example: "This club has working agreements with the following clubs" — naming them). (*If none, so state*.)

None

This certificate is executed and filed upon the basis of careful and complete examination and investigation of the certified facts by the undersigned, and with full knowledge that if this certificate is deliberately false in respect to any material fact above certified, there will be imposed a minimum fine of $1000 (if filed by a Major League Club) or $500 (if filed by a Minor League Club), any players involved will be declared free agents, and the official or employe responsible for the false statement will be placed on the ineligible list.

Executed at **Lumberton, N.C.**, **May 18**, 1950

Lumberton Baseball Club

By **John A. Cote**
Business Manager (Title)

STATE OF **North Carolina**
COUNTY OF **Robeson** } ss

John A. Cote, being first duly sworn, on oath deposes and says that he is **Business Mgr** (Official Title) and chief operating officer of the _____ Club, of the _____ League; that he has carefully read the foregoing certificate, particularly the concluding paragraph thereof; that he has executed said certificate upon the basis of careful and complete examination and investigation of the facts and matters therein certified; and that said certificate is in every respect a true and complete statement of all agreements, undertakings, pledges, relations, connections and understandings of every kind and nature, verbal or written, confidential or promulgated, of said Club and its officials, employes, stockholders and owners, with all other Major or Minor League Clubs, and the officials, employes, stockholders and owners thereof, directly or indirectly affecting players, managers, finances or operations of said Club and of such other Major or Minor League clubs, as known to, examined and investigated by affiant.

Subscribed and sworn to before me this **18** day of **May**, 1950.

Notary Public in and for the County and State aforesaid.
My Com Ex 10/24/51

(*If more space is needed, use reverse side of this sheet*)

Document signed by Lumberton owner Roy Dissinger certifying that he also owned a half-interest in the Greenville, North Carolina, club of the Coastal Plain League.

6. 1950: Newcomers and Attendance Struggles

clubs scheduled exhibition games on their free days. On August 22, Wilmington took on a team of All-Stars from the local semi-pro Cape Fear League. The Pirates prevailed, 9–3, over a team that featured several former Tobacco State League alumni.

As the season drew to a close, the Lumberton Auctioneers were locked in a battle for the pennant with Sanford's Spinners. With only three games remaining to be played the two teams were tied in the league standings. Lumberton prevailed in the end, however, and won the league by one-and-a-half games with a 92–43 record.

In the first round of the 1950 playoffs, pennant-winning Lumberton was matched up with fourth-place Rockingham, a team they finished 27 and-a-half games ahead of in the regular season. Surprisingly, Rockingham came away with a four games to two series victory, the final game going 17 innings before the Eagles pulled out a 7–6 victory. Ace Johnny Lagan took over on the mound for Lumberton in the tenth and the native of Bloomfield, Conn., who had been a workhorse all season with over 240 innings pitched, held the Eagles in check. He finally conceded in the 17th when he gave up a single to Billy Duffy, who then scored the winning run when Jim Fister followed with a double.

The other semi-final saw Sanford easily sweep Red Springs, four games to none. In the finals Rockingham again upset the favored team as they defeated Sanford in a hard-fought series that went the full seven games.

Final Standings

Club	W	L	Pct.	GB	Attend.
Lumberton	92	43	.682	—	42,796
Sanford	90	44	.672	1.5	19,686
Red Springs	68	61	.527	21	26,198
Rockingham	63	69	.477	27.5	31,806
Clinton	61	72	.459	30	29,060
Wilmington	56	75	.427	34	35,950
Whiteville	39	92	.298	51	20,839
*Smithfield-Selma	49	62	.441	NA	19,369

*Disbanded August 16

• 7 •

Requiem for a League

With the demise of the Smithfield franchise, the Tobacco State League was left with an awkward situation. It would be nearly impossible to carry on with an odd number of teams so either another team had to quit the league or a new member had to be found. The latter proposition would have proved difficult since every team in the league reportedly lost money in 1950. The situation was resolved in December, however, when representatives of the Sanford Spinners announced that their franchise could no longer continue to operate.

Six teams were left to continue in 1951 and team leaders met on January 28 to decide their plan of action. Already suffering from financial losses and faced with a looming player shortage due to the United States' growing involvement in the Korean War, there was uncertainty as to whether or not the league should continue. Because of these factors, Red Springs business manager Tom Cope introduced the idea of suspending operations for one season. A vote was held and while Whiteville and Rockingham voted to play, Wilmington, Clinton, Lumberton, and Red Springs were all in favor of the hiatus idea. A statement issued by league president Arthur Moore read: "We hope to resume operations again in 1952. Each member has paid his fee to protect territorial rights for 1951. The league merely suspends baseball for one year."

The Cincinnati Reds has already named veteran catcher Mike Blazo as Wilmington manager for 1951 but they shifted him to their Appalachian League club in Welch, West Virginia. Other players from Wilmington and Red Springs were also assigned to other clubs within the Reds' and Athletics' organizations. Lumberton players were part of Roy Dissinger's small group of minor league clubs and were dispersed

7. Requiem for a League

among them. The remaining independent clubs were given several weeks to sell their players as they could; if that wasn't possible, then the players would become free agents.

When the decision was announced, there was disappointment in league towns but not surprise. Wanting to continue on in the game but at a level with less of a financial burden, most of the league members returned to semi-pro baseball. In 1951, teams from Whiteville, Red Springs, Wilmington (Spofford Spinners) and Rockingham (Safie Rockets) entered teams in the semi-pro Eastern Carolina League. They joined with clubs from Bladenboro and the South Carolina town of McColl to form a six-team loop. Most teams were textile mill-sponsored.

Wilmington, on the other hand, unsuccessfully pursued membership into the Coastal Plain League. Even though the club had voted for the suspension of play in the Tobacco State League, team leaders tried to secure a place in what was considered an even more advanced professional league.

Though it was intended to just be temporary, the decision to suspend play proved to be permanent. At a director's meeting in November 1951 only two clubs, Red Springs and Clinton, committed to playing in 1952. Rockingham, on the other hand, reported loses of over $20,000 in 1950 and stated they could not possibly continue without a major league working agreement. In the end, it was decided that it just wasn't feasible to field teams at the professional level again.

It wasn't long before league name was revived for another semi-pro circuit. Much like the years before the war, it featured four to six teams and league membership often changed. That Tobacco State League carried on in one form or another until at least 1960. Some of the same towns that had been part of the Class D league were still involved at the end. The 1959 lineup included Angier, Fuquay Springs, Smithfield and Goldsboro, long a member of the neighboring Class D Coastal Plain League. Some of the same names from the glory years were also still involved: Smithfield's roster in 1959 included Ray Hardee, Virgil Payne and Amby Foote. In true semi-pro fashion, the local stars still turned out to play the game they loved.

In the Cape Fear League, a Wilmington-area semi-pro circuit, Johnie Edens (whose true career was as a construction engineer with the U.S. Army Corps of Engineers) could be found managing and pitching

Part I

for the Seagate Gators in the late '50s. He wasn't the only former Wilmington Pirate in the league; Freddy Townsend often took the mound for the Greenfield Tigers.

At times Whiteville also fielded a team in the semi-pro Border Belt League, as did Lumberton. As the name implies, that league featured teams from along the North-South Carolina border including Bladenboro, NC, and Dillon, SC. Though they didn't have the same fan support or the same level of play, the various semi-pro leagues of the region still provided area fans with baseball entertainment.

With the Class D Tobacco State League's official demise, the smaller towns of southeastern North Carolina were left without professional baseball, most of them forever. The only Tobacco State League towns to ever have baseball at that level again have been Wilmington, Fayetteville, and Red Springs.

1954 Fayetteville Hilanders of the Class B Carolina League (courtesy Bill Fowler).

7. Requiem for a League

Wilmington went more than forty years without a team until a homeless franchise in the AA Southern League moved to town for two seasons. For the 1995 and '96 seasons, the Port City Roosters, affiliates of the Seattle Mariners, played at UNC-Wilmington's Brooks Field before moving on to a permanent home in Mobile, Ala. In 2001, a South Atlantic League franchise, the Wilmington Waves, called the city home for one season but moved to Georgia when their hopes for a new stadium were dashed. Since 1997, the city has been home to the Wilmington Sharks, a member of the Coastal Plain League. That league, which bears the name of the old Class D league from the region, is comprised of top college players from around the country. The Wilmington club plays at Legion Stadium, the same ballpark–though much renovated and renamed–that its Tobacco State League predecessor used.

Fayetteville remained in baseball for several seasons after leaving the Tobacco State League. A team representing the city played through the 1956 season in the Carolina League before it, too, succumbed to poor attendance and financial difficulties. Finally in 1987 a new team, the Fayetteville Generals, was formed to play in the Class A South Atlantic League. Later named the Cape Fear Crocs, it lasted through the 2000 season, when the club was sold and moved to New Jersey. In 2001, Fayetteville was granted a franchise in the Coastal Plain League, one of the nation's top summer leagues for college players. Named the Swampdogs, the team has featured several top college players who have gone on to reach the major leagues, including reliever David Aardsma and slugger Mark Reynolds.

In 1969 the owner of the Carolina League's Wilson Tobs, a Minnesota Twins farm club, decided to move his team in search of better attendance. As an experiment, Red Springs, roughly 100 miles southwest, was chosen as the team's new home; the owner wanted to see if smaller towns with less competition for the entertainment dollar could support a team. Though attendance did nearly double, it was decided that it just wasn't feasible to have the team in such a small town and it was moved after that one season.

PART II

• 8 •

Managers

As was common in the lower minor leagues, managers in the Tobacco State League often came and went with surprising frequency. Sometimes this was because of conflicts with team ownership, and sometimes it was merely a matter of being offered more money elsewhere. Some managers were veterans hired specifically to guide the team while others were just players forced to fill in for interim periods. Some managers of clubs that were part of a farm system were assigned by the major league affiliate. Most managers, with a few exceptions, also served as players while guiding their teams.

1946

Dunn-Erwin

JAMES K. "JIMMY" GUINN
B: 1915
Professional debut: 1936
Teams played for: Americus Cardinals, Shelby Nationals, Charlotte Hornets, Greenville (SC) Spinners, Dunn-Erwin Twins, Sanford Spinners, Lumberton Auctioneers, Enterprise Boll Weevils

L. ALTON STEPHENSON
B: 1/16/11 Johnston County, North Carolina
Professional debut: 1937
Teams played for: Mayodan Senators, Dunn-Erwin Twins

C. DWIGHT WALL
B: 11/27/12 North Carolina

Part II

Played for Wake Forest College (Class of '36)
Professional debut: 1937
Teams played for: Snow Hill Billies, Greenville (NC) Greenies, Dunn-Erwin Twins

Wilmington

STANLEY P. "MICKEY" KATKAVECK
B: 1916 Manchester, Connecticut
Professional debut: 1936
Teams played for: Columbus (Ga.) Red Birds, Monessen Cardinals, Union City Greyhounds, Jacksonville Jax, Portsmouth (Ohio) Red Birds, Sacramento Solons, Asheville Tourists, Mobile Shippers, Hartford Bees, Wilmington Pirates, Albany (Ga.) Cardinals, Waycross Bears

JOHN E. WILBOURNE
B: 9/21/19 North Carolina
Professional debut: 1941
Teams played for: Salisbury (Md.) Cardinals, Greenville (SC) Spinners, Sanford Spinners, Wilmington Pirates, Montgomery Rebels, Rocky Mount Rocks

GUS BRITTAIN
B: 11/29/09 Wilmington, North Carolina
Professional debut: 1932
Teams played for: Wilmington

Wilmington native Gus Brittain began his professional career with his hometown Pirates in 1932. He spent two and a half seasons with the club before embarking on a career that saw him play for more than a dozen clubs across the country. The high point of Brittain's career came in 1937 when he spent the season as reserve catcher for the Cincinnati Reds. He was called on to pinch-hit twice during that season and started one game behind the plate. He returned to Wilmington to manage the Pirates for parts of the 1946 and '49 seasons (author's collection).

8. Managers—1946

Pirates, Beckley Black Knights, Tulsa Oilers, Fort Worth Cats, Cincinnati Reds, Trenton Senators, Greenville (SC) Spinners, Syracuse Chiefs, Springfield Nationals, Salisbury (Md.) Cardinals, Rocky Mount Leafs, Montreal Royals, Lexington A's, Montgomery Rebels

Sanford

GAITHER W. RILEY
B: 1/2/10 North Carolina
Professional debut: 1937
Teams played for: Williamson Colts, Ayden Aces, Wilson Tobs, South Boston Wrappers, New Bern Bears, Sanford Spinners, Angier-Fuquay Springs Bulls, Smithfield-Selma Leafs, Dunn-Erwin Twins

ZEB S. HARRINGTON
B: 5/31/06 Chatham County, NC
Played at Elon College (Class of '31)
Professional debut: 1941
Teams played for: Sanford Spinners

No. 125 PAUL DUNLAP

Angier-Fuquay Springs

J. PAUL DUNLAP
B: 4/4/13 Silver City, North Carolina
Played at the University of North Carolina (Class of '34)
Professional debut: 1934
Teams played for: Columbia

UNC graduate and Siler City native Paul Dunlap began his professional career in 1934 and quickly rose to the high minor leagues. He is seen here on a baseball card from Montreal, the top farm club of the Pittsburgh Pirates, where he played in 1937 and '38. After being replaced as manager of Angier in 1946 he signed with Portsmouth, Virginia, of the Piedmont League (author's collection).

Part II

Sandlappers, Asheville Tourists, Binghamton Triplets, Norfolk Tars, Indianapolis Indians, Montreal Royals, Birmingham Barons, Milwaukee Brewers, Wilkes-Barre Barons, Williamsport Grays, Wilmington (Del.) Blue Rocks, Albany (NY) Senators, Hartford Bees, Portsmouth (Va.) Cubs, Angier-Fuquay Springs Bulls, New Brunswick/Kingston Hubs

HERBERT C. "DOC" SMITH
B: 1898
Professional debut: 1920
Teams played for: Greensboro Patriots, New Orleans Pelicans, Atlanta Crackers, Little Rock Travelers, Fort Worth Panthers, Wichita Falls Spudders, Tulsa Oilers, Muskogee Chiefs, Clarksburg Generals, New Bern Bears

Smithfield-Selma

MICHAEL "MICKEY" BALLA
B: 6/4/19 Wilkes-Barre, Pennsylvania
Professional debut: 1937
Teams played for: Goldsboro Goldbugs, Martinsville Manufacturers, Lynchburg Senators, Allentown Cardinals, Scranton Miners, Albany Senators, Hagerstown Owls, Smithfield-Selma Leafs, Dunn-Erwin Twins, Franklin Cubs

GAITHER W. RILEY
B: 1/2/10 North Carolina
Professional debut: 1937
Teams played for: Williamson Colts, Ayden Aces, Wilson Tobs, South Boston Wrappers, New Bern Bears, Sanford Spinners, Angier-Fuquay Springs Bulls, Smithfield-Selma Leafs, Dunn-Erwin Twins

Clinton

MARVIN PETER LORENZ
B: 9/12/18 Illinois
Professional debut: 1937

8. Managers—1946

Teams played for: Clinton (Iowa) Owls, Tallahassee Capitals, Bluefield Blue-Grays, Angier-Fuquay Springs Bulls, Raleigh Capitals, Clinton-Sampson Blues

WILLIE E. DUKE
B: 7/5/09 Franklinton, North Carolina
Played for North Carolina State College (Class of '33)
Professional debut: 1934
Teams played for: Nashville Volunteers, Jackson Mississippians, Memphis Chickasaws, Minneapolis Millers, Atlanta Crackers, New Orleans Pelicans, Little Rock Travelers, Elmira Pioneers, Wilmington (Del.) Blue Rocks, Portsmouth (Va.) Cubs, Knoxville Smokies, Clinton Blues, Durham Bulls, Winston-Salem Cardinals, Danville Leafs, Rockingham Eagles, Greensboro Patriots, Raleigh Capitals

NICHOLAS L. "NICK" RHABE
B: 6/10/16 Detroit, Michigan
Professional debut: 1937
Teams played for: Mayodan Senators, Leaksville-Spray-Draper Triplets, Cooleemee Weavers, Durham bulls, Lynchburg Grays, Harrisonburg Turks, Williamston Martins, Salem-Roanoke Friends, Richmond Colts, Petersburg Rebels, Elmira Pioneers, Pulaski Counts, Winston-Salem Twins, Charlotte Hornets, Utica Braves, Hartford Bees, Newark Bears, Indianapolis Indians, Los Angeles Angels, Portland Beavers, Tarboro Tars, Concord Weavers, Pensacola Fliers, Gadsden Pilots, Fayetteville Scotties, Hickory Rebels, Statesville Owls, Clinton-Sampson Blues

VAN LINGLE MUNGO
B: 6/8/11 Pageland, South Carolina
Professional debut: 1929
Teams played for: Charlotte Hornets, Fayetteville Highlanders, Winston-Salem Twins, Hartford Senators, Brooklyn Robins, Brooklyn Dodgers, Montreal Royals, Minneapolis Millers, New York Giants, Clinton Blues

Part II

1947

The professional career of South Carolina native Van Mungo, who managed Clinton for parts of the 1946 and 47 seasons, began in Fayetteville in 1929. He made his big league debut with the Brooklyn Dodgers in 1931, went on win 120 games over 14 seasons and was named to three-time All-Star teams (courtesy Frank Dennison).

Sanford

ZEB S. HARRINGTON
B: 5/31/06 Chatham County, NC
Played at Elon College (Class of '31)
Professional debut: 1941
Teams played for: Sanford Spinners

Lumberton

CHARLES FRED "RED" LUCAS
B: 4/28/02 Columbia, Tennessee
Professional debut: 1921
Teams played for: Nashville Volunteers, Rome, Jackson Red Sox, Greenwood Indians, San Antonio Bears, New York Giants, Boston Braves, Seattle Indians, Cincinnati Reds, Pittsburgh Pirates, Chattanooga Lookouts, Montreal Royals, Newport Canners

Wilmington

NATHAN HARDY "NATE" ANDREWS
B: 9/30/13 Pembroke, North Carolina
Professional debut: 1934
Teams played for: Greensboro Patriots, Columbus (Ohio) Red Birds, Asheville Tourists, Wilkes-Barre Barons, Rochester Red Wings, Sacramento Solons, St. Louis Cardinals, St. Paul Saints, Cleveland Indians, Milwaukee Brewers, Syracuse Chiefs, Boston Braves, Wilmington Pirates, Cincinnati Reds, New York Giants, Florence Steelers

8. Managers—1947

Dunn-Erwin

EARL JACKSON "JACK" BELL
B: 1917
Professional debut: 1940
Teams played for: Kannapolis Towelers, Knoxville Smokies, Mobile Bears, Wilkes-Barre Barons, Wilmington (Del.) Blue Rocks, Norfolk Tars, Butler Yankees, Dunn-Erwin Twins, Clinton Blues, Jenkins Cavaliers

WILLIAM HUNT "BILL" AVERETTE, JR.
B: 1908 Oxford, North Carolina
Played for NC State College (Class of 1931)
Professional debut: 1931
Teams played for: Greensboro Patriots, Richmond Colts, Wilmington Pirates, Knoxville Smokies, New Bern Bears, Williamston Martins, Kinston Eagles, Bluefield Blue-Grays

Nate Andrews, Wilmington's manager in 1947, grew up in the Robeson County town of Rowland and was a star pitcher at Presbyterian Junior College in Laurinburg and the University of North Carolina in Chapel Hill. In the major leagues, he pitched for five teams over eight years and won 41 games (author's collection).

Warsaw

JAMES R. MILNER
B: 1919
Professional debut: 1938
Teams played for: Mooresville Moors, Leaksville-Spray-Draper Triplets, Fort Pierce Bombers, Miami Beach Flamingos, Dothan Browns, Richmond Colts, Warsaw Red Sox, Lexington A's, Concord Sports

Part II

Clinton

ROBERT HALL
B: ?
Professional debut: —
Teams played for: —

VAN LINGLE MUNGO
B: 6/8/11 Pageland, South Carolina
Professional debut: 1929
Teams played for: Charlotte Hornets, Fayetteville Highlanders, Winston-Salem Twins, Hartford Senators, Brooklyn Robins, Brooklyn Dodgers, Montreal Royals, Minneapolis Millers, New York Giants, Clinton Blues

SURVERN EDWARD WRIGHT
B: 5/25/19 South Carolina
Professional debut: 1939
Teams played for: Shelby Cardinals, Lexington Indians, Kannapolis Towelers, Wilmington Blue Rocks, Saginaw Athletics, Spartanburg Peaches, Clinton Blues, Rock Hill Chiefs, Chattanooga Lookouts, Charlotte Hornets

Red Springs

MANUEL CARSON "RED" NORRIS
B: 2/10/10 Whiteville, NC
Professional debut: 1937
Teams played for: Winston-Salem Twins, Elmira Pioneers, Montreal Royals

Smithfield-Selma

MICHAEL "MICKEY" BALLA
B: 6/4/19 Wilkes-Barre, Pennsylvania
Professional debut: 1937
Teams played for: Goldsboro Goldbugs, Martinsville Manufacturers, Lynchburg Senators, Allentown Cardinals, Scranton Miners, Albany Senators, Hagerstown Owls, Smithfield-Selma Leafs, Dunn-Erwin Twins, Franklin Cubs

8. Managers—1948

JOSEPH FRANCIS "JOE" EONTA
B: 1921 Pennsylvania
Professional debut: 1942
Teams played for: Sanford Spinners, Kinston Eagles, Smithfield-Selma Leafs

1948

Sanford

ZEB S. HARRINGTON
B: 5/31/06 Chatham County, North Carolina
Played at Elon College (Class of '31)
Professional debut: 1941
Teams played for: Sanford Spinners

Wilmington

JAMES C. "JIM" STATON
B: 1914
Professional debut: 1946
Teams played for: Wilmington Pirates

Red Springs

MANUEL CARSON "RED" NORRIS
B: 2/10/10 Whiteville, NC
Professional debut: 1937
Teams played for: Winston-Salem Twins, Elmira Pioneers, Montreal Royals

Most teams in the Tobacco State League changed managers every season, if not several times during the course of the season. The Sanford Spinners made only one managerial change in their five years in the league; they hired Zeb Harrington in midseason 1946 and he remained at the helm through the 1950 campaign (*Raleigh News and Observer*/North Carolina State Archives).

Part II

Smithfield-Selma

SAMUEL WOODY "SAM" NARRON
B: 8/25/13 Middlesex, North Carolina
Professional debut: 1934
Teams played for: Martinsville Manufacturers, Albany (Ga.) Travelers, St. Louis Cardinals, Sacramento Solons, Asheville Tourists, Rochester Red Wings, Houston Buffaloes, St. Paul Saints, Mobile Bears, Smithfield-Selma Leafs, Montreal Royals

HORACE VIRGIL PAYNE
B: 7/31/13 Whitley Co., Kentucky
Professional debut: 1938
Teams played for: Pennington Gap Lee Bears, Elizabethton Betsy Red Sox, Pennington Gap Miners, Superior Blues, Greenville (NC) Greenies, Goldsboro Goldbugs, Smithfield-Selma Leafs

Warsaw

VERNE CECIL BLACKWELL
B: 10/20/17 Larned, Kansas
Professional debut: 1939
Teams played for: Americus Pioneers, Superior Blues, Greenville (NC) Greenies, Portsmouth Cubs, Rocky Mount Leafs, Warsaw Red Sox, Goldsboro Goldbugs

SAMUEL BRAXTON "SAM" GIBSON
B: 8/5/1899 King, North Carolina
Professional debut: 1923
Teams played for: Danville (Va.) Tobacconists, Asheville Tourists, Toronto Maple Leafs, Detroit Tigers, New York Yankees, San Francisco Seals, New

Warsaw manager Sam Gibson won 32 games in the major leagues but found his greatest success in the Pacific Coast League. The North Carolina native won at least 20 games six times for the San Francisco Seals (author's collection).

8. Managers—1948

York Giants, Portland Beavers, Oakland Oaks, Bremerton Bluejackets, Reidsville Luckies, Radford Rockets, Warsaw Red Sox, Griffin Pimientos

Clinton

MARVIN PETER LORENZ
B: 9/12/18 Illinois
Professional debut: 1937
Teams played for: Clinton (Iowa) Owls, Tallahassee Capitals, Bluefield Blue-Grays, Angier-Fuquay Springs Bulls, Raleigh Capitals, Clinton-Sampson Blues

Lumberton

CHARLES F. "CHARLIE" JAMIN
B: 5/15/17 Jersey City, New Jersey
Professional debut: 1939
Teams played for: Akron Yankees, Butler Yankees, Amsterdam Rugmakers, Statesville Cubs, Fayetteville Cubs, Lumberton Cubs, Rockingham Eagles

Dunn-Erwin

JOSEPH CARL McQUILLEN
B: 7/27/22 Strasburg, Virginia
Professional debut: 1941

Clinton manager Marvin Lorenz gives the ball to pitcher Billy Price in 1949. As a 20-year-old in 1940, Lorenz hit .341 for Bluefield but spent the next five seasons in the army, where he attained the rank of sergeant. He found a home in the Tobacco State League after the war and played for or managed three teams (*Raleigh News and Observer*/North Carolina State Archives).

Part II

Teams played for: Orlando Senators, Sanford (Fla.) Seminoles, Augusta Tigers, Mooresville Moors, Norfolk Tars, Lancaster Red Roses, Binghamton Triplets, Montgomery Rebels, Dallas Rebels, Dunn-Erwin Twins, Greenville (NC) Greenies, Federalsburg Feds, Oil City Refiners, Pulaski Counts, Franklin Kildees, Hannibal Stags, St. Hyacinthe A's

Edwin McLeod "Babe" Bost
B: 5/28/12 Harnett County, North Carolina
Played for Duke University (Class of 1932)
Professional debut: NA
Teams played for: NA

Gaither W. Riley
B: 1/2/10 North Carolina
Professional debut: 1937
Teams played for: Williamson Colts, Ayden Aces, Wilson Tobs, South Boston Wrappers, New Bern Bears, Sanford Spinners, Angier-Fuquay Springs Bulls, Smithfield-Selma Leafs, Dunn-Erwin Twins

1949

Dunn-Erwin

James Clifford "Jim" Staton
B: 1914
Professional debut: 1946
Teams played for: Wilmington Pirates

Red Springs

Manuel Carson "Red" Norris
B: 2/10/10 Whiteville, NC
Professional debut: 1937
Teams played for: Winston-Salem Twins, Elmira Pioneers, Montreal Royals

Lumberton

CHARLES FRED "RED" LUCAS
B: 4/28/02 Columbia, Tennessee
Professional debut: 1921
Teams played for: Nashville Volunteers, Rome, Jackson Red Sox, Greenwood Indians, San Antonio Bears, New York Giants, Boston Braves, Seattle Indians, Cincinnati Reds, Pittsburgh Pirates, Chattanooga Lookouts, Montreal Royals, Newport Canners

JAMES K. "JIMMY" GUINN
B: 1915
Professional debut: 1936
Teams played for: Americus Cardinals, Shelby Nationals, Charlotte Hornets, Greenville (SC) Spinners, Dunn-Erwin Twins, Sanford Spinners, Lumberton Auctioneers, Enterprise Boll Weevils

Sanford

ZEB S. HARRINGTON
B: 5/31/06 Chatham County, NC
Played at Elon College (Class of '31)
Professional debut: 1941
Teams played for: Sanford Spinners

Smithfield-Selma

HORACE VIRGIL PAYNE
B: 7/3/13 Whitley County, Kentucky
Professional debut: 1938
Teams played for: Pennington Gap Lee Bears, Elizabethton Betsy Red Sox, Pennington Gap Miners, Superior Blues, Greenville (NC) Greenies, Goldsboro Goldbugs, Smithfield-Selma Leafs

CLAUDE W. WEAVER
B: 1905
Professional debut: 1937
Teams played for: Mayodan Senators, Leaksville-Spray-Draper Triplets, Mayodan Millers, Burlington Bees, Lynchburg Cardinals,

Part II

Smithfield-Selma manager Paul Kluk poses with club vice president J.N. Williams during the 1949 season. Kluk, a Pennsylvania native, had been a catcher in the Boston Red Sox system before naval service during the war. After two seasons with Newport News in the Class B Piedmont League he signed with the Leafs for 1949. He retired from baseball after the season (*Raleigh News and Observer*/North Carolina State Archives).

Durham Bulls, Montreal Royals, St. Paul Saints, Chattanooga Lookouts, Milwaukee Brewers, Vicksburg Billies, Shreveport Sports, Smithfield-Selma Leafs, Lawrenceville Robins, Suffolk Goobers, Reidsville Luckies

PAUL PETER KLUK
B: 2/29/20 Hudson, Pennsylvania
Professional debut: 1941
Teams played for: Owensboro Oilers, Scranton Red Sox, Greensboro Red Sox, Roanoke Red Sox, Newport News Dodgers, Smithfield-Selma Leafs

Fayetteville

JAMES CECIL "ZIP" PAYNE
B: 4/9/08 Swepsonville, NC
Professional debut: 1929
Teams played for: Goldsboro Goldbugs, Columbia Comers, Wichita Aviators, Henderson Gamecocks, Mayodan Senators, Mayodan Millers, Bassett Furnituremakers, Leaksville-spray-Draper Triplets, Lynchburg Cardinals, Rochester Red Wings, Winston Salem Cardinals, Fayetteville Scotties

8. Managers—1949

JOSEPH CARL "JOE" ROSEBERRY
B: 1/19/23 Marion, Ohio
Professional debut: 1946
Teams played for: Marion (Ohio) Cardinals, Winston-Salem Cardinals, Fayetteville Scotties, Mount Airy Graniteers

NICHOLAS L. "NICK" RHABE
B: 6/10/16 Detroit, Michigan
Professional debut: 1937
Teams played for: Mayodan Senators, Leaksville-Spray-Draper Triplets, Cooleemee Weavers, Durham bulls, Lynchburg Grays, Harrisonburg Turks, Williamston Martins, Salem-Roanoke Friends, Richmond Colts, Petersburg Rebels, Elmira Pioneers, Pulaski Counts, Winston-Salem Twins, Charlotte Hornets, Utica Braves, Hartford Bees, Newark Bears, Indianapolis Indians, Los Angeles Angels, Portland Beavers, Tarboro Tars, Concord Weavers, Pensacola Fliers, Gadsden Pilots, Fayetteville Scotties, Hickory Rebels, Statesville Owls, Clinton-Sampson Blues

JOHN R. HELMS
B: 1923
Professional debut: 1939
Teams played for: Spartanburg Spartans, Nashville Volunteers, Mobile Bears, Fayetteville Cubs, West Palm Beach Indians, Fayetteville Scotties, Clinton-Sampson Blues, Trois-Rivieres Phillies

The playing career of Cecil "Zip" Payne began with Goldsboro in 1929 and ended at Fayetteville two decades later. Shown here in the uniform of the Tri-City Triplets (Leaksville, NC) of 1940, Payne rose as high as Rochester in the International League. After three years as player-manager with Winston-Salem in the Carolina League he signed on to skipper Fayetteville in 1949. When a serious ankle injury ended his on-field career, the 41-year-old Payne felt he could no longer fulfill his role as a playing manager so he resigned in June (author's collection).

Part II

Clinton

MARVIN PETER LORENZ
B: 9/12/18 Illinois
Professional debut: 1937
Teams played for: Clinton (Iowa) Owls, Tallahassee Capitals, Bluefield Blue-Grays, Angier-Fuquay Springs Bulls, Raleigh Capitals, Clinton-Sampson Blues

Wilmington

ALBERT F. "AB" TIEDEMANN
B: 2/5/18 Baltimore, Maryland
Professional debut: 1943
Teams played for: Baltimore Orioles, Richmond Colts, Wilmington Pirates

JOHNIE ALTON EDENS
B: 7/13/21 Wilmington, North Carolina
Professional debut: 1946
Teams played for: Wilmington Pirates

GUS BRITTAIN
B: 11/29/09 Wilmington, North Carolina
Professional debut: 1932
Teams played for: Wilmington Pirates, Beckley Black Knights, Tulsa Oilers, Fort Worth Cats, Cincinnati Reds, Trenton Senators, Greenville (SC) Spinners, Syracuse Chiefs, Springfield Nationals, Salisbury (Md.) Cardinals, Rocky Mount Leafs, Montreal Royals, Lexington A's, Montgomery Rebels

HARGROVE BELLAMY "HOGGIE" DAVIS
B: 11/12/17 New Hanover County, North Carolina
Professional debut: 1941
Teams played for: Valdosta Trojans, Troy Dodgers, Tuskegee Airmen, Montgomery Rebels, Wilmington Pirates, Savannah Indians, Red Springs Red Robins

1950

Lumberton

JOHN STREZA
B: 4/7/20 Alliance, Ohio
Professional debut: 1938
Teams played for: Union springs Red Birds, Williamson Red Birds, Mobile Shippers, Houston Buffaloes, Columbus (Ga.) Red Birds, Durham Bulls, Shreveport Sports, Miami Beach Flamingos, Florence Steelers, Lumberton Auctioneers, Albany Senators, Harlan Smokies, Greenville (NC) Robins, Centralia Zeros, Fort Lauderdale Braves, Key West Conchs, Fort Walton Beach Jets, Wilkes-Barre Barons, Wausau Lumberjacks

Ohio native John Streza began his pro career in 1938 and was at Class B Columbus when the war interrupted his career. After four years of military service, the 6'3", 220-pound first baseman signed with the Durham Bulls of the Carolina League in 1946 and hit .299. After two good years with Florence in the Class B Tri-State League, Streza was lured to Lumberton with an offer to be playing-manager. It proved to be a good move for both club and manager as Streza batted .320 and guided the Auctioneers to the pennant with a 92–43 record (author's collection).

Sanford

ZEB S. HARRINGTON
B: 5/31/06 Chatham County, NC
Played at Elon College (Class of '31)
Professional debut: 1941
Teams played for: Sanford Spinners

Red Springs

ROBERT STERLING "DUCKY" DETWEILER
B: 2/5/19 Trumbauersville, Pennsylvania
Professional debut: 1939

Teams played for: Federalsburg A's, Wilmington (Del.) Blue Rocks, Bridgeport Bees, Boston Braves, Indianapolis Indians, Rochester Red Wings, Boston Braves, Red Springs Red Robins, Cordele A's, Salisbury Reds, Lexington Indians, Fayetteville A's

Rockingham

EARL JACKSON "JACK" BELL
B: 1917
Professional debut: 1940
Teams played for: Kannapolis Towelers, Knoxville Smokies, Mobile Bears, Wilkes-Barre Barons, Wilmington (Del.) Blue Rocks, Norfolk Tars, Butler Yankees, Dunn-Erwin Twins, Clinton Blues, Jenkins Cavaliers

Bob "Ducky" Detweiler made it into a handful of games for the Boston Braves before wartime service cost him three years of baseball. After the war he signed on with the Philadelphia Athletics organization. The A's saw Detweiler's potential as a playing manager and eventually assigned him to guide five teams, the second of which was Red Springs in 1950 (author's collection).

CECIL WASHINGTON "TURKEY" TYSON
B: 12/6/14 Wilson County, North Carolina
Professional debut: 1938
Teams played for: Tallahassee Capitals, Greenwood Dodgers, Winston-Salem Twins, Martinsville Manufacturers, Hagerstown Owls, Trenton Packers, Utica Blue Sox, Philadelphia Phillies, Durham Bulls, Rocky Mount Leafs, Raleigh Capitals, Lumberton Auctioneers, Rockingham Eagles, Colonial Heights-Petersburg Generals

8. Managers—1950

Clinton

ALVIN CLIFTON KLUTTZ
B: 1/13/22 Salisbury, North Carolina
Professional debut: 1941
Teams played for: Springfield Cardinals, Asheville Tourists, Lynchburg Cardinals, Houston Buffaloes, Carthage Cardinals, Omaha Cardinals, Richmond Colts, Kingsport Cherokees, Clinton-Sampson Blues, High Point-Thomasville Hi-Toms

NICHOLAS L. "NICK" RHABE
B: 6/10/16 Detroit, Michigan
Professional debut: 1937
Teams played for: Mayodan Senators, Leaksville-Spray-Draper Triplets, Cooleemee Weavers, Durham bulls, Lynchburg Grays, Harrisonburg Turks, Williamston Martins, Salem-Roanoke Friends, Richmond Colts, Petersburg Rebels, Elmira Pioneers, Pulaski Counts, Winston-Salem Twins, Charlotte Hornets, Utica Braves, Hartford Bees, Newark Bears, Indianapolis Indians, Los Angeles Angels, Portland Beavers, Tarboro Tars, Concord Weavers, Pensacola Fliers, Gadsden Pilots, Fayetteville Scotties, Hickory Rebels, Statesville Owls, Clinton-Sampson Blues

NICHOLAS "NICK" PURCHIA
B: 5/7/25 New York
Professional debut: 1949
Teams played for: Clinton-Sampson Blues, Richmond Colts

MARVIN PETER LORENZ
B: 9/12/18 Illinois
Professional debut: 1937
Teams played for: Clinton (Iowa) Owls, Tallahassee Capitals, Bluefield Blue-Grays, Angier-Fuquay Springs Bulls, Raleigh Capitals, Clinton-Sampson Blues

Wilmington

FRANK LOWELL "BULL" HAMONS
B: 1916 LaGrange, Georgia
Professional debut: 1937

Part II

Teams played for: New Bern Bears, Jacksonville Tars, Portsmouth Cubs, New Bern Bears, Concord Weavers, Sunbury Indians, Hagerstown Owls, Buffalo Bisons, Jamestown Falcons, New Orleans Pelicans, Syracuse Chiefs, Spartanburg Peaches, Tarboro Tars, Leaksville-Spray-Draper Triplets, Durham Bulls

DWIGHT EUGENE "RED" TEAGUE
B: 4/7/29 Alamance Co., North Carolina
Professional debut: 1947
Teams played for: Mount Airy Graniteers, Lockport Reds, Wilmington Pirates, Miami Sun Sox, Burlington-Graham Pirates

STEPHEN C. "STEVE" COLLINS
B: 1918
Professional debut: 1942
Teams played for: Burlington Bees, Rochester Red Wings, Knoxville Smokies, Mobile Bears, Toledo Mud hens, Atlanta Crackers, Kinston Eagles, Moultrie Cubs, Wilmington Pirates, Greenwood Tigers, Rocky Mount Leafs, New Bern Bears

Steve Collins, seen in the uniform of the Kinston team he managed in 1948 and '49, took over the reins of the Wilmington Pirates during the 1950 season. When the Tobacco State League foundered, he returned to the Coastal Plain League and skippered Rocky Mount in 1951 and New Bern in 1952 (author's collection).

Whiteville

JAMES CLIFFORD "JIM" STATON
B: 1914
Professional debut: 1946
Teams played for: Wilmington Pirates

8. Managers—1950

Smithfield-Selma

MARVIN PETER LORENZ
B: 9/12/18 Illinois
Professional debut: 1937
Teams played for: Clinton (Iowa) Owls, Tallahassee Capitals, Bluefield Blue-Grays, Angier-Fuquay Springs Bulls, Raleigh Capitals, Clinton-Sampson Blues

• 9 •

All-Star Selections

At the end of each season, the top player at each position was named to the official all-star team by league officials and managers.

In addition, all-star games were played in the middle of some seasons. The gate receipts from these games, as well as the special double headers on the Fourth of July and Labor Day, were pooled and split equally amongst all league members.

The league's first year saw a team representing the west (Sanford, Dunn-Erwin and Angier) face a team comprising players from the eastern part of the circuit (Smithfield-Selma, Clinton and Wilmington). The teams met at Clinton on July 16. The East, paced by the three RBIs of Bill Campau and strong pitching of George Brooks and Earl Mossor, defeated the West, 6–4.

In 1947, rather than have two all-star teams face each other, the league decided that the team in first place as of midnight on July 4

Opposite top: 1946 All-Star Teams: Angier-Fuquay Springs, Dunn-Erwin and Sanford: From left to right are (front row) Andrew Holliday, Phalti Shoffner, Shamrock Denning, Jimmy Guinn, Paul Crawford, Zeb Harrington (manager), Joe Nessing, Joe Mills, Ken Jackson and Paul Hunt; (back row) Doc Smith (coach), Marvin Lorenz, Ed Bass, Hank Nesselrode, Jim Taylor, Jim Stephenson, Jim House, Jim House, Howard Auman, Ray Hardee, Bob Pugh and Bruce Hedrick (courtesy late Howard Auman). *Opposite bottom:* Wilmington Clinton and Smithfield: From left to right are (front row) two unidentified, Mickey Balla, Gaither Riley, Willie Duke (manager), Earl Mossor, Griffin Staples, unidentified; Bill Campau, unidentified; (back row) Pete Howard, Dick Woodard, Hearn Robinson, three unidentified, Leo Niezgoda and unidentified. Unidentified players include John Larrieu, Andrew Cullen, Lonnie Smith, George Brooks, Bobby Keane, Andrew Poklemba, William Harrison, Roy Lamb, Bob Skinner, and Alex Daniels (courtesy Gaither Riley).

9. All-Star Selections

Part II

would face a team comprising select players from the other seven members. That leading team proved to be Sanford and the game was set for Monday, July 21, at 7:45 at Temple Park.

To face the Spinners, players were chosen by ballot by all the club managers. The line-up was:

Manager: Red Lucas (Lumberton)
Right-handed pitchers: Bob Spicer (Lumberton) and Suvern Wright (Clinton)
Left-handed pitcher: Richard Whitmire (Warsaw)
Catcher: Bill Kivett (Lumberton)
1B: Jim Milner (Warsaw)
2B: Jerry Cabaniss (Lumberton)
Shortstop: Pete Howard (Smithfield)
OF: Kenneth Jackson (Dunn-Erwin), Shamrock Denning (Dunn-Erwin) and Carl McQuillen (Dunn-Erwin)
3B: Ed Kukulka (Clinton)
Utility infielders: Micky Balla (Smithfield-Selma)

To assist Manager Lucas as coaches. President A.T. Moore named Nate Andrews of Wilmington, Red Norris of Red Springs, and Bill Averette of Dunn-Erwin. All eight of the league's umpires worked the All Star game.

Despite the potent line-up, Lucas' squad could not overcome the hometown team. An overflow crowd of 2700 saw the Spinners rally in the bottom of the eighth and then hold on for a 6–5 victory. Bill Stone got credit for the win.

In 1948 it was decided that no all-star game would be played but in 1949 the league decided to return to the format of two all-star teams, each representing four teams, playing each other. The game was played in Dunn on July 27 and a reported 2300 fans turned out to watch the South squad, which featured players from Clinton, Lumberton, Wilmington and Red Springs, defeat the North, 2–0. Clinton's Billy Price started on the mound for the South and teamed up with Ray Flaim of Lumberton and Bill Harrington of Red Springs for the shutout.

At the league meeting before the 1950 season, officials decided that teams would play special double-headers at mid-season rather than hold one all-star game.

9. All-Star Selections

ROSTER SOUTH			ALL STAR 1949 BOX SCORE							ROSTER NORTH		
Red Norris Mgr.		Red Springs	South	Ab	R	H	North	Ab	R	H	Jim Staten Mgr.	Dunn-Erwin
Balogh	ss	Lumberton	Balogh, ss 3	0	2		Snek 2b-3b 4	0	0		Haithcock ... of	Dunn-Erwin
Campbell	ss	Red Springs	Campbell, ss 1	0	0		Haithcock, ef 4	0	0		Miller ... 3b	Dunn-Erwin
Guinn	2b	Lumberton	Guinn 2b 4	2	0		Miller, 3b 2	0	1		Cooper ... p	Smithfield-Selma
Scrobola	of	Clinton	Scrobola, ef 2	0	0		Cooper, p 1	0	0		Smith ... p	Dunn-Erwin
Weineswki	of	Red Springs	Winewski, ef 2	0	0		Smith, p 2	0	0		Woodard ... of	Smithfield-Selma
Davis	of	Wilmington	Davis, rf 1	0	1		Woodard, rf 1	0	0		Denning ... rf	Dunn-Erwin
Spaine	cf	Clinton	Spaine, rf 2	0	1		Denning, rf 2	0	0		Richards ... of	Dunn-Erwin
Lorenz	1b	Clinton	Lorenz, 1b 4	0	0		Richards, lf 4	0	0		Marko ... c	Dunn-Erwin
Delworth	3b	Lumberton	Dulworth, 3b 1	0	0		Marko, c 0	0	0		Helms ... c	Fayetteville
Brockman	3b	Red Springs	Brockman, 3b 1	0	0		Helms, c 3	0	0		Kittrell ... 1b	Fayetteville
Edens	of	Wilmington	Edens, lf 2	0	0		Kittrell, 1b 2	0	0		Roseberry ... of	Fayetteville
Stern	of	Clinton	Stern, lf 1	0	0		Roseberry, 1b 2	0	0		Mason ... ss	Fayetteville
Pettit	c	Wilmington	Haswell, c 1	0	0		Mason, ss 1	0	0		Clayton ... 2b	Sandford
Vojesik	c	Red Springs	Pettit, c 0	0	0		Clayton, 2b 2	0	0		Barr ... p	Dunn-Erwin
Haswell	c	Clinton	Vojesik, c 1	0	0		Barr, p 1	0	0		Musumeci ... 3b	Fayetteville
Price	p	Clinton	Price, p 1	0	0		Musumeci, 3b 2	0	0			
Harrington	p	Red Springs	Flaim, p 1	0	0		Totals 31	0	5			
Flaim	p	Lumberton	Harrington, p 1	0	0							
			Totals 30	2	4							

Rosters and box score from the 1949 All Star game played in Dunn (author's collection).

Post-Season All-Star Teams
1946

1B: Phalti Shoffner, Sanford
2B: Mickey Balla, Smithfield-Selma
3B: Lonnie Smith, Clinton
SS: Andrew Cullen, Wilmington
OF: Willie Duke, Clinton
OF: Edward Bass, Dunn-Erwin
OF: Hank Nesselrode, Sanford
C: William Campau, Clinton
UTIL: William Ratteree, Angier-Fuquay Springs
P: Robert Keane, Clinton
P: George Bortz, Sanford
Manager: Zeb Harrington, Sanford

1947

1B: Elzer Marx, Lumberton
2B: Jimmy Guinn, Sanford
3B: Edmond Kukulka, Clinton
SS: Pete Howard, Smithfield-Selma

Part II

The opposing teams from the 1949 All Star game (author's collection).

9. All-Star Selections

OF: Carl McQuillen, Dunn-Erwin
OF: James Wilson, Sanford
OF: Hank Nesselrode
C: Bruce Hedrick, Sanford
UTIL: Mickey Balla, Dunn-Erwin
UTIL: Andrew Scrobola, Wilmington
P: Bobby Spicer, Lumberton
P: Lewis Cheshire, Wilmington
Manager: Charles "Red" Lucas, Lumberton

1948

1B: Joe Mangini, Red Springs
2B: Edward Hardiskey, Wilmington
3B: Curtis Lowry, Clinton
SS: Robert Keane, Sanford
OF: Tom Clayton, Red Springs
OF: William Benton, Wilmington
OF: Hank Nesselrode, Sanford
UTIL: Virgil Payne, Smithfield-Selma
UTIL: Andrew Scrobola, Warsaw
P: Lewis Cheshire, Wilmington
P: John McFadden, Sanford
Manager: Red Norris, Red Springs

1949

1B: Marvin Lorenz, Clinton
2B: Jimmy Guinn, Lumberton
3B: Hoggie Miller, Dunn-Erwin
SS: Thomas Campbell, Red Springs
OF: John Richards, Dunn-Erwin
OF: Bill Bohlender, Lumberton
OF: Hargrove Davis, Wilmington
C: Steve Marko, Dunn-Erwin
P: Clancy Condit, Dunn-Erwin
P: Gordon McDonald, Lumberton

Part II

1950

1B: Marvin Lorenz, Smithfield-Selma / Clinton
2B: Nick Purchia, Clinton
3B: Johnie, Wilmington
SS: Mike Milosevich, Lumberton
OF: Jim Francoline, Lumberton
OF: Shamrock Denning, Whiteville
OF: Herb May, Sanford
C: James Petit, Sanford
UTIL: Ducky Detweiler, Red Springs
UTIL: Bill Kay, Clinton
P: Hoyt Clegg, Sanford
P: Bill Bernier, Lumberton
P: John Lagan, Lumberton
P: George Vereault, Red Springs
Manager: Zeb Harrington, Sanford

• 10 •

Umpires

Like players, umpires started at the bottom and worked their way up. Quite a few of the Tobacco State League's umps did advance and ended up working circuits such as the Carolina or Piedmont Leagues. Andrew Mitchell called games in the Southern Association and spent three seasons working the AAA International League. In fact, the Tobacco State alumnus with the longest involvement in the major leagues was an umpire. Jim Odom, who began his career behind the plate in the dusty and poorly lit high school ballparks of the Tobacco State League, went on to call games in the American League from 1965 to 1974 and even worked the 1971 World Series.

1946

Roland L. Adcox
Blanchard
Frazier (John Fraser?)
J. C. Freeman
Pat P. Fragile

J. W. Gill
James R. Godwin
Robert H. Mann
Vincent Moneyhun
Roper

1947

James A. Baker
William L. Bauer
Eugene H. Chandler
Emil Davidzuk
Paul C. Kircher
Jason T. House

Howard V. Gaskill
Kenneth K. Ouzts
Andrew A. Mitchell
Roy E. Raby
Nick J. Reveille
Douglas E. Ruch

Part II

June H. Stallings
James C. Taylor

Richard R. Wilson
Alex B. Woodard

1948

James A. Baker
Eugene H. Chandler
Thomas A. Coffman
Daniel Hritzko
Dale P. Hughes
Carl Kieffer

Douglas E. Ruch
Paul D. Kratsch
Al J. Matulionis
Dominick Monterose
David Schreiber
Alex B. Woodard

1949

Frank J. Anasti
James A. Baker
William J. Cash
Eugene H. Chandler
Edward J. Cuneo
Tony Grillo
Daniel Hritzko
John Magna
James C. Odom
John T. Mazur
Dominick Monterose
Alex B. Woodard

Name	Position	Bats	Throws
Monterose, Dominick	P-Umpire		
Born-Place	**Date**		**Married**
Archbald, Pa.	Oct. 11, 1921		yes
Address 1421 Summitt Ave.,		**Height**	**Weight**
Fayetteville, N. Car.		5'11	190

Teams Played With Bill McGowan Umpire School
Player--Shelby 5/46-rel. to Fayetteville 5/46-
rel. 5/46-Dunn-Erwin 7/46-rel. 7/46-Angier-Fuquay
7/46-rel. 7/46-Salisbury, N.C. 7/46-rel. 8/46-
Smithfield 4/2/47-rel. 4/25/47-
Umpire Tobacco State League 6/16/48-49-rel. to
Piedmont League 10/4/49- res. for 51 RES FOR 1952- **RES. FOR 1953**

Married Ruby Hall, Nov. 9, 1944.
Medical Corps Oct. 1942-Feb. 1946.

10. Umpires

1950

William J. Cash
John T. Mazur
Welden D. O'Brien
James C. Odom
Brice R. Wrenn
Joseph Francis "Fax" Healy

George John Popp
Herman Richard Ziruolo
Darrell L. Sayre
Ivan S. Moore
Alex B. Woodard

Opposite top: Umpire Jim Odom, a native of South Carolina, worked games in the minor leagues for 18 years before being promoted to the majors. During a 10-year career in the in the American League he umpired 1597 games and worked the 1968 Major League All-Star Game and the 1971 World Series. *Opposite bottom:* The information card for umpire Dominick Monterose. After trials with several teams as a pitcher, Monterose turned to umpiring. He called games in the Tobacco State League for two seasons before moving up to the Piedmont League (author's collection).

♦ 11 ♦

League and Team Information

1946

Office of the League: 205 Princess St. Wilmington, NC
President: James E. L. Wade
Vice President: A. D. Moore
Secretary/Treasurer: J. M. Wade
Directors: Brodie Smith, Lewis D. Isenhour, J. E. Jackson, Langdon C. Kerr, W. H. Hamilton, L. M. Pollock
Official League Scorer: Edward Sachs
Salary Limit: $1800
Player Limit: 15 (three, class men, eight limited service, and four rookies), includes manager.

Angier-Fuquay Springs

President: W. H. Hamilton
Vice President: W. B. "Red" Williams
Business Manager: Herbert "Doc" Smith

Clinton

President: Langdon Chevis Kerr
Vice President: Jack Poole
Secretary: Jeff D. Johnson
Treasurer: Norwood Price Parker
Traveling Secretary: George E. Rackley

11. League and Team Information—1947

Dunn-Erwin

President: J. E. Jackson
Vice President: Grover Henderson
Business Manager: Sam Bear
Secretary/Treasurer: Charles H. Adams
Public Relations: J. M. Wade

Sanford

President: Lewis D. Isenhour
Vice President: S. L. Stack
Secretary/Treasurer: Zeb Harrington
Business Manager: Hillman E. "Sam" Allen

Smithfield-Selma

President: Brodie Smith
Vice President: John Best
Secretary/Treasurer: James Boone
Business Manager: James E. Overby

Wilmington

President: L. M. Pollock
Vice President: Vic S. Stefano
Business Manager: Bert Kite

1947

Office of the League: P.O. Box 566, Fayetteville, NC
President: Arthur T. Moore
Vice President: Langdon C. Kerr
Secretary/Treasurer: J. Morris Wade
League Statistician: J. L. Wade
Directors: Lewis D. Isenhour, J. E. Jackson, Langdon C. Kerr, L. M. Pollock, Jack Sheehan, Connie Mack, Hubert Johnson, S. W. Marriner

Salary Limit: $2250
Player Limit: 15 (four class men, seven limited service, four rookies), includes manager

Clinton

President: Langdon C. Kerr
Vice President: R. A. "Jack" Poole
Secretary/Treasurer: Norwood P. Parker
Directors: Langdon C. Kerr, R. A. "Jack" Poole, N. B. Hill, R. C. Carter, George E. Rackley, Gordon W. Love, H. B. Barwick. Clarence Clayton Tart, Sr., Jeff D. Johnson, Jr.
Business Manager: K. D. Barnes
Official Scorer: James H. Register

George Trautman, who been president of the American Association, took over as president of the National Association of Professional Baseball Leagues in 1947 and moved the office from Durham, NC, to his home city, Columbus, Ohio. Trautman remained in office until his death in 1963 (minor league program, author's collection).

Dunn-Erwin

President: J. E. Jackson
Vice President: E. M. Bost
Secretary/Treasurer: Charles H. Adams
Official Scorer: John Ingram

Lumberton

President: John T. Sheehan
Vice Presidents: James T. Gallagher, Harold K. George
Secretary: Margaret Donahue
Treasurer: Earl W. Nelson

11. League and Team Information—1947

Business Manager: Elton "Buddy" Frazier
Official Scorer: George Knudson

Red Springs

President: Connie Mack
Vice President: Arthur Ehlers
Secretary: Robert Schroeder
Treasurer: Roy Mack
Business Manager: Tom Cope
Official Scorer: James Davis

Sanford

President: Lewis D. Isenhour
Business Manager: Hillman E. "Sam" Allen
Official Scorer: Roby Hillard

Smithfield-Selma

President: H. G. Johnson
Vice President: John W. Best
Secretary/Business Manager: Peggy Johnson
Official Scorer: Joe Padget

Warsaw

President: Sterling W. Marriner
Vice President/Business Manager: Arthur Apple
Secretary: Robert L. West
Treasurer/Official Scorer: Paul B. Potter
Directors: Allen Draughon, Gilbert Alphin, Jr., W. E. Currie, Mosley Phillips, C. A. Precythe, Caswell Moore, H. C. Dail

Wilmington

President: L.M. Pollack
Vice President: Vic A. Stefano

Part II

Secretary: Odell Bridges
Business Manager: J. Morris Wade
Official Scorer: Rufus Powell
Groundskeeper: Rhodie Farrow

1948

Office of the League: P.O. Box 566, Fayetteville, NC
President/Secretary/Treasurer: Arthur T. Moore
Vice President: Lewis D. Isenhour
Directors: Lewis D. Isenhour, J. E. Jackson, Jack Sheehan, Connie Mack, Hubert Johnson, C. H. Caison, W. P. Sutton, A. J. Jenkins
Salary Limit: $2600
Player Limit: 17 (three class men, nine limited service, five rookies), does not include manager

Clinton

President: C. Hillary Caison
Vice President: P. S. Carr
Secretary/Treasurer/
   Business Manager:
   Norwood P. Parker

Dunn-Erwin

President: J. E. Jackson
Vice President: Sam Bear
Secretary/Treasurer: Earl McD. Westbrook

Lumberton

President: John T. Sheehan
Vice Presidents: James T. Gallagher, Harold K. George

League President A. T. Moore in his Fayetteville office in 1948 (*Raleigh News and Observer*/North Carolina State Archives).

Secretary: Margaret Donahue
Treasurer: Earl W. Nelson
Business Manager: Elton "Buddy" Frazier

Red Springs

President: Connie Mack
Vice President: Arthur Ehlers
Secretary: Robert Schroeder
Treasurer: Roy Mack
Business Manager: Tom Cope

Sanford

President: Lewis D. Isenhour
Secretary/Business Manager: Hillman E. "Sam" Allen
Scorekeeper: Kyle Cox

Smithfield-Selma

President/Treasurer: E. W. Mayton
Vice President: John W. Best
Secretary/Business Manager: Peggy Johnson

Warsaw

President: A. J. Jenkins
Vice President: George D. Bennett
Secretary: A. L. Cavenaugh
Treasurer: O. S. Carroll
Business Manager: Claude L. Hepler

Wilmington

President: W. P. Sutton
Vice Presidents: M. A. Rooks, Vic S. Stefano
Business Manager: J. Lewis Chesire
Radio Broadcaster: Lou Essick on WGNI

Part II

1949

Office of League: P.O. Box 566, Fayetteville, NC
President/Secretary/Treasurer: Arthur T. Moore
Vice President: Lewis D. Isenhour
Directors: Connie Mack, C. H. Caison, Dr. W. W. Stansfield, Mike Boosalis, Dr. E. L. Bowman, E. W. Fields, E. W. Mayton, W. P. Sutton
Salary Limit: $2,600
Player Limit: 17 (three class men, nine limited service, five rookies), does not include manager

Clinton

President: C. Hillary Caison
Vice-President: Melton O. Register
Secretary/Treasurer/Business Manager: Norwood P. Parker
Pop.: 6,000

Dunn-Erwin

President: Dr. W. W. Stanfield
Vice President: W. H. Miley
Secretary/Treasurer: J. E. Jackson
Pop.: 8,000

Fayetteville

Business Manager: Michael G. "Mike" Boosalis
Pop.: 60,000

Lumberton

President: William Murphy Bowman
Vice-President: R. A. "Rom" Hedgepeth
Treasurer: A. M. Hartley
Business Manager: Elton "Buddy" Frazier
Pop.: 12,000

11. League and Team Information—1949

Red Springs

President: Connie Mack
Vice President: Arthur Ehlers
Secretary: Robert Schroeder
Treasurer: Roy Mack
Business Manager: Tom Cope
Pop.: 4,000

Sanford

President: E. W. Fields
Vice President: J. C. Pittman
Secretary/Treasurer: P. L. Johnson
Business Manager: Zeb Harrington
Pop.: 10,000

Arthur Ehlers, director of the Philadelphia Athletics' farm system, discusses prospects with Manager Red Norris during a visit to Red Springs in 1949. Ehlers later served as general manager of the Athletics and the Baltimore Orioles (*Raleigh News and Observer*/North Carolina State Archives).

Part II

Smithfield-Selma

President: Dixon Wallace
Vice President: J. Noah Williams
Secretary/Treasurer: J. A. Jones
Business Manager: Willard E. Lawrence
Pop.: 8,000

Wilmington

President: W. P. Sutton
Vice Presidents: M. A Rooks, Vic S. Stefano
Secretary/Treasurer/Business Manager: J. Lewis Cheshire
Business Manager: Michael V. Conte
Pop.: 50,000

1950

Office of League: P.O. Box 566, Fayetteville, NC
President/Secretary/Treasurer: Arthur T. Moore
Vice President: Lewis D. Isenhour
Directors: Dr. W. W. Stansfield, Dr. E. L. Bowman, J. B. Williams, Jr., Tom Cope, W. G. Pittman, Dixon Wallace, J. Lewis Cheshire
Salary Limit: $2,600
Player Limit: Seventeen, not including manager

Clinton

President: John Blaney Williams, Jr.
Vice-President: P. S. Carr
Business Manager: Dr. M. L. O'Brian
Pop.: 6,000

Dunn-Erwin

President: Dr. W. W. Stanfield
Vice President: W. H. Miley

11. League and Team Information—1950

Secretary/Treasurer: J. E. Jackson
Business Manager: Herbert B. Taylor
Pop.: 8,000

Lumberton

President/Secretary/Treasurer: Roy Dissinger
General Manager: James J. Francoline
Business Manager: Russell B. Filley/John A. Cote
Pop.: 11,000

Red Springs-Laurinburg

President: Connie Mack
Vice Presidents: Arthur Ehlers, Earle Mack
Secretary: Connie Mack, Jr.
Treasurer: Roy Mack
Business Manager: Tom Cope
Red Springs pop.: 3,500
Laurinburg pop.: 8,000

Rockingham

Office Address: Manufacturers Building
President: Heath Penegar
Vice President: Henry Smithey
Secretary/Treasurer: John Gore
Business Manager: Matt F. Gettings
Pop.: 3,500

Sanford

President: Lewis D. Isenhour
Vice President: J.C. Pittman
Secretary/Treasurer: Annie F. Thomas
Business Manager: Zeb Harrington
Pop.: 10,000

Part II

Smithfield-Selma

President: Dixon Wallace
Vice President: J. Noah Williams
Secretary/Treasurer: J. A. Jones
Business Manager: Willard E. Lawrence
Pop.: 8,000

Wilmington

President: W. P. Sutton
Vice Presidents: M. A. Rooks, Vic S. Stefano
Secretary/Treasurer/Business Manager: J. Lewis Cheshire
Business Manager: Michael V. Conte
Pop.: 50,000

Whiteville

President: Paul J. Williamson
Vice President: X. Brown, Jr.
Secretary/Treasurer: Felix M. Smith
Board of Directors: Hyman Kramer, Josiah A. Maultsby, Cary H. Fleming, J. Rufus Marks
Pop.: 4,200

Ballparks

ANGIER-FUQUAY
Angier Baseball Park
Seating capacity 1,900

CLINTON
Clinton High School Park
Seating capacity 2,000 in 1946 and 2,500 in 1950

DUNN-ERWIN
Dunn High School Park
Seating capacity 2,000 in 1946 and 1,600 in 1949

11. League and Team Information—Ballparks

FAYETTEVILLE
Cumberland Memorial Stadium
Seating capacity 4,800

LUMBERTON
Armory Field
Seating capacity 1,600 in 1948, 2,500 in 1949 and 3,000 in 1950

RED SPRINGS
Robbins Park
Seating capacity 3,000 in 1949 and 2,000 in 1950
Dimensions: 350' to left, 395' to center, 350' to right
Some games at American Legion Park (Laurinburg)
Seating capacity 2,000

ROCKINGHAM
Rockingham Baseball Park
Seating capacity 3,500

SANFORD
Temple Park
Corner of McIver and Seventh Streets
Seating capacity 2,500

Our Concession Handles The Following Name Brand ITEMS

Cigars — 2 for 15c	Cracker Jacks — 10c
Cigarettes — 20c	Ice Cream — 10c
Chewing Tobacco — 10c	Pillows — 10c
B. C. Powders — 5c	Popcorn — 10c
Aspirins — 10c	Peanuts — 10c
Tums — 10c	Soft Drinks — 10c
Gum — 10c	Candies — 10c
Cookies — 10c	Hot Dogs — 15c

GROUND RULES
LUMBERTON ARMORY FIELD

1.—Ball in play off dugout ledge.
2.—One base in the dugout.
3.—One base in the drinking fountain.
4.—Fair catch off bats.
5.—One base if ball gets lodged in the back-stop, otherwise in play.
6.—Fair catch off the wire above home plate.
7.—Fair catch off the wires in left center and right center field.
8.—Score board out of the park.
9.—2 Bases on any ball going under the left field and right field foul line fences.
10.—2 bases if a ball hits a foul line post and goes behind fence.
11.—If the ball hits the foul line marker and bounces in the ball is in play.
12.—Ball in play on overthrows to first and third.

From the 1950 Lumberton scorecard (author's collection).

Part II

Two views of Temple Park in Sanford, circa late 1930s (courtesy Jimmy Haire).

11. League and Team Information—Agreements

SMITHFIELD-SELMA
Legion Park
Seating capacity 4,000

WARSAW
Warsaw High School Park
Seating capacity 1,500

WHITEVILLE
Legion Field
Seating capacity 1,000+

WILMINGTON
American Legion Stadium (1946–May 1949)
Seating capacity 5,000 in 1946
Dimensions: 340' to right, 340' to left, 420' to center
New Hanover War Memorial Park (late May 1949–1950)
Seating capacity 3,000
Dimensions: 328' to left, 328' to right

Working Agreements

(with Major League or higher-level minor league clubs)

1946

None

Top: Shortstop Pete Howard takes practice swings in front of the Smithfield grandstand in 1946 (courtesy Pete Howard). *Bottom:* An unidentified Clinton player with the Smithfield ballpark in the background (*Raleigh News and Observer*/North Carolina State Archives).

Whiteville Ballpark as it looks today. The facility is still in use and well maintained. (author's photographs).

11. League and Team Information—Spring Training

```
Meeting of January 3, 1949 continued.

A summery of operations of Legion Stadium for period December 1, 1947, to
November 30, 1948, requested of the County Auditor, was received and
discussed.
Upon motion of Mr. Gardner, seconded by Mr. Trask, the Board granted the
Pirate's Baseball Club the use of Legion Stadium for its 1949 season on
the same basis as last year, requested by Mr. Lewis Cheshire. With the
exception of the dates to be reserved for the New Hanover High School commencement
exercises and games, to be arranged with Mr. T. T. Hamilton, Principal of the
school.
```

Discussion of Legion Field in the minutes of Wilmington City Council's meeting in January on 1949 (courtesy Special Collections Department, New Hanover County Public Library).

1947
Lumberton—Chicago Cubs
Red Springs—Philadelphia Athletics

1948
Red Springs—Philadelphia Athletics
Lumberton—Chicago Cubs
Clinton—Buffalo Bisons

1949
Red Springs—Philadelphia Athletics
Lumberton—Chicago Cubs
Clinton—Buffalo Bisons
Fayetteville—Reidsville Luckies
Wilmington—Baltimore Orioles

1950
Red Springs—Philadelphia Athletics
Wilmington—Cincinnati Reds
Sanford—Greensboro Patriots

Spring Training Sites *(Other than at home)*

1949
Sanford—Bartow, Florida
Red Springs—Moultrie, Georgia

1950
Lumberton—Melbourne, Florida
Red Springs—West Palm Beach, Florida

Part III

• 12 •

Player Register

Introduction

Though it is probably the dream of every minor league player to one day reach the big leagues, few ever make it. This was particularly true in the late 1940s, when there were many more minor league teams than today and only sixteen big league teams. The odds of making it were very slim. In all, around a dozen Tobacco State League players appeared on major league rosters. Most of these, however, made their big league appearances before coming to the tobacco towns of North Carolina, continuing in the game as minor league player-managers after their careers had peaked. The most well-known of these was South Carolina native Van Lingle Mungo. A three-time All-Star with the Brooklyn Dodgers in the 1930s, he retired from the majors after the 1945 season.

Of the players in the Tobacco State League working their way up in the game, it is probable that

A 1952 baseball card featuring Bob Spicer of the AAA Los Angeles Angels. A rookie with Lumberton in 1947, he appeared in the big leagues with Kansas City in 1955 and 1956. With his final season in 1961, he was probably the last Tobacco State League alumnus active as a player (author's collection).

12. Player Register—Introduction

Left: A star rookie in 1946, Earl Mossor spent a dozen years in professional baseball during which he pitched for 15 clubs. He made it to the major leagues briefly with the Brooklyn Dodgers early in the 1951 season and retired in 1959. *Right:* Duane "Duke" Maas, seen here with the Durham Bulls in 1953, was a rookie when he pitched for Dunn—Erwin in 1949. He went on to spend six seasons in the major leagues and even made an appearance in the 1960 World Series for the New York Yankees (author's collection).

pitchers Bill Harrington of Red Springs, Bob Spicer of Lumberton, Duke Maas of Dunn-Erwin and Earl Mossor of Clinton were the only ones who made it to the big leagues. Harrington pitched two full seasons as a reliever for the Kansas City Athletics in the mid–'50s. Spicer joined him in Kansas City for a few games during those same seasons. Maas spent much of eight seasons in the big leagues with the Tigers, Athletics, and Yankees while Mossor made it into three games for the Brooklyn Dodgers in 1951 before spending the next nine seasons at the highest level of the minor leagues.

Part III

Quite a few players did go on to play professional ball at higher levels in leagues including the Southern Association and the Pacific Coast League and a few also became minor league managers. Pierre Ethier excelled with various minor league teams but never rose above AAA. His grandson Andre, however, debuted in the outfield for the Los Angeles Dodgers in 2006. It was a similar story for Smithfield-Selma pitcher Amby Foote. He played six seasons in the minors with teams including Winston-Salem and Burlington in the Carolina League, but his son Barry spent a decade as a big leagues catcher. Sam Narron, who had appeared in the big leagues before playing at Smithfield, returned to the majors and spent thirteen seasons as the bullpen coach for the Pittsburgh Pirates. John Streza managed in the minors for several seasons then worked as a scout for the Chicago Cubs and California Angels. Marvin Lorenz retired from playing and managing after the 1950 season but eventually spent many years as general manager of the Asheville Tourists of the Western Carolinas League.

Sanford pitcher Howard Auman was a star at Campbell College and got in one minor league season before the war took him away for three seasons. Returning to baseball at age 24, he had a phenomenal 22-win season with his hometown Spinners. Signed by the Cubs, he won 20 games the following season at Macon and eventually had a stint with Los Angeles in 1948. By 1951, however, wear and tear began to take a toll on his arm and Auman retired after spending that season with Shreveport in the Texas League.

Verlon Walker, still a teenager when caught for Lumberton in 1948, never made it to the big leagues as a player, unlike his big brother Rube, who caught in the majors for more than a decade. Verlon remained in the Chicago Cubs farm system where he played for and managed various minor league clubs until 1961. That year his loyalty to the organization paid off when he was hired to join the coaching staff in Chicago. He was still a member of the Cubs staff when he tragically died of leukemia in 1971 at age 42.

Pitcher Bill Narleski, who turned in an 8–11 record for Fayetteville in 1949, came from a baseball family. His father, Bill, Sr., played a couple seasons as a shortstop for the Boston Red Sox and had a long minor league career that included stays in Raleigh and Rocky Mount, NC in the 1920s. Ray Narleski, younger brother of Bill, Jr., would also make

12. Player Register—Introduction

the major leagues; he pitched five seasons for Cleveland and one for Detroit. A two-time All-Star, Ray was one of the American League's best relief pitchers in the late 1950s. Another brother, Ted, was an infielder in the Indians' minor league system for three seasons in the 1950s. Ray's son, Steve, also played professional baseball and spent eight seasons in the minor leagues, reaching as high as the AAA level.

George "Buck" Hardee, who played less than 30 games for Whiteville in 1950, went on to have a huge impact on the game in southeastern North Carolina, He was head baseball coach at New Hanover High School in Wilmington for 24 years as well as head coach of Wilmington's American Legion Post 10 baseball team from 1959–84. The field at Legion Stadium in Wilmington was named after Hardee in 1984 and he was elected to the NC High School Athletic Association Hall of Fame in 1994.

Willie Duke, who played 14 minor league seasons in cities including Nashville, Atlanta, Memphis and Durham—and retired with an impressive career .331 average—was actively involved with the game of baseball until his death in 1993. Duke founded the Raleigh Hot Stove League and today the organization's lifetime achievement award for service to the game is named to honor him.

Hargrove Davis, one of the league's top hitters, became a successful college coach, spending many years at Campbell College in Buies Creek, North Carolina. He was the school's assistant baseball coach from 1947 to 1953 then served as head coach from 1954 to 191969. His greatest coaching successes with Campbell came in the game of golf, however, and he led his team to the school's only national championship, the 1970 NAIA crown.

Charlie Moir, who played outfield for Wilmington in 1950, also made his name as a coach in a sport other than baseball. He spent 31 seasons as a high school and college basketball coach, including eleven (1976–87) as head coach of the men's team at Virginia Tech. Moir led Roanoke College to a NCAA Div. II National Championship in 1972.

Peanut Doak, who spent two seasons with Red Springs, carried on a family tradition when he also turned to coaching. Doak's father, Chick, had coached baseball at North Carolina State College for 16 seasons and even served as president of the Tobacco State League it its early semi-pro years. He also coached basketball at the University

Part III

of North Carolina and Trinity College (now Duke University) in the 1910s. The younger Doak was coach and athletic director at Presbyterian Junior College (now St. Andrew's University in Laurinburg) for several years. He later served in the athletic department of NC State and was the first head coach of that school's women's basketball team. Doak was instrumental in hiring the legendary Kay Yow to succeed him in the role in 1975.

Johnie Edens, versatile star of the Wilmington Pirates for five seasons, had a big impact on the game in his hometown—not only because of his own feats on the field, but those of his son and grandson as well. Like his father, Larry Edens was a star athlete at New Hanover High School. He went on to play collegiate baseball at Wilmington College (now UNC-Wilmington) and at Virginia Tech. Larry, Jr., carried on the family tradition by being named first-team all-Atlantic Coast Conference while playing for North Carolina State University. Drafted by the Chicago Cubs in 1994, he played one season of professional baseball.

Leo Katkaveck, who starred in both baseball and basketball at North

A two—sport star at North Carolina State, Leo Katkaveck was selected in the 1948 professional basketball draft by the Washington Capitols. That same year he also signed a professional baseball contract and played a handful of games for both Warsaw and Raleigh of the Carolina League. Katkaveck went on to play two seasons of professional basketball. In minor league baseball he also played for Goldsboro in 1949 and Roanoke Rapids in 1950 and '51. (Courtesy North Carolina State Archives).

12. Player Register—Introduction

Carolina State, also played two sports at the professional level. He made his professional baseball debut with Warsaw in 1948 and spent parts of five seasons in the minor leagues. In basketball, however, he reached a higher level and spent two seasons in the NBA playing guard for the Washington Capitals.

Fred Schubach, who caught for Red Springs in 1948, chose the sport of football as his career after spending two seasons in the Athletics farm system. Schubach worked for the Baltimore Colts for 30 years, beginning as the team's equipment manager and eventually rising to director of player personnel. He later worked as a scout for the Buffalo Bills and Kansas City Chiefs before retirement.

The Tobacco State League alum who found the greatest success in a sport other than baseball was, without a doubt, Red Springs pitcher/utility infielder Don Carter. In 1947, his only year in professional baseball, the St. Louis native turned in a 3–7 record on the mound and hit a very respectable .302. After the season Carter decided to trade his spikes for bowling shoes and he went on to become one of the greatest bowlers of all time. During his career he won seven Professional Bowlers Association titles and was the first athlete from any sport to secure a $1 million endorsement deal when he signed with bowling manufacturer Ebonite in 1964.

In a *Bowlers Journal* interview in 1970, Carter recalled the team played 128 games in 112 days and–thanks to Southern heat and flannel uniforms–he lost 30 pounds from his 180-pound frame. "I got $150 a month plus room and board," he remembered. "Riding that bus all over the countryside to games was too much. I quit after a season."

Though many alumni of the Tobacco State League certainly had an impact on the world of sports, most players left professional baseball to return to "normal" lives. Most men never really intended to pursue baseball as a long-term career. Instead it was just a way to make a living for a few years playing a game they loved. Many league players were also fresh home from military service so a simple joy like playing baseball was probably a welcome way to put the war behind them. After baseball most of these men turned to new careers and became things like teachers, farmers, mill workers, insurance salesmen, mechanics, etc. Just to name a few, Vernon Mustian became of doctor or neurology, Duncan Futrelle was ordained as a Baptist minister, George Erath

Part III

founded a veneer company that supplied the furniture industry, Otis Stephens was a plant manager at a textile mill, Emmett Williams was a successful tobacco farmer, Pete Howard retired from the U.S. Postal Service, and Hank Nesselrode owned a service station.

Jim Fister, who played second base for Wilmington and Rockingham in 1950, was one of several former Tobacco State League players drafted into the military. Fister, a once-promising Cincinnati Reds prospect, was drafted after the 1950 season, went on to rise to the rank of sergeant, and served with distinction while fighting in the Korean War. Afterwards, he returned to his native Missouri and embarked upon a long career in the insurance industry.

Roxboro, NC, native Otis Stephens began his pro baseball career as a teenager in 1946 when he spent part of a season with Angier—Fuquay. At Warsaw the following season he began to develop into solid hitter also know for his speed. Stephens worked his way up the minor league ladder and eventually played for teams including Hickory (where he hit 32 homeruns in 1948), Williamsport and Savannah. In 1952, while playing for Macon, he unfortunately suffered a broken leg that cut short his career (courtesy the late Otis Stephens).

12. Player Register—Abernathy

The Register

Names in bold italics indicate appearance in the major leagues.

Abernathy, Talmadge Lafayette "Tal"

Year	Club	G	CG	W	L	IP	H	R	BB	SO	ERA
1950	Rockingham	3	1	2	0	—	—	—	—	—	—

Other teams played for: Philadelphia Athletics (ML), Wilmington, Del. (B), Memphis (AA), Leaksville (C), Reidsville (C), Burlington (C), Greensboro (B)

Aiken,

Year	Club	G	CG	W	L	IP	H	R	BB	SO	ERA
1946	Angier-Fuquay	2	—	0	0	6	—	—	—	—	—

Other teams played for: Unknown

Akens, James M. "Jim"

Year	Club	POS	G	AB	R	H	2B	3B	HR	BB	SB	RBI	BA
1948	Clinton	p	27	56	5	13	3	0	1	6	0	2	.232
1949	Clinton	p	18	33	3	9	2	0	0	4	0	4	.273

Year	Club	G	CG	W	L	IP	H	R	BB	SO	ERA
1948	Clinton	21	13	10	9	129	116	59	62	68	3.14
1949	Clinton	17	7	3	7	86	97	58	50	43	5.44

Other teams played for: None

Albert, John J.

Year	Club	POS	G	AB	R	H	2B	3B	HR	BB	SB	RBI	BA
1950	Red Springs	c	20	62	9	17	0	1	0	14	1	10	.274

Other teams played for: Gainesville (D), Sanford, Fla. (D)

Alexander, (Theodore?)

Year	Club	POS	G	AB	R	H	2B	3B	HR	BB	SB	RBI	BA
1946	Smith-Selma	of	34	123	15	31	2	1	1	—	0	16	.252

Other teams played for: Unkown

Allegue, Manuel

Year	Club	POS	G	AB	R	H	2B	3B	HR	BB	SB	RBI	BA
1948	Warsaw	3b	45	161	19	35	1	1	0	25	5	12	.217

Other teams played for: Martinsville (C), Lancaster (B), Lincoln (C), High Point-Thomasville (D)

12. Player Register—Allen

Allen, Oliver "Snag"

Year	Club	POS	G	AB	R	H	2B	3B	HR	BB	SB	RBI	BA
1946	Wilmington	3b	15	67	9	17	5	1	0	—	2	8	.254

Year	Club	G	CG	W	L	IP	H	R	BB	SO	ERA
1946	Wilmington	2	0	0	1	4	9	13	8	4	—

Other teams played for: Newton-Conover (D)

Allen, William "Bill"

Year	Club	POS	G	AB	R	H	2B	3B	HR	BB	SB	RBI	BA
1949	Fayetteville	of	3	8	1	3	0	0	0	—	0	1	.375

Other teams played for: Unknown

Alsenauer, William E. "Bill"

Year	Club	POS	G	AB	R	H	2B	3B	HR	BB	SB	RBI	BA
1947	Wilmington	c	57	205	12	41	3	0	0	3	3	20	.200
1948	Smith.-Selma	c	19										
	Wilmington	c	39										
	totals:	c	58	188	30	40	5	0	0	14	1	16	.213

Other teams played for: Washington, Penn. (D), Jamestown (D)

Ammons, Wallace

Year	Club	POS	G	AB	R	H	2B	3B	HR	BB	SB	RBI	BA
1948	Red Springs	p	43	91	13	19	1	1	0	6	0	13	.209
1949	Red Springs	p	—	—	—	—	—	—	—	—	—	—	—
1950	Red Springs	p	26	51	8	9	2	0	0	5	0	1	.176

Year	Club	G	CG	W	L	IP	H	R	BB	SO	ERA
1948	Red Springs	35	17	16	17	233	199	122	157	198	3.52
1949	Red Springs	7	7	7	0	61	52	26	36	59	2.51
1950	Red Springs	14	8	7	6	97	71	44	71	65	3.34

Other teams played for: Martinsville (B)

Andrews, Clayton C. "Jack"

Year	Club	POS	G	AB	R	H	2B	3B	HR	BB	SB	RBI	BA
1949	Sanford	p	23	59	4	6	0	0	0	14	0	5	.102
1950	Sanford	p	31	77	7	13	2	0	0	11	0	4	.169

Year	Club	G	CG	W	L	IP	H	R	BB	SO	ERA
1949	Sanford	22	16	11	8	171	171	82	26	95	2.68
1950	Sanford	31	21	15	12	212	202	93	44	100	2.63

Other teams played for: None

12. Player Register—Askew

Andrews, Nathan Hardy "Nate"

Year	Club	POS	G	AB	R	H	2B	3B	HR	BB	SB	RBI	BA
1946	Wilmington	p	13	36	1	3	0	0	0	—	0	3	.083
1947	Wilmington	p	12	25	2	6	0	0	0	4	0	3	.240

Year	Club	G	CG	W	L	IP	H	R	BB	SO	ERA
1946	Wilmington	13	12	9	2	98	83	32	27	90	—
1947	Wilmington	12	4	4	3	70	84	45	18	40	4.37

Other teams played for: Greensboro (B), Asheville (B), Wilkes-Barre (A), Rochester (AA), Columbus (AA), St. Louis Cardinals (ML), Cleveland (ML), Sacramento (AA), Boston Braves (ML), St. Paul (AA), Syracuse (AA), Milwaukee (AA), Cincinnati (ML), New York Giants (ML), Florence (B)

Andrews, Winfred "Wink"

Year	Club	POS	G	AB	R	H	2B	3B	HR	BB	SB	RBI	BA
1947	Warsaw	ss	44	172	34	42	2	1	0	13	11	18	.244

Other teams played for: None

Arakelian, Zaven Joseph

Year	Club	POS	G	AB	R	H	2B	3B	HR	BB	SB	RBI	BA
1946	Smith.-Selma	—	<10	—	—	—	—	—	—	—	—	—	—

Other teams played for: Mount Airy (D), Tarboro (D), St. Augustine (D), Palatka (D), Galax (D), Concord (D), Reidsville (D), Bridgeport (B), Watertown (C), Augusta (A), Shelby (D),

Armbruster, Eugene R. "Gene"

Year	Club	POS	G	AB	R	H	2B	3B	HR	BB	SB	RBI	BA
1947	Red Springs	of	37	116	12	31	6	4	1	5	2	20	.267
1948	Red Springs	of	133	487	113	162	24	13	11	79	23	103	.333

Other teams played for: Federalsburg (D), Kewanee (C), Martinsville (B), Sunbury (B), Lexington (D), Fayetteville (B)

Askew,

Year	Club	G	CG	W	L	IP	H	R	BB	SO	ERA
1946	Smith.-Selma	3	3	2	1	27	34	11	4	11	—

Other teams played for: Unkown

Askew, Charles F.

Year	Club	POS	G	AB	R	H	2B	3B	HR	BB	SB	RBI	BA
1947	Clinton	of	56	228	48	76	11	4	4	14	4	46	.333

Other teams played for: Concord (D), Wilson (D)

12. Player Register—Auman

Auman, Howard Claude

Year	Club	POS	G	AB	R	H	2B	3B	HR	BB	SB	RBI	BA
1946	Sanford	p	35	110	11	29	3	0	2	—	0	25	.264

Year	Club	G	CG	W	L	IP	H	R	BB	SO	ERA
1946	Sanford	33	28	22	8	256	234	115	81	167	—

Other teams played for: Leaksville (D), Macon (A), Shreveport (AA), Los Angeles (AAA), Texarkana (B)

Backner, Thomas A.

Year	Club	POS	G	AB	R	H	2B	3B	HR	BB	SB	RBI	BA
1946	Clint./S.-S.	—	<10	—	—	—	—	—	—	—	—	—	—

Other teams played for: Goldsboro (D), Youngstown (C), Lawrence (B), Lowell (B), New London (B)

Baham, Carl Alton

Year	Club	POS	G	AB	R	H	2B	3B	HR	BB	SB	RBI	BA
1949	Smith.-Selma	2b	74	220	40	56	12	4	0	41	1	31	.255
1950	Smith.-Selma	of	45	125	22	32	5	5	1	32	3	15	.256

Year	Club	G	CG	W	L	IP	H	R	BB	SO	ERA
1949	Smith.-Selma	25	—	11	5	158	136	65	113	—	3.25
1950	Smith.-Selma	16	7	5	5	85	76	61	82	70	5.61

Other teams played for: Hammond (D)

Balikes, Nicholas "Nicky"

Year	Club	POS	G	AB	R	H	2B	3B	HR	BB	SB	RBI	BA
1948	Clinton	c	55	184	24	41	10	1	0	15	2	24	.223

Other teams played for: Rome (C)

Balla, Michael "Mickey"

Year	Club	POS	G	AB	R	H	2B	3B	HR	BB	SB	RBI	BA
1946	Smithfield	2b	103	347	78	98	10	8	0	—	6	42	.282
1947	Smith.-Selma	2b	63										
	Dunn-Erwin	2b	40										
	totals:	2b	103	321	71	80	17	3	0	95	7	29	.249

Other teams played for: Goldsboro (D), Martinsville (D), Lynchburg (D), Scranton (A), Albany (A), Hagerstown (B), Allentown (B), Franklin (D)

12. Player Register—Bare

Ballerini, John Frank

Year	Club	POS	G	AB	R	H	2B	3B	HR	BB	SB	RBI	BA
1946	Clinton	ss	60	213	30	45	4	2	0	—	6	25	.211

Other teams played for: Hickory (D), Danville (C)

Ballinger, William H.

Year	Club	POS	G	AB	R	H	2B	3B	HR	BB	SB	RBI	BA
1950	Sanford	ss	123	417	83	114	18	1	3	98	10	72	.273

Other teams played for: Rutherford County (D), Greensboro (B), Reidsville (B), Bluefield (D), Charleston (A), Raleigh (B), Winston-Salem (B)

Balogh, James E. "Jimmy"

Year	Club	POS	G	AB	R	H	2B	3B	HR	BB	SB	RBI	BA
1948	Lumberton	3b	125	483	86	112	17	2	2	31	21	43	.232
1949	Lumberton	ss	103	409	76	116	21	2	0	72	4	48	.284

Other teams played for: Rutherford County (D), St. Cloud (C), Gloversville-Johnstown (C), Cocoa (D), Fort Lauderdale (B), Key West (B)

Bangs, Lester Meredith Jr.

Year	Club	POS	G	AB	R	H	2B	3B	HR	BB	SB	RBI	BA
1946	Clinton	ss	<10	—	—	—	—	—	—	—	—	—	—

Other teams played for: Danville (C), Wilson (D), Newton-Conover (D), Hendersonville (D), Petersburg (D), Hopewell (D)

Bankhead, Walter

Year	Club	POS	G	AB	R	H	2B	3B	HR	BB	SB	RB	BA
1950	Rockingham	c	29	101	13	28	3	0	0	6	0	14	.277

Other teams played for: None

Barbee, Walter "Bud"

Year	Club	G	CG	W	L	IP	H	R	BB	SO	ERA
1946	Angier-Fuquay	4	0	0	1	5	5	6	4	3	—

Other teams played for: Unknown

Bare, Frank Burman

Year	Club	POS	G	AB	R	H	2B	3B	HR	BB	SB	RBI	BA
1946	Sanford	—	<10	—	—	—	—	—	—	—	—	—	—
1947	Clinton	3b	16										
	Smith.-Selma	3b	18										
	totals:	3b	34	154	20	33	5	1	1	15	4	23	.214

12. Player Register—Barnett

Other teams played for: Canton (C), Rocky Mount (B), Welch (D), Snow Hill (D), Tucson (C), Durham (B), Thomasville (D), Riverside (C), Pensacola (B), Burlington (C), Landis (D),

Barnett, Gilmus

Year	Club	G	CG	W	L	IP	H	R	BB	SO	ERA
1949	Lumberton	—	—	—	—	<45	—	—	—	—	—

Other teams played for: Unknown

Barnes, Jack J.

Year	Club	POS	G	AB	R	H	2B	3B	HR	BB	SB	RBI	BA
1949	Fayetteville	of	26	73	13	21	2	0	4	16	1	22	.288

Other teams played for: New Bern (D), Savannah (B), Charleston, SC (B), Knoxville (A), Elmira (A), Greenville, SC (A), Wilson (D)

Barneycastle, Michael "Mike"

Year	Club	G	CG	W	L	IP	H	R	BB	SO	ERA
1950	Rockingham	<10	—	—	—	—	—	—	—	—	—

Other teams played for: Unknown

Barnham, Ovie C.

Year	Club	POS	G	AB	R	H	2B	3B	HR	BB	SB	RBI	BA
1948	Smith.-Selma	2b	22	66	9	20	0	2	0	1	0	6	.303

Other teams played for: None

Barr, James "Jim"

Year	Club	POS	G	AB	R	H	2B	3B	HR	BB	SB	RBI	BA
1948	Dunn-Erwin	p	22	49	7	10	1	1	0	5	0	2	.204
1949	Dunn-Erwin	p	50	112	10	20	7	1	2	11	1	15	.179

Year	Club	G	CG	W	L	IP	H	R	BB	SO	ERA
1948	Dunn-Erwin	16	9	6	8	107	108	60	45	100	3.70
1949	Dunn-Erwin	30	23	14	13	216	206	127	118	168	3.75

Other teams played for: Pittsfield (C), Quebec (C), Moline (C), Lancaster (B)

Barrett, William Joseph "Billy"

Year	Club	POS	G	AB	R	H	2B	3B	HR	BB	SB	RBI	BA
1950	Smith.-Selma	2b	26										
	Clinton	2b	6										
	totals:	2b	32	108	29	26	3	1	0	33	4	15	.241

Other teams played for: Landis (D), Lafayette (C), Thibodaux (C), Miami Beach (B), Hagerstown (B), Atlanta (AA), New Iberia (C)

12. Player Register—Becker

Basile, Peter

Year	Club	POS	G	AB	R	H	2B	3B	HR	BB	SB	RBI	BA
1950	Wilmington	p	34	42	3	4	0	1	0	4	0	5	095

Year	Club	G	CG	W	L	IP	H	R	BB	SO	ERA
1950	Wilmington	29	1	5	5	84	100	77	73	46	6.75

Other teams played for: None

Bass, Earl C.

Year	Club	POS	G	AB	R	H	2B	3B	HR	BB	SB	RBI	BA
1947	Dunn-Erwin	of	33	117	21	31	3	2	3	1	3	19	.265

Other teams played for: Raleigh (C), Eau Claire (C), Evansville (B), Jackson (B), Hartford (A), Wilson (D).

Bass, Edward Oliver

Year	Club	POS	G	AB	R	H	2B	3B	HR	BB	SB	RBI	BA
1946	Dunn-Erwin	of	109	446	75	144	30	9	19	—	2	110	.323

Other teams played for: Anniston (B), Bluefield (D), Macon (B), Miami (C), Lakeland (C), DeLand (D), Fort Lauderdale (B), Shelby (D), St. Hyacinthe (C), Portsmouth, Va. (B).

Bassler, Robert E.

Year	Club	POS	G	AB	R	H	2B	3B	HR	BB	SB	RBI	BA
1948	Red Springs	p	20	76	14	10	2	0	0	7	0	8	.132
1949	Red Springs	p	11	12	0	0	0	0	0	2	0	0	.000

Year	Club	G	CG	W	L	IP	H	R	BB	SO	ERA
1948	Red Springs	30	16	14	7	228	234	126	110	158	3.99
1949	Red Springs	11	—	—	—	<45	—	—	—	—	—

Other teams played for: Youngstown (C).

Bauder, Raymond Thomas "Ray"

Year	Club	POS	G	AB	R	H	2B	3B	HR	BB	SB	RBI	BA
1949	Red Springs	1b	97	349	53	93	17	2	0	60	8	43	.266

Other teams played for: Portsmouth, Ohio (D), Tarboro (D).

Becker, Henry C.

Year	Club	POS	G	AB	R	H	2B	3B	HR	BB	SB	RBI	BA
1947	Smith.-Selma	of	26	110	23	39	5	8	1	9	3	13	.355

Other teams played for: Lancaster (B), Albany (A), Utica (A), Tarboro (D), Suffolk (D).

12. Player Register—Beeson

Beeson, Harry Leon

Year	Club	POS	G	AB	R	H	2B	3B	HR	BB	SB	RBI	BA
1948	Warsaw	of	28	103	21	26	4	0	0	14	2	12	.245

Other teams played for: Goldsboro (D)

Belcher, Neil Edwin

Year	Club	G	CG	W	L	IP	H	R	BB	SO	ERA
1946	Angier-Fuquay	4	0	0	2	12	19	15	4	5	—

Other teams played for: Thomasville, Ga. (D), Mooresville (D)

Bell, Earl Jackson "Jack"

Year	Club	POS	G	AB	R	H	2B	3B	HR	BB	SB	RBI	BA
1947	Dunn-Erwin	2b	42										
	Clinton	2b	2										
	totals:	2b	44	165	29	41	9	1	1	26	3	24	.248

Other teams played for: Kannapolis (D), Wilmington, Del, (B), Knoxville (A), Mobile (A), Wilkes-Barre (A), Norfolk (B), Butler (C), Jenkins (D)

Bell, Luby Francis

Year	Club	POS	G	AB	R	H	2B	3B	HR	BB	SB	RBI	BA
1948	Warsaw	p	15	24	2	5	0	0	0	1	0	0	.208

Other teams played for: None

Year	Club	G	CG	W	L	IP	H	R	BB	SO	ERA
1948	Warsaw	14	2	2	7	55	70	55	49	24	7.04

Other teams played for:

Bennett, John Wilber "Jack"

Year	Club	POS	G	AB	R	H	2B	3B	HR	BB	SB	RBI	BA
1949	Smith.-Selma	p	26	66	9	19	0	0	0	5	0	8	.288
1950	Smith.-Selma	p	25	74	3	7	0	0	0	2	0	1	.095

Year	Club	G	CG	W	L	IP	H	R	BB	SO	ERA
1949	Smith.-Selma	17	7	10	3	122	125	65	77	58	3.91
1950	Smith.-Selma	22	14	8	12	173	177	91	106	77	3.54

Other teams played for: Oak Ridge (D), Hazard), Cambridge (D), Big Stone Gap (D)

Benson, Archie

Year	Club	G	CG	W	L	IP	H	R	BB	SO	ERA
1946	Wilmington	1	—	0	0	4	—	—	—	—	—

Other teams played for: None

12. Player Register—Bernstein

Benton, Clint D.

Year	Club	POS	G	AB	R	H	2B	3B	HR	BB	SB	RBI	BA
1946	Smithfield	p	10	23	6	3	1	0	0	—	0	0	.130
1947	Smith.-Selma	p	17	34	3	3	0	0	0	0	0	2	.088

Year	Club	G	CG	W	L	IP	H	R	BB	SO	ERA
1946	Smithfield	10	5	2	6	61	90	68	31	13	—
1947	Smith.-Selma	17	3	3	7	78	105	71	29	33	5.54

Other teams played for: None

Benton, William E. "Billy"

Year	Club	POS	G	AB	R	H	2B	3B	HR	BB	SB	RBI	BA
1947	Wilmington	of	126	539	100	159	22	10	10	54	24	73	.295
1948	Wilmington	of	137	555	120	195	37	15	17	77	19	123	.351

Other teams played for: Savannah (A)

Berger, Eugene W. "Gene"

Year	Club	POS	G	AB	R	H	2B	3B	HR	BB	SB	RBI	BA
1947	Lumberton	ss	11	44	7	6	0	0	1	6	0	3	.136

Other teams played for: Centralia (D), Iola (D)

Bernardini, Ralph Frank

Year	Club	POS	G	AB	R	H	2B	3B	HR	BB	SB	RBI	BA
1949	Sanford	c	<10	—	—	—	—	—	—	—	—	—	—
1950	Rockingham	c	10	37	4	9	1	0	0	4	0	4	.243

Other teams played for: Rocky Mount (D), Wilson (D), Roanoke Rapids (D), Raleigh (B), Granite Falls (D), Hagerstown (B)

Bernier, William Joseph

Year	Club	POS	G	AB	R	H	2B	3B	HR	BB	SB	RBI	BA
1950	Lumberton	p	36	64	9	7	2	0	1	15	0	7	.109

Year	Club	G	CG	W	L	IP	H	R	BB	SO	ERA
1950	Lumberton	34	12	18	5	170	129	70	138	98	3.07

Other teams played for: Mooresville (D), Americus (D), Winston-Salem (b)

Bernstein, Leonard (or Burnstein) "Lenny"

Year	Club	POS	G	AB	R	H	2B	3B	HR	BB	SB	RBI	BA
1946	Wilmington	of	10										
	Sanford	of	17										
	totals:	of	27	90	20	23	6	0	0	—	3	12	.256

12. Player Register—Bidwell

Year	Club	POS	G	AB	R	H	2B	3B	HR	BB	SB	RBI	BA
1947	Smith.-Selma	of	92	244	43	79	16	5	3	37	8	34	.324

Other teams played for: DeLand (D)

Bidwell, Alonzo William

Year	Club	POS	G	AB	R	H	2B	3B	HR	BB	SB	RBI	BA
1950	Clinton	p	14										
	Rockingham	p	17										
	totals:	p	31	57	11	13	3	0	0	14	1	7	.228

Year	Club	G	CG	W	L	IP	H	R	BB	SO	ERA
1950	Clinton	14									
	Rockingham	17									
	totals:	31	15	16	10	196	202	114	123	130	4.04

Other teams played for: Johnson City (D), Elizabethton (D), Greenville, SC (B), Lexington, Ky. (C)

Bird, Alton G., Sr.

Year	Club	POS	G	AB	R	H	2B	3B	HR	BB	SB	RBI	BA
1946	Smithfield	p	40	74	8	13	1	1	0	—	0	4	.176
1947	Smith.-Selma	p	22										
	Warsaw	p	15										
	totals:	p	37	67	1	6	1	0	0	2	0	3	.090
1948	Smith.-Selma	p	19	37	3	9	0	0	0	2	0	3	.243

Year	Club	G	CG	W	L	IP	H	R	BB	SO	ERA
1946	Smithfield	40	11	12	8	187	206	124	85	70	—
1947	Smith.-Selma	22									
	Warsaw	15									
	totals:	37	10	7	12	169	218	136	55	59	5.00
1948	Smith.-Selma	17	7	4	6	92	116	70	26	43	4.40

Other teams played for: None

Blackwell, Vernon C.

Year	Club	POS	G	AB	R	H	2B	3B	HR	BB	SB	RBI	BA
1948	Warsaw	1b	41	147	18	46	10	0	1	20	1	20	.313

Other teams played for: Americus (D), Superior (C), Greenville (D), Rocky Mount (D), Portsmouth, Va. (B), Goldsboro (D)

Blair, Robert Burns

Year	Club	POS	G	AB	R	H	2B	3B	HR	BB	SB	RBI	BA
1950	Red Springs	p	21	48	2	10	0	0	0	6	0	3	.208

12. Player Register—Bold

Year	Club	G	CG	W	L	IP	H	R	BB	SO	ERA
1950	Red Springs	21	7	8	6	118	92	59	120	65	3.43

Other teams played for: Youngstown (C), Lexington (D)

Blake, Dean P.

Year	Club	POS	G	AB	R	H	2B	3B	HR	BB	SB	RBI	BA
1948	Smith.-Selma	3b	103	359	65	90	20	4	0	71	2	38	.251

Other teams played for: Winston-Salem (B), Topeka (C), Hutchinson (C), Durham (C), Waterbury (B), Helena (C)

Bland, Edward Bernard

Year	Club	POS	G	AB	R	H	2B	3B	HR	BB	SB	RBI	BA
1948	Clinton	2b	125	465	77	132	17	4	0	72	1	55	.284
1949	Fayetteville	2b	57	216	55	57	9	3	0	53	10	22	.264

Other teams played for: Lenoir (D), Rome, NY (C), Watertown (C), Greenville, NC (D), Hammond (C), Anderson (B), Edenton (D)

Bohannon, Elmer Leroy "Bo"

Year	Club	POS	G	AB	R	H	2B	3B	HR	BB	SB	RBI	BA
1947	Warsaw	of	103	348	83	97	25	3	14	77	16	82	.279

Other teams played for: Columbia (B), Troy (D), Thomasville, NC (D), Mooresville (D), Dothan (D)

Bohlender, William Lee

Year	Club	POS	G	AB	R	H	2B	3B	HR	BB	SB	RBI	BA
1949	Lumberton	of	134	513	101	157	29	11	3	86	21	88	.305

Other teams played for: Marion, Ohio (D), Sioux Falls (C), Macon (A), Beaumont (AA), Topeka (A), Auston (AA), Tulsa (AA), Colorado Springs (A), Schenectady (A)

Bohonko, John J.

Year	Club	POS	G	AB	R	H	2B	3B	HR	BB	SB	RBI	BA
1946	Clinton	2b	17	51	10	16	5	2	0	—	3	9	.314
1947	Clinton	2b	30	120	24	24	1	4	2	30	3	14	.200

Other teams played for: Cordele (D), Olean (D), Lynchburg (C), Newport News (C), Wilson (B), Goldsboro (D), Springfield, Il, (B), Elmira (A), Suffolk (D)

Bold, Bernard

Year	Club	POS	G	AB	R	H	2B	3B	HR	BB	SB	RBI	BA
1948	Lumberton	of	10	34	1	2	0	0	0	3	2	0	.059

Other teams played for: None

12. Player Register—Bollinger

Bollinger, William

Year	Club	POS	G	AB	R	H	2B	3B	HR	BB	SB	RBI	BA
1949	Sanford	ss	74	238	52	52	11	3	0	78	10	16	.218

Other teams played for: None

Bomar, Raymond E.

Year	Club	POS	G	AB	R	H	2B	3B	HR	BB	SB	RBI	BA
1946	Angier-Fuquay	p	40	84	10	15	4	0	0	—	1	10	.179

Year	Club	G	CG	W	L	IP	H	R	BB	SO	ERA
1946	Angier-Fuquay	28	9	11	8	150	213	135	43	32	—

Other teams played for: Leaksville (D)

Bonds, Kenneth Lee

Year	Club	POS	G	AB	R	H	2B	3B	HR	BB	SB	RBI	BA
1950	Clinton	c	73	219	31	63	14	2	0	39	3	39	.288

Other teams played for: Americus (D), Roanoke Rapids (D), Charlotte (B)

Boos, Minor Herschel

Year	Club	G	CG	W	L	IP	H	R	BB	SO	ERA
1946	Dunn-Erwin	4	0	1	1	19	28	24	20	11	—

Other teams played for: Kinston (D)

Borneman, Henry D.

Year	Club	POS	G	AB	R	H	2B	3B	HR	BB	SB	RBI	BA
1948	Wilminton	p	10										
	Dunn-Erwin	p	2										
	totals:	p	12	17	3	2	1	0	0	1	0	2	.118

Other teams played for: Hendersonville (D)

Bortz, George W.

Year	Club	POS	G	AB	R	H	2B	3B	HR	BB	SB	RBI	BA
1946	Sanford	p	31	97	6	13	1	1	0	—	0	9	.134
1947	Sanford	p	30	86	12	10	3	0	0	7	0	9	.116

Year	Club	G	CG	W	L	IP	H	R	BB	SO	ERA
1946	Sanford	31	21	14	14	237	220	116	108	193	—
1947	Sanford	27	15	13	8	195	196	124	92	180	3.65

Other teams played for: Mayodan (D0, Elizabethton (D), South Boston (D), Mouint Airy (D), Burlington (C)

12. Player Register—Brenner

Bosley, Arthur Roland

Year	Club	POS	G	AB	R	H	2B	3B	HR	BB	SB	RBI	BA
1949	Wilmington	util	19	40	7	9	2	1	0	4	1	1	.225

Other teams played for: None

Bosser, Melvin Edward "Mel"

Year	Club	POS	G	AB	R	H	2B	3B	HR	BB	SB	RBI	BA
1949	Lumberton	p	10	25	2	6	0	0	0	1	1	1	.240

Year	Club	G	CG	W	L	IP	H	R	BB	SO	ERA
1949	Lumberton	10	6	2	4	62	88	37	29	25	4.50

Other teams played for: Dover (D), Thomasville, Ga. (D), Selma (B) Syracuse (AA), Cincinnati (ML), Carrollton (D), Memphis (AA), Burlington, NC (B), Augusta (A)

Bowen, Warren J.

Year	Club	POS	G	AB	R	H	2B	3B	HR	BB	SB	RBI	BA
1950	Lumberton	of	129	476	115	137	12	9	4	127	11	74	.288

Other teams played for: Ardmore (D)

Bowman,

Year	Club	POS	G	AB	R	H	2B	3B	HR	BB	SB	RBI	BA
1946	Angier-Fuquay	—	<10	—	—	—	—	—	—	—	—	—	—

Other teams played for: Unkown

Boyco,

Year	Club	POS	G	AB	R	H	2B	3B	HR	BB	SB	RBI	BA
1946	Clinton	c	7	19	2	3	1	0	0	1	—	0	.158

Other teams played for: Unknown

Brady, Richard T.

Year	Club	POS	G	AB	R	H	2B	3B	HR	BB	SB	RBI	BA
1947	Smith.-Selma	p	12	24	0	5	1	0	0	5	1	2	.208

Year	Club	G	CG	W	L	IP	H	R	BB	SO	ERA
1947	Smith.-Selma	11	3	2	5	61	81	51	32	26	5.02

Other teams played for: None

Brenner, John Andrew "Jack"

Year	Club	POS	G	AB	R	H	2B	3B	HR	BB	SB	RBI	BA
1948	Lumberton	ss	59	223	32	47	3	1	0	28	10	10	.211

Other teams played for: Springfield, Mass. (B), Quebec (C)

12. Player Register—Brewer

Brewer, Orbie Lee

Year	Club	POS	G	AB	R	H	2B	3B	HR	BB	SB	RBI	BA
1948	Warsaw	3b	29	111	15	31	4	1	0	15	4	14	.279

Other teams played for: Johnson City (D), Erwin (D), Statesville (D), Nashville (A), Elizabethton (D), Moultrie (D)

Brickner, Arthur J.

Year	Club	POS	G	AB	R	H	2B	3B	HR	BB	SB	RBI	BA
1949	Wilmington	c	62	182	16	43	5	1	0	25	0	21	.236

Other teams played for: Marion, NC (D)

Bridges, Harry

Year	Club	POS	G	AB	R	H	2B	3B	HR	BB	SB	RBI	BA
1947	Wilmington	1b	112	449	65	140	25	7	2	41	5	94	.312

Other teams played for: None

Bridgman, Newton Boyce

Year	Club	POS	G	AB	R	H	2B	3B	HR	BB	SB	RBI	BA
1948	Lumberton	p	8	—	—	—	—	—	—	—	—	—	—

Year	Club	G	CG	W	L	IP	H	R	BB	SO	ERA
1948	Lumberton	8	5	5	1	57	47	17	20	16	1.58

Other teams played for: None

Brisson, Virgil Evans

Year	Club	POS	G	AB	R	H	2B	3B	HR	BB	SB	RBI	BA
1950	Wilmington	p	17	12	1	2	0	0	0	1	0	2	.167

Year	Club	G	CG	W	L	IP	H	R	BB	SO	ERA
1950	Wilmington	17	—	—	—	<45	—	—	—	—	—

Other teams played for: Cordele (D), Pauls Valley (D), Mayfield (D)

Britt, John W.

Year	Club	POS	G	AB	R	H	2B	3B	HR	BB	SB	RBI	BA
1950	Clinton	of	19	79	12	15	2	5	1	5	1	11	.190

Other teams played for: Wilson (D), DeLand (D), St. Augustine (D), Palatka (D)

Brittain, August Schuster "Gus"

Year	Club	POS	G	AB	R	H	2B	3B	HR	BB	SB	RBI	BA
1946	Wilmington	of	61	201	29	64	13	0	7	—	3	40	.318

Other teams played for: Beckley (C), Tulsa (A), Fort Worth (A), Cincinnati (ML),

Greenville, SC (B), Trenton (A), Syracuse (AA), Springfield, Mass. (A), Salisbury, Md. (D), Rocky Mount (D), Montreal (B), Lexington, NC (D), Montgomery (B)

Brockman, Irwin Ernest "Ernie"

Year	Club	POS	G	AB	R	H	2B	3B	HR	BB	SB	RBI	BA
1948	Red Springs	ss	117	430	78	135	12	6	0	72	24	65	.314
1949	Red Springs	2b	137	484	103	124	16	7	1	61	23	59	.256

Other teams played for: None

Brooks, George J.

Year	Club	POS	G	AB	R	H	2B	3B	HR	BB	SB	RBI	BA
1946	Wilmington	util	42	90	7	13	0	0	0	—	1	4	.144

Other teams played for: Daytona Beach (D), Gastonia (D)

Brooks, Kenneth C.

Year	Club	POS	G	AB	R	H	2B	3B	HR	BB	SB	RBI	BA
1949	Fayetteville	p	1										
	Wilmington	p	17										
	totals:	p	18	34	0	4	1	0	0	1	0	0	.118

Year	Club	G	CG	W	L	IP	H	R	BB	SO	ERA
1949	Fayetteville	1									
	Wilmington	16									
	totals:	17	3	1	6	83	116	69	38	33	5.53

Other teams played for: Greenville, NC (D)

Broseker, Gordon H.

Year	Club	POS	G	AB	R	H	2B	3B	HR	BB	SB	RBI	BA
1949	Wilmington	c	18	34	7	5	2	0	0	5	0	8	.147

Other teams played for: None

Brown,

Year	Club	POS	G	AB	R	H	2B	3B	HR	BB	SB	RBI	BA
1946	Smith.-Selma	—	<10	—	—	—	—	—	—	—	—	—	—

Other teams played for: Unknown

Brown, Lawrence R.

Year	Club	POS	G	AB	R	H	2B	3B	HR	BB	SB	RBI	BA
1948	Red Springs	util	19	39	6	8	4	0	0	10	1	4	.205

Other teams played for: None

12. Player Register—Brown

Brown, Richard I.

Year	Club	POS	G	AB	R	H	2B	3B	HR	BB	SB	RBI	BA
1947	Red Springs	of	106	347	45	82	15	8	2	24	12	34	.236

Other teams played for: Portsmouth, Ohio (D), Austin (B)

Brown, Wade Andrew "Weenie"

Year	Club	POS	G	AB	R	H	2B	3B	HR	BB	SB	RBI	BA
1949	Sanford	p	16	13	1	1	1	0	0	6	0	2	.077

Year	Club	G	CG	W	L	IP	H	R	BB	SO	ERA
1949	Sanford	16	4	2	9	58	63	47	50	28	5.48

Other teams played for: Lincolnton (D), Shelby (D), Gastonia (D), Statesville, NC (D)

Bryant,

Year	Club	POS	G	AB	R	H	2B	3B	HR	BB	SB	RBI	BA
1946	Smith.-Selma	—	<10	—	—	—	—	—	—	—	—	—	—

Other teams played for: Unknown

Budzin, (Joe?)

Year	Club	POS	G	AB	R	H	2B	3B	HR	BB	SB	RBI	BA
1946	Smith.-Selma	util	10	32	3	9	1	1	0	—	0	4	.281

Other teams played for:

Bullock, Frank N.

Year	Club	POS	G	AB	R	H	2B	3B	HR	BB	SB	RBI	BA
1947	Red Springs	c	51	161	20	47	11	1	1	19	2	28	.292

Other teams played for: Martinsville (D), Satunton (C), Lexington, NC (D)

Burch, Alfred D.

Year	Club	POS	G	AB	R	H	2B	3B	HR	BB	SB	RBI	BA
1947	Red Springs	p	52	101	16	31	2	0	0	7	0	7	.307
1948	Red Springs	p	57	127	15	45	8	0	0	5	0	14	.354

Year	Club	G	CG	W	L	IP	H	R	BB	SO	ERA
1947	Red Springs	37	13	9	12	213	235	150	73	96	4.19
1948	Red Springs	39	26	18	9	266	272	123	90	172	2.84

Other teams played for: Savannah (A), Buffalo (AAA), Lancaster (B), Ottawa (AAA)

Burda, William J.

Year	Club	POS	G	AB	R	H	2B	3B	HR	BB	SB	RBI	BA
1949	Smith.-Selma	2b	19	71	14	20	1	0	0	17	1	16	.282

Other teams played for: Johnson City (D), Duluth (C), Lynchburg (B), Columbus, Ohio (AAA), Miami Beach (B), Selma, Al. (B)

Burgess, Lewis

Year	Club	G	CG	W	L	IP	H	R	BB	SO	ERA
1946	Dunn-Erwin	1	0	0	0	1	—	—	—	—	—

Other teams played for: None

Burk, Ronald Edward

Year	Club	POS	G	AB	R	H	2B	3B	HR	BB	SB	RBI	BA
1948	Dunn-Erwin	2b	49	190	39	53	6	3	1	24	5	14	.279

Other teams played for: Blackstone (D), Fond du Lac (D), La Grange (D)

Burnham, John Edward

Year	Club	POS	G	AB	R	H	2B	3B	HR	BB	SB	RBI	BA
1949	Wilmington	util	11	28	6	8	0	2	0	4	0	3	.286
1950	Red Springs	3b	107	434	52	121	19	8	2	47	19	53	.279

Other teams played for: Federalsburg (D), Salisbury, Md. (D)

Burns,

Year	Club	G	CG	W	L	IP	H	R	BB	SO	ERA
1946	Smith.-Selma	1	0	0	0	1/3	—	—	—	—	—

Other teams played for: Unknown

Burris, Carl Jackson

Year	Club	POS	G	AB	R	H	2B	3B	HR	BB	SB	RBI	BA
1950	Clinton	of	107	356	91	86	9	3	2	109	17	42	.242

Other teams played for: Troy (D)

Burrows, John

Year	Club	G	CG	W	L	IP	H	R	BB	SO	ERA
1946	Clinton	2	0	0	1	5	6	5	7	0	—

Other teams played for: York (A), Alexandria (D), Opelousas (D), Gladewater (C), San Antonio (A), Selma, Al. (B), Chattanooga (A), Wilmington, Del. (B), Philadelphia Ahtletics (ML), Chicago Cubs (ML), Atlanta (A), Buffalo (AA), Thiboduax (D), Anniston (B), Birmingham (AA), Phoenix (C)

12. Player Register—Butcher

Butcher, Edward "Ned"

Year	Club	POS	G	AB	R	H	2B	3B	HR	BB	SB	RBI	BA
1946	Smith.-Selma	of	30	94	11	20	3	1	1	—	2	18	.213
1947	Sanford	ss	34	104	26	25	4	1	1	39	4	12	.240

Other teams played for: None

Butler, Lester

Year	Club	G	CG	W	L	IP	H	R	BB	SO	ERA
1946	Dunn-Erwin	1	0	0	1	0	0	3	3	0	—

Other teams played for: None

Byrd, Carl L.

Year	Club	G	CG	W	L	IP	H	R	BB	SO	ERA
1946	Dunn-Erwin	3	1	1	1	20	31	16	8	14	—

Other teams played for: Portsmouth, Va. (B), Williamsport (A), Sanford, NC (D-Bi-State Lg.)

Cabaniss, Proctor Eugene "Jerry"

Year	Club	POS	G	AB	R	H	2B	3B	HR	BB	SB	RBI	BA
1947	Lumberton	2b	119	507	87	161	27	11	8	15	10	100	.318

Other teams played for: Tallahassee (D), Davenport (B)

Calo, Antonio

Year	Club	POS	G	AB	R	H	2B	3B	HR	BB	SB	RBI	BA
1946	Sanford	—	<10	—	—	—	—	—	—	—	—	—	—

Other teams played for: None

Campau, William J.

Year	Club	POS	G	AB	R	H	2B	3B	HR	BB	SB	RBI	BA
1946	Clinton	c	108	437	70	147	22	5	16	—	4	85	.336

Other teams played for: Tiffin (D), Zanesville (D), Portsmouth, Va. (B), Des Moines (A)

Campbell, Thomas Carl "Bud"

Year	Club	POS	G	AB	R	H	2B	3B	HR	BB	SB	RBI	BA
1949	Red Springs	ss	74	302	52	75	15	5	5	27	6	40	.248

Other teams played for: Galax (D), Martinsville (B), Fayetteville (B), Lexington, NC (D), High Point-Thomasville (D)

12. Player Register—Castagna

Carabba, David

Year	Club	POS	G	AB	R	H	2B	3B	HR	BB	SB	RBI	BA
1950	Whiteville	of	42	158	28	33	4	3	1	27	0	27	.209

Other teams played for: None

Cardillo, Joseph

Year	Club	POS	G	AB	R	H	2B	3B	HR	BB	SB	RBI	BA
1950	Clinton	1b	128	449	82	117	20	6	6	119	25	72	.261

Other teams played for: None

Carpenter, Wallace Reid

Year	Club	POS	G	AB	R	H	2B	3B	HR	BB	SB	RBI	BA
1949	Red Springs	p	38	85	22	25	4	4	0	15	0	9	.294

Year	Club	G	CG	W	L	IP	H	R	BB	SO	ERA
1949	Red Springs	18	11	10	5	130	124	75	89	75	3.32

Other teams played for: Bristol (D), Johnson City (D), Martinsville (B), Hammond (C), Granite Falls (D), Statesville, NC (D)

Carrabus, Rudolph

Year	Club	POS	G	AB	R	H	2B	3B	HR	BB	SB	RBI	BA
1950	Whiteville	ss	29	74	10	11	0	0	0	25	1	3	.149

Other teams played for: Wytheville/Bassett (D)

Carroll, Preston Welch

Year	Club	POS	G	AB	R	H	2B	3B	HR	BB	SB	RBI	BA
1947	Smith.-Selma	of	68	277	46	91	5	2	1	23	22	22	.329
1948	Smith.-Selma	of	98	403	71	130	23	2	1	64	65	38	.323

Other teams played for: Burlington (C), Greensboro (C)

Carter, Donald James "Don"

Year	Club	POS	G	AB	R	H	2B	3B	HR	BB	SB	RBI	BA
1947	Red Springs	p	38	96	17	29	6	5	1	5	0	9	.302

Year	Club	G	CG	W	L	IP	H	R	BB	SO	ERA
1947	Red Springs	15	6	3	7	97	110	64	32	31	4.19

Other teams played for: None

Castagna, Vincent

Year	Club	POS	G	AB	R	H	2B	3B	HR	BB	SB	RBI	BA
1950	Red Springs	3b	21	65	7	10	3	1	0	9	2	4	.154

Other teams played for: Tarboro (D)

12. Player Register—Castleberry

Castleberry, Hoyt Gold

Year	Club	G	CG	W	L	IP	H	R	BB	SO	ERA
1946	Smith.-Selma	1	—	0	0	3	—	—	—	—	—

Other teams played for:

Catapano, Joseph Anthony

Year	Club	G	CG	W	L	IP	H	R	BB	SO	ERA
1946	Clinton	3	0	1	0	18	18	12	14	7	—

Other teams played for: Pittsfield (C)

Causey, Richard Douglas "Rick"

Year	Club	POS	G	AB	R	H	2B	3B	HR	BB	SB	RBI	BA
1949	Sanford	p	53	135	16	36	8	1	2	12	1	26	.267
1950	Sanford	p	27	82	6	14	3	0	1	5	1	6	.171

Year	Club	G	CG	W	L	IP	H	R	BB	SO	ERA
1949	Sanford	31	18	13	12	234	218	136	145	152	3.04
1950	Sanford	25	14	12	8	179	161	95	124	148	3.37

Other teams played for: Wilson (D), Kinston (D), Goldsboro (D), Leesburg (D), Lincolnton (D), Newton-Conover (D)

Chafin, Loran

Year	Club	POS	G	AB	R	H	2B	3B	HR	BB	SB	RBI	BA
1947	Lumberton	util	11	46	5	11	2	0	0	1	0	9	.239

Other teams played for: Eastman (D), St. Augustine (D), Macon (A), Greenville, SC (B), Columbia (A), Burlington, Ill. (B), Tifton (D), Jacksonville Beach (D), Portsmouth, Va. (B), Macon (A)

Chambers, George

Year	Club	G	CG	W	L	IP	H	R	BB	SO	ERA
1950	Rockingham	<10	—	—	—	—	—	—	—	—	—

Other teams played for: Unknown

Cheshire, John Lewis

Year	Club	POS	G	AB	R	H	2B	3B	HR	BB	SB	RBI	BA
1947	Wilmington	p	35	100	11	28	3	2	0	7	0	16	.280
1948	Wilmington	p	42	108	19	34	4	1	0	12	1	14	.315
1949	Wilmington	p	20	52	8	19	3	1	1	6	0	12	.365

Year	Club	G	CG	W	L	IP	H	R	BB	SO	ERA
1947	Wilmington	35	24	19	8	251	207	115	109	214	2.83
1948	Wilmington	38	24	19	11	268	208	97	150	258	2.35

12. Player Register—Cieply

Year	Club	G	CG	W	L	IP	H	R	BB	SO	ERA
1949	Wilmington	13	5	6	5	82	92	70	53	47	5.49

Other teams played for: Danville-Schoolfield (D), Roanoke (B)

Childers, John G.

Year	Club	POS	G	AB	R	H	2B	3B	HR	BB	SB	RBI	BA
1948	Lumberton	of	45	142	15	32	4	2	0	14	4	15	.225

Other teams played for: Erwin, Tenn. (D), Wyhteville/Bassett (D), North Wilkesboro (D), Lenoir (D)

Childs, William Brown

Year	Club	POS	G	AB	R	H	2B	3B	HR	BB	SB	RBI	BA
1948	Smith.-Selma	util	21	53	5	8	2	0	0	7	1	1	.151

Other teams played for: None

Chinnis, Warner M.

Year	Club	G	CG	W	L	IP	H	R	BB	SO	ERA
1946	Angier-Fuquay	3	—	0	0	4	—	—	—	—	—

Other teams played for: Welch (D), Galax (D)

Chorbora, Michael

Year	Club	POS	G	AB	R	H	2B	3B	HR	BB	SB	RBI	BA
1947	Red Springs	of	25	102	15	26	4	2	3	5	3	20	.255

Other teams played for: None

Chute, William Elwin Jr. "Charlie"

Year	Club	POS	G	AB	R	H	2B	3B	HR	BB	SB	RBI	BA
1949	Sanford	of	50	189	37	57	11	2	2	25	1	29	.302

Other teams played for: West Palm Beach (D), Greenville, NC (D), New Bern (D),

Ciani, Nicholas Joseph "Nick"

Year	Club	POS	G	AB	R	H	2B	3B	HR	BB	SB	RBI	BA
1947	Smith.-Selma	of	14	42	11	11	2	1	0	4	3	6	.262

Other teams played for: Lenoir (D), Goldsboro (D), Hamilton (D), Tallassee (D)

Cieply, Walter

Year	Club	POS	G	AB	R	H	2B	3B	HR	BB	SB	RBI	BA
1950	Rockingham	of	52	176	21	39	5	3	0	14	3	28	.222

Other teams played for: Rocky Mount (D)

12. Player Register—Cieslinski

Cieslinski (aka Cecil), Henry E.

Year	Club	POS	G	AB	R	H	2B	3B	HR	BB	SB	RBI	BA
1947	Clinton	util	100	425	71	120	17	7	4	40	9	59	.282

Other teams played for: Danville-Schoolfield (D), Radford (D), Galax(D),

Clayton, John E.

Year	Club	POS	G	AB	R	H	2B	3B	HR	BB	SB	RBI	BA
1949	Sanford	2b	74	239	52	55	16	0	1	98	2	29	.230

Other teams played for: Burlington (C)

Clayton, Thomas Hill

Year	Club	POS	G	AB	R	H	2B	3B	HR	BB	SB	RBI	BA
1947	Red Springs	of	84	315	52	90	18	6	3	40	6	63	.286
1948	Red Springs	of	37	118	21	29	7	2	6	25	1	28	.246
1949	Red Springs	of	17										
	Sanford	of	57										
	totals:	of	74	218	43	48	6	1	4	49	5	31	.220

Other teams played for: Martinsville (C), Savannah (A),

Clegg, Hoyt

Year	Club	POS	G	AB	R	H	2B	3B	HR	BB	SB	RBI	BA
1947	Sanford	p	31	87	10	17	1	0	1	6	1	9	.195
1948	Sanford	p	44	91	20	24	4	1	3	10	0	13	.264
1949	Sanford	p	36	106	8	25	3	1	0	5	1	11	.236
1950	Sanford	p	41	109	15	27	2	1	3	17	0	27	.248

Year	Club	G	CG	W	L	IP	H	R	BB	SO	ERA
1947	Sanford	28	15	15	7	195	210	120	82	86	4.29
1948	Sanford	31	18	15	6	208	215	109	78	132	3.50
1949	Sanford	31	26	19	9	242	222	105	81	194	2.57
1950	Sanford	29	24	24	5	235	237	108	92	147	3.22

Other teams played for: Marion (D)

Clemmer,

Year	Club	POS	G	AB	R	H	2B	3B	HR	BB	SB	RBI	BA
1946	Angier-F.	—	<10	—	—	—	—	—	—	—	—	—	—

Other teams played for:

Clinard, Cloris H.

Year	Club	G	CG	W	L	IP	H	R	BB	SO	ERA
1946	Angier-Fuquay	7	3	5	2	37	41	19	15	30	—

Other teams played for: Mount Airy (D)

12. Player Register—Colones

Coakley, John B.

Year	Club	POS	G	AB	R	H	2B	3B	HR	BB	SB	RBI	BA
1947	Red Springs	p	11	19	2	3	0	0	0	0	0	2	.158

Year	Club	G	CG	W	L	IP	H	R	BB	SO	ERA
1947	Red Springs	11	1	3	3	46	45	32	36	38	5.09

Other teams played for: Federalsburg (D), Aberdeen (C), Springfield, Ill. (B), Gloversville-Johnstown (C)

Colclough, John C. "Julius"

Year	Club	G	CG	W	L	IP	H	R	BB	SO	ERA
1946	Angier-Fuquay	6	0	0	1	8	12	12	14	5	—

Other teams played for: Newport News (B), Zanesville (D), Durham (C)

Collins, Fleet Marion

Year	Club	POS	G	AB	R	H	2B	3B	HR	BB	SB	RBI	BA
1947	Dunn-Erwin	ss	64	265	57	64	15	5	1	33	6	26	.242

Other teams played for: Gainesville (D), Palatka (D)

Collins, Leonard Thomas

Year	Club	POS	G	AB	R	H	2B	3B	HR	BB	SB	RBI	BA
1949	Fayetteville	p	31	52	7	9	3	0	0	9	0	5	.173

Year	Club	G	CG	W	L	IP	H	R	BB	SO	ERA
1949	Fayetteville	30	8	6	13	148	188	119	63	59	4.74

Other teams played for: Mount Airy (D), Morganton (D)

Collins, Stephen C. "Steve"

Year	Club	POS	G	AB	R	H	2B	3B	HR	BB	SB	RBI	BA
1950	Wilmington	ss	100	375	50	108	30	3	1	51	6	50	.288

Other teams played for: Burlington (D), Knoxville (A), Rochester (AA), Mobiel (A), Toledo (AA), Atlanta (AA), Kinston (D), Moultrie (D), Rocky Mount (D), Greenwood (B), New Bern (D)

Colones, John

Year	Club	POS	G	AB	R	H	2B	3B	HR	BB	SB	RBI	BA
1947	Smith.-Selma	util	29	101	20	30	1	0	1	15	8	10	.297

Other teams played for: None

12. Player Register—Condit

Condit, Clarence L. Jr. "Clancy"

Year	Club	POS	G	AB	R	H	2B	3B	HR	BB	SB	RBI	BA
1948	Dunn-Erwin	p	21	52	11	11	1	0	0	6	0	3	.212
1949	Dunn-Erwin	p	53	104	21	24	2	0	0	26	0	15	.231

Year	Club	G	CG	W	L	IP	H	R	BB	SO	ERA
1948	Dunn-Erwin	14	10	7	5	102	109	61	47	94	3.71
1949	Dunn-Erwin	33	19	20	9	225	198	123	157	264	3.60

Other teams played for: Zanesville (D), Newport News (B), Danville, Ill. (B), Pueblo (A), Roanoke Rapids (D), Durham (B)

Conn, Hampton T.

Year	Club	POS	G	AB	R	H	2B	3B	HR	BB	SB	RBI	BA
1947	Warsaw	p	38	77	11	13	0	0	0	13	0	7	.169

Year	Club	G	CG	W	L	IP	H	R	BB	SO	ERA
1947	Warsaw	34	18	9	17	216	263	153	69	130	4.64

Other teams played for: Paducah (D), Hot Srpings (C), Welch (D), Bridgeport (B), Raleigh (C), Jackson (B)

Conn, James C.

Year	Club	POS	G	AB	R	H	2B	3B	HR	BB	SB	RBI	BA
1949	Sanford	p	12	15	0	1	0	0	0	3	0	0	.067

Year	Club	G	CG	W	L	IP	H	R	BB	SO	ERA
1949	Sanford	12	—	—	—	<45	—	—	—	—	—

Other teams played for: None

Connelly, William F.

Year	Club	POS	G	AB	R	H	2B	3B	HR	BB	SB	RBI	BA
1946	Dunn-Erwin	—	<10	—	—	—	—	—	—	—	—	—	—

Other teams played for: Kingsport (D)?, Bridegeport (B)?

Cooper, Kenneth Wilson

Year	Club	POS	G	AB	R	H	2B	3B	HR	BB	SB	RBI	BA
1948	Sanford	p	12	13	1	3	0	0	0	2	0	0	.231
1949	Smith.-Selma	p	10	16	2	2	0	0	0	1	0	1	.125
1950	Whiteville	p	29	54	7	16	2	3	0	6	0	8	.296

Year	Club	G	CG	W	L	IP	H	R	BB	SO	ERA
1948	Sanford	12	—	—	—	<45	—	—	—	—	—
1949	Smith.-Selma	—	—	—	—	<45	—	—	—	—	—

12. Player Register—Cotten

Year	Club	G	CG	W	L	IP	H	R	BB	SO	ERA
1950	Whiteville	18	10	6	9	109	110	92	111	86	5.78

Other teams played for: Lawrenceville (D)

Corbett, Charles Sprunt Jr. "Charlie"

Year	Club	POS	G	AB	R	H	2B	3B	HR	BB	SB	RBI	BA
1948	Clinton	p	27	65	3	8	1	0	0	8	0	7	.123
1949	Clinton	p	33	80	10	23	0	0	0	9	0	13	.288
1950	Clinton	p	5										
	Smith.-Selma	p	22										
	Wilmington	p	11										
	totals:	p	38	62	7	20	1	0	0	7	0	10	.323

Year	Club	G	CG	W	L	IP	H	R	BB	SO	ERA
1948	Clinton	27	15	13	10	174	198	102	80	79	4.24
1949	Clinton	32	17	11	14	205	202	115	92	117	4.04
1950	Clinton	5									
	Smith.-Selma	22									
	Wilmington	8									
	totals:	35	9	8	8	163	184	107	83	101	3.75

Other teams played for: None

Costinette, Robert H.

Year	Club	POS	G	AB	R	H	2B	3B	HR	BB	SB	RBI	BA
1950	Wilmington	p	23	24	5	2	0	1	0	5	0	2	.083

Year	Club	G	CG	W	L	IP	H	R	BB	SO	ERA
1950	Wilmington	22	1	0	7	66	70	95	132	65	11.86

Other teams played for: Muncie (D)

Costler,

Year	Club	G	CG	W	L	IP	H	R	BB	SO	ERA
1946	Clinton	7									
	Smith.-Selma	1									
	totals:	8	0	0	4	22	36	28	15	11	—

Other teams played for: None

Cotten, Cecil H.

Year	Club	POS	G	AB	R	H	2B	3B	HR	BB	SB	RBI	BA
1949	Sanford	of	86	263	42	78	9	2	5	45	2	39	.297

Other teams played for: None

12. Player Register—Covahay

Covahay, William "Billy"

Year	Club	G	CG	W	L	IP	H	R	BB	SO	ERA
1949	Wilmington	—									
	Dunn-Erwin	—									
	totals:	8	3	3	2	51	59	36	25	20	5.12

Other teams played for: None

Cowan, James H.

Year	Club	POS	G	AB	R	H	2B	3B	HR	BB	SB	RBI	BA
1949	Lumberton	c	23	60	6	5	0	0	0	8	0	1	.083

Other teams played for: Rutherford County (D), Moultrie (D)

Coward, Clarence Wesley "Dink"

Year	Club	POS	G	AB	R	H	2B	3B	HR	BB	SB	RBI	BA
1948	Wilmington	of	22	81	17	18	3	2	0	10	1	8	.222

Other teams played for: None

Craddock, William W. "Bill"

Year	Club	POS	G	AB	R	H	2B	3B	HR	BB	SB	RBI	BA
1946	Dunn-Erwin	p	6										
	Sanford	p	8										
	totals:	p	14	16	1	0	0	0	0	—	0	1	.000

Year	Club	G	CG	W	L	IP	H	R	BB	SO	ERA
1946	Dunn-Erwin	6									
	Sanford	7									
	totals:	13	4	2	4	53	70	44	17	11	—

Other teams played for: Newport News (C)

Crawford, Paul Louis

Year	Club	POS	G	AB	R	H	2B	3B	HR	BB	SB	RBI	BA
1946	Sanford	c	102	376	67	107	22	1	8	—	6	71	.285

Other teams played for: Erwin, Tenn. (D), Leaksville (C), Durham (C), Petersburg (D), Elizabeth City (D), Norfolk (B), Plataka (D), Lakeland (D), Hickory (D), St. Petersburg (B), West Palm Beach (B), Norfolk (B), Colonial Heights-Petersburg (B)

Crocker, Thomas G.

Year	Club	POS	G	AB	R	H	2B	3B	HR	BB	SB	RBI	BA
1946	Smithfield	of	17	61	6	17	1	0	1	—	0	10	.279

Other teams played for: Raleigh (C)

12. Player Register—Cross

Cronin, Francis Michael

Year	Club	POS	G	AB	R	H	2B	3B	HR	BB	SB	RBI	BA
1948	Dunn-Erwin	p	14	19	1	5	0	0	0	1	0	2	.263

Year	Club	G	CG	W	L	IP	H	R	BB	SO	ERA
1948	Dunn-Erwin	14	4	3	5	60	75	58	27	23	5.55

Other teams played for: Waycross (D), Atlanta (A), Savannah (B), Durham (B), Mobile (A), Toronto (AA), Columbus (AA), Kinston (D).

Cropcho, John

Year	Club	G	CG	W	L	IP	H	R	BB	SO	ERA
1946	Dunn-Erwin	2									
	Wilmington	1									
	totals:	3	—	0	0	5	—	—	—	—	—

Other teams played for: None

Cross, Jack R.

Year	Club	POS	G	AB	R	H	2B	3B	HR	BB	SB	RBI	BA
1949	Dunn-Erwin	2b	38	110	30	23	0	2	0	26	7	3	.209

Other teams played for: Houma (C), West Palm Beach (D).

Catcher Paul Crawford hit .285 in 102 games for Sanford in 1946 before being sold to the Durham Bulls of the Carolina League in August. His career saw him play for many teams from Virginia to Florida. He is seen here in the uniform of the Elizabeth City, NC team he managed in 1950 and '51 (courtesy the late Pete Howard).

12. Player Register—Crouch

Crouch, George

Year	Club	POS	G	AB	R	H	2B	3B	HR	BB	SB	RBI	BA
1948	Dunn-Erwin	util	11	36	4	4	1	0	0	3	0	0	.111

Other teams played for: None

Crummie, Arthur T.

Year	Club	POS	G	AB	R	H	2B	3B	HR	BB	SB	RBI	BA
1946	Angier-Fuquay	—	<10	—	—	—	—	—	—	—	—	—	—

Other teams played for: None

Crummie, William E. "Willie"

Year	Club	POS	G	AB	R	H	2B	3B	HR	BB	SB	RBI	BA
1947	Lumberton	3b	27	93	15	17	2	1	0	9	0	1	.183

Other teams played for: Rutherford County (D)

Cudemo, Michael N.

Year	Club	POS	G	AB	R	H	2B	3B	HR	BB	SB	RBI	BA
1948	Dunn-Erwin	c	109	330	32	88	10	2	1	54	6	50	.267

Other teams played for: Newnan (D), Dublin (D), Rome (D)

Cullen, Andrew A. Jr. "Andy"

Year	Club	POS	G	AB	R	H	2B	3B	HR	BB	SB	RBI	BA
1946	Wilmington	ss	115	453	95	128	22	8	3	—	30	42	.283

Other teams played for: San Jose (C), Oneonta (C)

Cummings, Joseph

Year	Club	G	CG	W	L	IP	H	R	BB	SO	ERA
1946	Clinton	9	2	1	3	51	73	51	10	7	—

Other teams played for: Pittsfield (C), Galax (D), Leaksville (C)

Curry,

Year	Club	G	CG	W	L	IP	H	R	BB	SO	ERA
1946	Smithfield	1	—	0	0	1	—	—	—	—	—

Other teams played for: Unknown

Dalton, William M.

Year	Club	POS	G	AB	R	H	2B	3B	HR	BB	SB	RBI	BA
1947	Lumberton	p	22	26	7	9	1	0	0	2	0	3	.346
1948	Lumberton	of	110	416	68	123	8	5	2	34	16	42	.296

12. Player Register—Davis

Year	Club	G	CG	W	L	IP	H	R	BB	SO	ERA
1947	Lumberton	22	2	2	2	76	86	62	66	50	7.10

Other teams played for: None

Damon, Robert

Year	Club	POS	G	AB	R	H	2B	3B	HR	BB	SB	RBI	BA
1947	Lumberton	c	19	63	8	14	1	2	0	1	0	12	.222

Other teams played for: None

Daniels, Alexander D. "Alex"

Year	Club	POS	G	AB	R	H	2B	3B	HR	BB	SB	RBI	BA
1946	Smithfield	c	96	318	63	93	14	9	4	—	15	57	.292

Other teams played for: Goldsboro (D), Greenville, NC (D), Ottawa (C), Martinsville (D), Elmira (A), Hagerstown (B), York (B), Albany (A), Harrisburg (B)

Daniels, William "Bill"

Year	Club	G	CG	W	L	IP	H	R	BB	SO	ERA
1946	Angier-Fuquay	1	—	0	0	1	—	—	—	—	—

Other teams played for: Unknown

Dardes, Nicholas

Year	Club	POS	G	AB	R	H	2B	3B	HR	BB	SB	RBI	BA
1950	Lumberton	c	74	196	37	44	9	1	1	72	2	27	.224

Other teams played for: Hazlehurst-Baxley (D), Mooresville (D), Anderson (B), New Iberia (C)

Davis, Hargrove Bellamy "Hoggie"

Year	Club	POS	G	AB	R	H	2B	3B	HR	BB	SB	RBI	BA
1946	Wilmington	of	66	258	41	84	12	2	6	—	2	55	.326
1947	Wilmington	of	90	372	68	119	27	6	12	21	4	77	.320
1948	Wilmington	of	101	404	63	148	31	2	11	32	4	92	.366
1949	Wilmington	of	107	436	72	178	42	5	9	40	6	106	.408
1950	Red Springs	1b	38	141	24	51	13	2	1	19	1	30	.362

Other teams played for: Troy (D), Tuskegee (D), Valdosta (D), Montgomery (B), Savannah (A)

Davis, Jesse O.

Year	Club	POS	G	AB	R	H	2B	3B	HR	BB	SB	RBI	BA
1950	Whiteville	p	47	63	9	7	2	0	0	9	0	3	.111

12. Player Register—Davis

Year	Club	G	CG	W	L	IP	H	R	BB	SO	ERA
1950	Whiteville	31	3	5	8	129	125	107	150	59	5.86

Other teams played for: None

Davis, Walter

Year	Club	G	CG	W	L	IP	H	R	BB	SO	ERA
1946	Dunn-Erwin	1	0	0	1	6	13	9	5	0	—

Other teams played for: Unknown

DeLapp, Royal Stokes Jr. "Mike"

Year	Club	POS	G	AB	R	H	2B	3B	HR	BB	SB	RBI	BA
1949	Fayetteville	of	24										
	Dunn-Erwin	of	19										
	totals:	of	43	105	14	27	20	7	6	22	5	11	.257
1950	Whiteville	of	16										
	Clinton	of	19										
	totals:	of	35	122	24	28	5	1	0	20	1	12	.230

Other teams played for: None

Dellinger, Francis William

Year	Club	G	CG	W	L	IP	H	R	BB	SO	ERA
1946	Dunn-Erwin	1	0	0	1	4	7	6	4	—	—

Other teams played for: Kingsport (D), New Bern (D), Albemarle (D)

Del Piano, (Ronald J.?)

Year	Club	G	CG	W	L	IP	H	R	BB	SO	ERA
1949	Smith.-Selma	—	—	—	—	<45	—	—	—	—	—

Other teams played for: *Goldsboro (D), Moultrie (D), Harlan (D), Eau Claire (C)?*

Dendy, Robert Gerald "Bobby"

Year	Club	POS	G	AB	R	H	2B	3B	HR	BB	SB	RBI	BA
1949	Smith.-Selma	2b	20	65	9	10	1	0	0	14	0	3	.154

Other teams played for: Hazlehurst-Baxley (D), Valdosta (D)

Denning, Elmer Parker "Mickey Mouse"

Year	Club	G	CG	W	L	IP	H	R	BB	SO	ERA
1949	Wilmington	<10	—	—	—	—	—	—	—	—	—

Other teams played for: None

12. Player Register—Dicola

Denning, Granville Morrison "Shamrock"

Year	Club	POS	G	AB	R	H	2B	3B	HR	BB	SB	RBI	BA
1946	Dunn-Erwin	of	101	385	74	117	14	5	11	—	18	80	.304
1947	Dunn-Erwin	of	123	481	101	160	19	9	5	67	25	96	.333
1948	Dunn-Erwin	of	139	524	105	171	30	13	10	97	18	92	.326
1949	Dunn-Erwin	of	133	523	118	185	32	7	7	93	21	119	.354
1950	Whiteville	of	125	470	176	176	35	8	3	98	7	95	.374

Other teams played for: Jamestown (D), Lynchburg (B), Raleigh (C), Jackson (B), Goldsboro (D), Fayetteville (B)

DePriest, Fay E.

Year	Club	POS	G	AB	R	H	2B	3B	HR	BB	SB	RBI	BA
1947	Smith.-Selma	p	15	37	5	9	2	0	0	7	0	8	.243

Other teams played for: Kinston (D), Wilson (D), Danville-Schoolfield (D), Pulaski (D), Salem (D), Lenoir (D), Greensboro (C), Radford (D)

Detweiler, Robert Sterling "Ducky"

Year	Club	POS	G	AB	R	H	2B	3B	HR	BB	SB	RBI	BA
1950	Red Springs	1b	110	398	92	136	21	19	11	90	30	95	.342

Other teams played for: Federalsburg (D), Wilmington, Del. (B), Bradford (D), Bridgeport (B), Evensville (B), Boston Braves (ML), Rochester (AAA), Indianapolis (AAA), Cordele (D), Lexington, NC (D), Salisbury, Md. (B), Fayetteville (B)

Diaz, Amado Quintana

Year	Club	POS	G	AB	R	H	2B	3B	HR	BB	SB	RBI	BA
1949	Fayetteville	p	40	87	12	19	4	0	0	11	1	1	.218

Year	Club	G	CG	W	L	IP	H	R	BB	SO	ERA
1949	Fayetteville	29	14	11	12	169	189	103	83	94	4.31

Other teams played for: Florence (B), Wytheville (D), Leaksville (D), Abingdon (D)

Dichara, Walter (DiChiara?)

Year	Club	POS	G	AB	R	H	2B	3B	HR	BB	SB	RBI	BA
1947	Warsaw	2b	29	118	23	25	3	1	0	17	2	14	.212

Other teams played for: None

Dicola, Charles G. "Chick"

Year	Club	POS	G	AB	R	H	2B	3B	HR	BB	SB	RBI	BA
1949	Sanford	3b	15	57	7	15	4	1	0	7	1	6	.263

Other teams played for: Salisbury, Md. (D), Greensboro (C), Miami Beach (C)

12. Player Register—Diehl

Diehl, Leonard E. Jr.

Year	Club	POS	G	AB	R	H	2B	3B	HR	BB	SB	RBI	BA
1950	Whiteville	ss	52	196	29	45	3	4	1	45	3	24	.230

Other teams played for: Newnan (D)

Diem, Arthur A.

Year	Club	G	CG	W	L	IP	H	R	BB	SO	ERA
1946	Clinton	1	0	1	0	5	7	6	3	1	—

Other teams played for: Bentonville (D), Wiiliamston (D)

Dietrich, Raymond Allen

Year	Club	POS	G	AB	R	H	2B	3B	HR	BB	SB	RBI	BA
1949	Dunn-Erwin	p	20	39	3	9	0	0	0	4	0	1	.231

Year	Club	G	CG	W	L	IP	H	R	BB	SO	ERA
1949	Dunn-Erwin	19	4	6	3	101	81	60	89	70	4.37

Other teams played for: Tarboro (D)

Dillard, Rudolph W. "Rudy"

Year	Club	POS	G	AB	R	H	2B	3B	HR	BB	SB	RBI	BA
1949	Smith.-Selma	p	13	26	4	7	1	0	0	3	0	4	.269

Year	Club	G	CG	W	L	IP	H	R	BB	SO	ERA
1949	Smith.-Selma	13	4	2	4	64	74	65	79	41	7.45

Other teams played for: Jesup (D), Port Arthur (B), Asheville (B), Elmira (A)

Dillinger, Francis

Year	Club	G	CG	W	L	IP	H	R	BB	SO	ERA
1946	Dunn-Erwin	1	0	0	1	4	7	6	4	3	—

Other teams played for: None

DiOrio, Lawrence "Larry"

Year	Club	POS	G	AB	R	H	2B	3B	HR	BB	SB	RBI	BA
1946	Wilmington	of	49	141	25	36	4	2	2	—	1	20	.255
1947	Wilmington	of	6										
	Smith.-Selma	of	18										
	totals:	of	24	62	11	23	0	0	4	9	2	16	.371

Other teams played for: Hickory (D)

Dixon, Ralph William

Year	Club	POS	G	AB	R	H	2B	3B	HR	BB	SB	RBI	BA
1947	Lumberton	of	115	446	78	130	14	11	6	25	8	67	.291
1948	Lumberton	of	91	345	54	101	12	7	7	34	19	47	.293

Other teams played for: Statesville (D), Forest City (D), Selma, Ala. (B), Rutherford County (D), Anderson (B), Rock Hill (B), Greenville, SC (B), Marion (D), Hickory (D), Scranton (A).

Dixon, Robert M.

Year	Club	POS	G	AB	R	H	2B	3B	HR	BB	SB	RBI	BA
1948	Warsaw	c	29	83	14	25	5	3	0	7	0	15	.301

Other teams played for:

Doak, Robert Renfrow "Peanut"

Year	Club	POS	G	AB	R	H	2B	3B	HR	BB	SB	RBI	BA
1948	Red Springs	of	79	198	28	56	5	4	0	23	4	30	.283
1949	Red Springs	of	120	415	70	130	26	8	3	65	10	76	.313

Other teams played for: Scranton (A), Elmira (A), Williamsport (A), Greensboro (C), Hagerstown (B), New Bern (D).

Dobias, John E.

Year	Club	POS	G	AB	R	H	2B	3B	HR	BB	SB	RBI	BA
1950	Red Springs	of	125	502	86	134	21	9	5	69	9	77	.267

Other teams played for: Federalsburg (D), Cordele (D), Fayetteville (B).

Dominic, Raymond

Year	Club	POS	G	AB	R	H	2B	3B	HR	BB	SB	RBI	BA
1950	Clinton	c	11	29	3	5	2	0	0	7	0	2	.172

Other teams played for: Newark, Ohio (D), Fond du Lac (D).

Dopkin, John P. "Lefty"

Year	Club	POS	G	AB	R	H	2B	3B	HR	BB	SB	RBI	BA
1948	Warsaw	p	34	81	10	14	1	1	0	10	0	6	.173

Year	Club	G	CG	W	L	IP	H	R	BB	SO	ERA
1948	Warsaw	34	17	17	8	213	189	110	102	174	3.76

Other teams played for: Goldsboro (D), Quebec (C).

Dornbusch, John William

Year	Club	POS	G	AB	R	H	2B	3B	HR	BB	SB	RBI	BA
1949	Wilmington	of	54	196	35	57	14	4	1	40	9	35	.291

12. Player Register—Dosch

Other teams played for: Baltimore (AA), Wilkes-Barre (A), Centreville (D), St. Petersburg (C), Spartanburg (B), High Point-Thomasville (D), Florence (B)

Dosch, Dean Anthony

Year	Club	POS	G	AB	R	H	2B	3B	HR	BB	SB	RBI	BA
1949	Fayetteville	util	10	27	6	3	1	0	0	11	3	0	.111

Other teams played for: Mount Airy (D), Franklin (D), Kinston (D)

Drew, John A.

Year	Club	POS	G	AB	R	H	2B	3B	HR	BB	SB	RBI	BA
1949	Sanford	util	10	40	4	12	1	0	0	1	1	4	.300

Other teams played for: Bristol (D), Easton (D), Stroudsburg (D), Amsterdam (D)

Duffy, William I. "Bill"

Year	Club	POS	G	AB	R	H	2B	3B	HR	BB	SB	RBI	BA
1950	Rockingham	of	124	467	99	135	18	10	1	122	10	60	.289

Other teams played for: Kinsrton (D), Franklin (D), Edenton (D), Statesville (D)

Dugan, James J.

Year	Club	POS	G	AB	R	H	2B	3B	HR	BB	SB	RBI	BA
1948	Dunn-Erwin	util	18	47	8	6	0	0	0	4	0	5	.128

Other teams played for: None

Duke, Willie Eleanor

Year	Club	POS	G	AB	R	H	2B	3B	HR	BB	SB	RBI	BA
1946	Clinton	of	96	328	106	129	29	6	27	—	15	109	.393
1950	Rockingham	of	38	138	37	48	11	3	4	30	2	35	.348

Other teams played for: Jackson (C), Nashville (A), Memphis (A), Minneapolis (AA), New Orleans (A), Atlanta (A), Little Rock (A), Elmira (A), Wilmington, Del. (B), Portsmouth (B), Knoxville (A), Memphis (A), Durham (C), Winston-Salem (B), Danville, Va. (B), Raleigh (B), Greensboro (B)

Dulworth, Randall "Randy"

Year	Club	POS	G	AB	R	H	2B	3B	HR	BB	SB	RBI	BA
1949	Lumberton	3b	135	532	98	149	30	13	8	52	7	102	.280

Other teams played for: None

Duncan, Romas Hicks Jr.

Year	Club	POS	G	AB	R	H	2B	3B	HR	BB	SB	RBI	BA
1948	Lumberton	c	19	60	5	15	1	0	0	6	0	6	.250

Other teams played for: St. Augustine (D), Rutherford County (D), Portsmouth (B)

12. Player Register—Eager

Dunkleburger, Charles H.

Year	Club	POS	G	AB	R	H	2B	3B	HR	BB	SB	RBI	BA
1947	Red Springs	of	15	47	9	9	3	4	0	4	1	3	.191

Other teams played for: Nyack (D), Martinsville (C)

Dunlap, Joseph Paul

Year	Club	POS	G	AB	R	H	2B	3B	HR	BB	SB	RBI	BA
1946	Angier-Fuquay	of	76	296	60	107	14	3	11	—	0	81	.361

Other teams played for: Columbia (B), Asheville (B), Norfolk (B), Binhamton (A), Indianapolis (AA), Montreal (AA), Birmingham (A), Milwaukee (AA), Williamsport (A), Wilkes-Barre (A), Wilmington, Del. (B), Albany (A), Hartford (A), Portsmouth (B), New Brunswick/Kingston (B)

Dunmore, John G.

Year	Club	POS	G	AB	R	H	2B	3B	HR	BB	SB	RBI	BA
1948	Lumberton	3b	16	66	8	9	0	0	0	5	0	6	.136

Other teams played for: None

Duvall, Benjamin

Year	Club	POS	G	AB	R	H	2B	3B	HR	BB	SB	RBI	BA
1950	Red Springs	util	2										
	Whiteville	util	8										
	totals:	util	10	8	3	2	0	0	0	4	0	0	.250

Other teams played for: None

Dykema, Jack

Year	Club	G	CG	W	L	IP	H	R	BB	SO	ERA
1946	Dunn-Erwin	1	0	0	0	1	—	—	—	—	—

Other teams played for: None

Dziengielewski, Eugene L.

Year	Club	POS	G	AB	R	H	2B	3B	HR	BB	SB	RBI	BA
1950	Clinton	3b	28	98	18	21	1	1	0	16	1	14	.214

Other teams played for: None

Eager, Jack

Year	Club	POS	G	AB	R	H	2B	3B	HR	BB	SB	RBI	BA
1946	Angier-Fuquay	—	<10	—	—	—	—	—	—	—	—	—	—

Other teams played for: None

12. Player Register—Eames

Eames, Paul Edward

Year	Club	POS	G	AB	R	H	2B	3B	HR	BB	SB	RBI	BA
1947	Smith.-Selma	c	94	297	39	72	14	3	3	37	2	39	.242
1948	Smith.-Selma	c	104	306	43	93	16	4	2	41	8	44	.304
1949	Smith.-Selma	c	25	81	22	23	2	1	0	21	4	11	.284

Other teams played for: Kinston (D), Goldsboro (D), Albany, Ga. (D), Johnson City (D), Lynchburg (B), Thomasville, Ga. (D), Harlingen (B), Waycross (D), Tifton (D)

Earich, Jerome Roderic "Rod"

Year	Club	POS	G	AB	R	H	2B	3B	HR	BB	SB	RBI	BA
1949	Lumberton	of											
	Clinton	of											
	totals:	of	48	164	25	43	12	2	0	17	2	32	.262

Other teams played for: Clinton, Iowa (C)

Earl, Leslie Leroy "Les"

Year	Club	POS	G	AB	R	H	2B	3B	HR	BB	SB	RBI	BA
1948	Lumberton	c	20	66	4	15	3	0	0	4	2	7	.227

Other teams played for: Janesville (D), Big Stone Gap (D), Clovis (C), Moultrie (D)

Edens, John Alton "Johnie"

Year	Club	POS	G	AB	R	H	2B	3B	HR	BB	SB	RBI	BA
1946	Wilmington	3b	34	112	13	37	9	0	0	—	1	20	.330
1947	Wilmington	p	53	133	21	47	7	3	1	9	0	21	.353
1948	Wilmington	1b	95	254	44	89	19	2	6	27	10	60	.350
1949	Wilmington	3b	98	315	62	114	21	6	6	44	5	70	.362
1950	Wilmington	3b	120	451	89	155	27	5	4	69	24	65	.344

Year	Club	G	CG	W	L	IP	H	R	BB	SO	ERA
1946	Wilmington	7	5	3	3	50	47	27	24	46	—
1947	Wilmington	30	22	15	11	204	230	116	85	152	3.39
1948	Wilmington	32	19	14	11	194	194	101	87	144	3.66
1949	Wilmington	25	17	11	10	173	186	118	103	140	4.53
1950	Wilmington	11	8	5	4	79	69	31	51	49	2.85

Other teams played for: None

Edwards, James Robert

Year	Club	POS	G	AB	R	H	2B	3B	HR	BB	SB	RBI	BA
1948	Wilmington	p	15										
	Clinton	p	2										
	totals:	p	17	30	5	10	1	0	1	2	0	10	.333

12. Player Register—Ellis

Year	Club	G	CG	W	L	IP	H	R	BB	SO	ERA
1948	Wilmington	15									
	Clinton	2									
	totals:	17	5	8	3	73	81	43	35	38	4.32

Other teams played for: Hopewell (D)

Edwards, Presley James

Year	Club	POS	G	AB	R	H	2B	3B	HR	BB	SB	RBI	BA
1947	Clinton	p	22	37	5	4	0	0	0	5	0	2	.108
1948	Clinton	p	16	34	5	5	2	0	0	6	0	5	.147

Year	Club	G	CG	W	L	IP	H	R	BB	SO	ERA
1947	Clinton	20	4	3	7	84	103	66	31	35	5.46
1948	Clinton	16	5	4	8	88	110	81	46	38	6.03

Other teams played for: None

Ehrhardt, Willard H. "Billy"

Year	Club	POS	G	AB	R	H	2B	3B	HR	BB	SB	RBI	BA
1947	Lumberton	ss	61	244	40	47	8	3	3	25	4	28	.193
1948	Lumberton	ss	62	238	39	66	9	3	2	34	17	28	.277

Other teams played for: St. Augustine (D), Clovis (C), Greensboro (B)

Einsel, William C.

Year	Club	POS	G	AB	R	H	2B	3B	HR	BB	SB	RBI	BA
1947	Red Springs	c	12	17	0	4	1	0	0	2	0	0	.235

Other teams played for: Federalsburg (D)

Ellington, Paul W.

Year	Club	POS	G	AB	R	H	2B	3B	HR	BB	SB	RBI	BA
1947	Smith.-Selma	1b	14	46	11	16	5	0	1	11	2	13	.348

Other teams played for: Roanoke (B), Raleigh (C), Pulaski (D), Mooresville (D), Burlington, NC (C), Abbeville (D), Concord (D)

Ellis,

Year	Club	POS	G	AB	R	H	2B	3B	HR	BB	SB	RBI	BA
1946	Dunn-Erwin	—	<10	—	—	—	—	—	—	—	—	—	—

Other teams played for: Unknown

Ellis, James N. Jr.

Year	Club	POS	G	AB	R	H	2B	3B	HR	BB	SB	RBI	BA
1947	Warsaw	of	12	28	7	8	3	0	0	6	0	7	.286

Other teams played for: Kinston (D)

12. Player Register—Enogh

Enogh,

Year	Club	POS	G	AB	R	H	2B	3B	HR	BB	SB	RBI	BA
1946	Smithfield	—	<10	—	—	—	—	—	—	—	—	—	—

Other teams played for: Unknown

Eonta, Joseph Francis "Joe"

Year	Club	POS	G	AB	R	H	2B	3B	HR	BB	SB	RBI	BA
1946	Sanford	p	6										
	Smithfield	p	34										
	totals:	p	40	140	24	36	4	4	2	—	1	17	.257
1947	Smith.-Selma	of	106	382	67	104	17	6	6	36	4	54	.272
1948	Smith.-Selma	of	72										
	Sanford	of	12										
	totals:	of	84	312	43	94	22	5	6	30	1	59	.301

Year	Club	G	CG	W	L	IP	H	R	BB	SO	ERA
1946	Sanford	4									
	Smith.-Selma	13									
	totals:	17	11	8	7	131	120	67	60	49	—

Other teams played for: Kinston (D)

Eraca, Francis Joseph "Frank"

Year	Club	POS	G	AB	R	H	2B	3B	HR	BB	SB	RBI	BA
1949	Red Springs	c	54	177	24	39	6	4	0	16	2	23	.220

Other teams played for: Nazareth (D), Poughkeepsie (B)

Erath, George Snider

Year	Club	POS	G	AB	R	H	2B	3B	HR	BB	SB	RBI	BA
1948	Lumberton	p	30	72	7	11	2	0	0	2	0	2	.153

Year	Club	G	CG	W	L	IP	H	R	BB	SO	ERA
1948	Lumberton	29	14	8	14	192	215	135	79	88	4.64

Other teams played for: Carthage (D), Sioux Falls (C), St. Augustine (D), Greensboro (B), Sioux City (A), Richmond (B), Danville, Va. (B), Lancaster (B)

Estes, John Leo "Jack"

Year	Club	POS	G	AB	R	H	2B	3B	HR	BB	SB	RBI	BA
1946	Wilmington	p	21	21	2	4	1	0	0	—	0	2	.190

Year	Club	G	CG	W	L	IP	H	R	BB	SO	ERA
1946	Wilmington	18	1	1	7	53	94	71	36	19	—

Other teams played for: Springfield, Ohio (D), Bridgeport (B), Stamford (B), Auburn (C), Waterbury (B), Norton (D), Headland (D)

12. Player Register—Evans

Estevez, J. Ernesto

Year	Club	POS	G	AB	R	H	2B	3B	HR	BB	SB	RBI	BA
1948	Dunn-Erwin	ss	15	58	9	12	3	0	1	13	1	4	.207

Other teams played for: Portsmouth (B), Atlanta (A), Franklin (D), Suffolk (D)

Estill, Anthony "Tony"

Year	Club	POS	G	AB	R	H	2B	3B	HR	BB	SB	RBI	BA
1950	Red Springs	1b	2										
	Whiteville	1b	68										
	totals:	1b	70	213	44	46	9	2	4	72	9	32	.216

Other teams played for: Mattoon (D), Wisconsin Rapids (D), Canton/Vincennes (D), Lewiston (B)

Ethier, Pierre Leo "Pete"

Year	Club	POS	G	AB	R	H	2B	3B	HR	BB	SB	RBI	BA
1950	Lumberton	2b	128	506	146	152	30	12	13	135	43	68	.300

Other teams played for: Mooresville (D), Hopewell (D), Columbus, Ga. (A), Lynchburg (B), Allentown (A), Harlingen (B), Phoenix (C), Savannah (A), Havana (AAA), Albuquerque (A)

Eubanks, Ruie Arizona Jr.

Year	Club	POS	G	AB	R	H	2B	3B	HR	BB	SB	RBI	BA
1946	Angier-Fuquay	—	<10	—	—	—	—	—	—	—	—	—	—

Other teams played for: Durham (C)

Eury, Fred Lee

Year	Club	POS	G	AB	R	H	2B	3B	HR	BB	SB	RBI	BA
1950	Rockingham	p	35	53	4	12	3	1	0	1	0	4	.226

Year	Club	G	CG	W	L	IP	H	R	BB	SO	ERA
1950	Rockingham	35	6	5	8	134	138	92	111	77	5.10

Other teams played for: Emporia (D), Newton-Conover (D), Concord (D)

Evans, Theron Odell

Year	Club	POS	G	AB	R	H	2B	3B	HR	BB	SB	RBI	BA
1947	Clinton	ss	92	392	71	131	22	2	3	34	5	60	.334

Other teams played for: Spartanburg (B), Goldsboro (D), Concord (D), Hendersonville (D), Rutherford County (D)

12. Player Register—Everette

Everette,

Year	Club	G	CG	W	L	IP	H	R	BB	SO	ERA
1946	Angier-Fuquay	4	0	0	2	14	14	14	10	4	—

Other teams played for: Unknown

Faircloth, James Sykes

Year	Club	POS	G	AB	R	H	2B	3B	HR	BB	SB	RBI	BA
1947	Warsaw	p	34	81	13	18	6	0	0	17	0	19	.222

Year	Club	G	CG	W	L	IP	H	R	BB	SO	ERA
1947	Warsaw	28	19	17	6	212	217	117	61	98	3.10

Other teams played for: Goldsboro (D), Rome (C)

Fasano, Benjamin "Benny"

Year	Club	POS	G	AB	R	H	2B	3B	HR	BB	SB	RBI	BA
1950	Lumberton	of/p	11	30	5	8	2	0	1	3	0	2	.267

Other teams played for: Hazlehurst-Baxley (D), Landis (D), Mooresville (D), Americus (D), New Iberia (C), Winston-Salem (B)

Fassler, Leonard

Year	Club	POS	G	AB	R	H	2B	3B	HR	BB	SB	RBI	BA
1948	Wilmingtonp	17	35	7	4	0	0	0	2	0	0	.114

Year	Club	G	CG	W	L	IP	H	R	BB	SO	ERA
1948	Wilmington	17	4	4	5	88	80	66	89	90	5.83

Other teams played for: Lawrenceville (D), Bristol (D), St. Cloud (C), Lawton (D), Enid (C), Sioux City (A)

Fauci, Vincent F.

Year	Club	POS	G	AB	R	H	2B	3B	HR	BB	SB	RBI	BA
1946	Smith.-Selma	—	<10	—	—	—	—	—	—	—	—	—	—

Other teams played for: Wellsville (D), Kingsport (D), Erwin, Tenn. (D), Lancaster (B), Trenton (B), Hagerstown (B)

Fernandez, (possibly Frank)

Year	Club	POS	G	AB	R	H	2B	3B	HR	BB	SB	RBI	BA
1946	Smith.-Selma	—	<10	—	—	—	—	—	—	—	—	—	—

Other teams played for:

12. Player Register—Foote

Fernandez, Frank

Year	Club	POS	G	AB	R	H	2B	3B	HR	BB	SB	RBI	BA
1946	Dunn-Erwin	util	11	35	6	5	1	0	1	—	0	1	.143

Other teams played for:

Fish, Walter Pate "Archie"

Year	Club	POS	G	AB	R	H	2B	3B	HR	BB	SB	RBI	BA
1946	Wilmington	—	—										
	Angier-Fuquay	—	—										
	totals:	—	<10	—	—	—	—	—	—	—	—	—	—

Other teams played for: Danville-Schoolfield (D), Montgomery (B)

Fister, James Peter "Jim"

Year	Club	POS	G	AB	R	H	2B	3B	HR	BB	SB	RBI	BA
1950	Wilmington	2b	85										
	Rockingham	2b	36										
	totals:	2b	121	444	81	119	14	9	7	95	4	65	.268

Other teams played for: Muncie (D), Rockford (C), Leavenworth (C)

Flaim, Raymond S.

Year	Club	POS	G	AB	R	H	2B	3B	HR	BB	SB	RBI	BA
1949	Lumberton	p	29	65	5	10	0	0	0	5	0	4	.154

Year	Club	G	CG	W	L	IP	H	R	BB	SO	ERA
1949	Lumberton	29	15	10	10	173	174	97	83	82	3.49

Other teams played for: Janesville (D)

Fleming, Eugene E. Jr.

Year	Club	POS	G	AB	R	H	2B	3B	HR	BB	SB	RBI	BA
1950	Wilmington	c	22	75	6	14	2	0	2	2	0	11	.187

Other teams played for: Muncie (D), Lockport (D)

Flint,

Year	Club	POS	G	AB	R	H	2B	3B	HR	BB	SB	RBI	BA
1946	Smith.-Selma	—	<10	—	—	—	—	—	—	—	—	—	—

Other teams played for: Unknow

Foote, Ambrose Clifton "Amby"

Year	Club	POS	G	AB	R	H	2B	3B	HR	BB	SB	RBI	BA
1948	Smith.-Selma	p	44	61	14	12	3	1	0	10	4	9	.197
1949	Smith.-Selma	p	48	107	16	22	5	1	0	10	0	12	.206

12. Player Register—Forbess

Year	Club	G	CG	W	L	IP	H	R	BB	SO	ERA
1948	Smith.-Selma	31	5	9	9	144	167	109	85	73	5.06
1949	Smith.-Selma	37	20	18	12	236	251	135	120	135	3.24

Other teams played for: Burlington, NC (B), Greenville, NC (D), Rocky Mount (D), Waycross (D), Reidsville (B), Winston-Salem (B)

Forbess, James H. "Jim"

Year	Club	POS	G	AB	R	H	2B	3B	HR	BB	SB	RBI	BA
1948	Clinton	p	18	38	3	5	1	0	0	6	0	3	.132
1949	Clinton	p	12	22	3	6	0	1	0	6	0	3	.273

Year	Club	G	CG	W	L	IP	H	R	BB	SO	ERA
1948	Clinton	17	8	7	4	100	117	65	45	45	4.68
1949	Clinton	11	4	3	3	57	69	46	50	18	5.84

Other teams played for: Rome (C), Corpus Christi (D), McAllen (C)

Ford, Donald Thomas "Don"

Year	Club	POS	G	AB	R	H	2B	3B	HR	BB	SB	RBI	BA
1949	Sanford	c	57	201	29	50	9	1	6	25	10	35	.249

Other teams played for: Leesburg (D), Lakeland (C), La Grange (D), Tallassee (D), Sanford, Fla. (D), Orlando (D), Gadsden (B), Chattanooga (AA), Greensboro (B), Waycross (D), St. Augustine (D), Jacksonville Beach (D), Cocoa (D)

Fortuna, Justin James

Year	Club	POS	G	AB	R	H	2B	3B	HR	BB	SB	RBI	BA
1949	Dunn-Erwin	2b	52										
	Wilmington	2b	38										
	totals:	2b	90	345	50	76	9	6	0	44	6	36	.220

Other teams played for: Gainesville (D)

Fortune, Harry T.

Year	Club	POS	G	AB	R	H	2B	3B	HR	BB	SB	RBI	BA
1946	Angier-Fuquay	p	11	17	2	3	0	0	1	—	0	2	.176
1947	Warsaw	util	12	23	9	8	0	0	0	7	0	6	.348

Year	Club	G	CG	W	L	IP	H	R	BB	SO	ERA
1946	Angier-Fuquay	8	0	0	3	29	31	32	30	30	—

Other teams played for: New River (D)

Foster, Arthur

Year	Club	POS	G	AB	R	H	2B	3B	HR	BB	SB	RBI	BA
1946	Dunn-Erwin	p	29	45	13	18	2	0	0	—	0	5	.400

12. Player Register—Frazier

Year	Club	POS	G	AB	R	H	2B	3B	HR	BB	SB	RBI	BA
1948	Smith.-Selma	p	9										
	Clinton	p	4										
	totals:	p	13	15	2	3	0	0	0	3	0	1	.200

Year	Club	G	CG	W	L	IP	H	R	BB	SO	ERA
1946	Dunn-Erwin	27	5	6	7	132	186	109	33	54	—
1948	Smith.-Selma	9									
	Clinton	4									
	totals:	13	—	—	—	<45	—	—	—	—	—

Other teams played for: None

Fowler,

Year	Club	POS	G	AB	R	H	2B	3B	HR	BB	SB	RBI	BA
1946	Smith.-Selma	—	<10	—	—	—	—	—	—	—	—	—	—

Other teams played for: Unknown

Fox, James L. "Jimmie"

Year	Club	POS	G	AB	R	H	2B	3B	HR	BB	SB	RBI	BA
1946	Wilmington	of	51	155	24	38	4	1	0	—	6	19	.245

Other teams played for: None

Francoline, James J. "Jim"

Year	Club	POS	G	AB	R	H	2B	3B	HR	BB	SB	RBI	BA
1950	Lumberton	of	106	392	71	129	35	10	12	78	7	98	.329

Other teams played for: Greensburg (D), New Iberia (D), Monett (D), Tallahassee (D), Winston-Salem (B), Clinton, Iowa (B), Bradford (D), Hartford (A), Anderson (B), Geneva (D) Anniston (B), Americus (D), West Palm Beach (B), Hartford (A)

Franz, William P. "Bill"

Year	Club	POS	G	AB	R	H	2B	3B	HR	BB	SB	RBI	BA
1949	Sanford	c	53	172	23	41	7	1	0	16	9	17	.238

Other teams played for: None

Frazier,

Year	Club	POS	G	AB	R	H	2B	3B	HR	BB	SB	RBI	BA
1946	Smithfield	2b	36	117	21	25	4	1	1	—	1	17	.214

Other teams played for: Unknown

12. Player Register—Frazier

Frazier, William C.

Year	Club	POS	G	AB	R	H	2B	3B	HR	BB	SB	RBI	BA
1950	Sanford	p	21	46	8	10	2	0	0	10	0	4	.217

Year	Club	G	CG	W	L	IP	H	R	BB	SO	ERA
1950	Sanford	20	5	7	3	102	90	61	98	47	4.76

Other teams played for: Mooresville (D), Reidsville (B)

Freiberger, Arthur Lewis

Year	Club	POS	G	AB	R	H	2B	3B	HR	BB	SB	RBI	BA
1948	Smith.-Selma	2b	44	132	23	29	4	2	0	28	2	20	.220

Other teams played for: Burlington, NC (C), New Bern (D), Rocky Mount (D), Emporia (D), Elizabeth City (D), Gastonia (B)

Futrelle, Duncan Lacy Jr.

Year	Club	POS	G	AB	R	H	2B	3B	HR	BB	SB	RBI	BA
1949	Wilmington	1b	42	172	23	55	6	2	2	7	1	25	.320

Other teams played for: Landis (D), Albemarle (D)

Gailes, Elwood Lonnie

Year	Club	POS	G	AB	R	H	2B	3B	HR	BB	SB	RBI	BA
1950	Rockingham	c	37	118	12	17	1	0	0	18	2	7	.144

Other teams played for: Sanford (D), Mooresville (D)

Gales, James

Year	Club	POS	G	AB	R	H	2B	3B	HR	BB	SB	RBI	BA
1946	Sanford	of	102	362	72	105	24	5	2	—	5	68	.290

Other teams played for: None

Gallo, Anthony

Year	Club	POS	G	AB	R	H	2B	3B	HR	BB	SB	RBI	BA
1950	Smith.-Selma	—	11	32	3	5	1	0	0	4	0	1	.156

Other teams played for: None

Gallo, Ernest

Year	Club	POS	G	AB	R	H	2B	3B	HR	BB	SB	RBI	BA
1946	Angier-F.	p	17										
	Clinton	p	6										
	totals:	p	23	40	2	6	2	0	0	—	0	2	.150

12. Player Register—Garrett

Year	Club	G	CG	W	L	IP	H	R	BB	SO	ERA
1946	Angier-F.	15									
	Clinton	6									
	totals:	21	5	4	8	100	116	96	69	55	—

Other teams played for: None

Gallo, Joseph "Joe"

Year	Club	POS	G	AB	R	H	2B	3B	HR	BB	SB	RBI	BA
1946	Smithfield	ss	22	76	13	11	2	0	0	—	0	5	.145

Other teams played for: None

Gamache, Ray John

Year	Club	POS	G	AB	R	H	2B	3B	HR	BB	SB	RBI	BA
1948	Smith.-Selmap	10	20	2	2	1	0	1	0	0	3	.100

Year	Club	G	CG	W	L	IP	H	R	BB	SO	ERA
1948	Smith.-Selma	8	3	1	5	48	61	34	22	26	4.13

Other teams played for: Superior (C), Grand Forks (C), Duluth (C), Decatur (B), Burlington, NC (C), Durham (C)

Garcia, Manuel R.

Year	Club	POS	G	AB	R	H	2B	3B	HR	BB	SB	RBI	BA
1947	Lumbertonp	37	94	16	21	4	1	2	3	0	15	.223

Year	Club	G	CG	W	L	IP	H	R	BB	SO	ERA
1947	Lumberton	28	20	15	8	198	175	114	120	133	4.27

Other teams played for: None

Gardner,

Year	Club	G	CG	W	L	IP	H	R	BB	SO	ERA
1946	Angier-Fuquay	3	0	0	0	2	—	—	—	—	—

Other teams played for: Unknown

Garrett, Edward Franklin

Year	Club	POS	G	AB	R	H	2B	3B	HR	BB	SB	RBI	BA
1948	Lumbertonp	33	68	10	12	1	0	0	4	1	5	.176

Year	Club	G	CG	W	L	IP	H	R	BB	SO	ERA
1948	Lumberton	29	8	7	11	172	159	109	92	96	4.50

Other teams played for: Carthage (D), Clovis (C), Decatur (D), Danville, Ill. (D)

12. Player Register—Garris

Garris, Reid Gay

Year	Club	G	CG	W	L	IP	H	R	BB	SO	ERA
1950	Rockingham	<10	—	1	3	—	—	—	—	—	—

Other teams played for: Mooresville (D)

Gay, Frederick Leonard "Fred"

Year	Club	G	CG	W	L	IP	H	R	BB	SO	ERA
1946	Smithfield	4	1	0	2	19	26	13	19	11	—

Other teams played for: Norfolk (B), Binghamton (A), Canton (C), Kansas City (AA), Holywood (AA), Tacoma (B), Seattle (AAA)

Gentry, Roscoe

Year	Club	POS	G	AB	R	H	2B	3B	HR	BB	SB	RBI	BA
1946	Angier-Fuquay	2b	57	228	43	75	10	3	6	—	3	41	.329

Other teams played for: Kinston (D)

Gerace, John J.

Year	Club	POS	G	AB	R	H	2B	3B	HR	BB	SB	RBI	BA
1950	Lumberton	p	36	78	17	15	2	0	0	17	0	12	.192

Year	Club	G	CG	W	L	IP	H	R	BB	SO	ERA
1950	Lumberton	35	16	15	9	214	165	103	160	142	3.57

Other teams played for: Americus (D), New Iberia (C), Fargo-Moorehead (C), Houma (C), Ardmore (D), Harlingen (B)

Geresy, Donald S.

Year	Club	POS	G	AB	R	H	2B	3B	HR	BB	SB	RBI	BA
1949	Lumberton	of	66	239	80	52	6	4	1	37	6	29	.218

Other teams played for: Ozark (D), Nazareth (D), Clovis (C), Grand Rapids (A), Blackwell (D), Macon (A)

Ghant, Roland Thomas

Year	Club	POS	G	AB	R	H	2B	3B	HR	BB	SB	RBI	BA
1950	Rockingham	p	20	45	7	10	0	1	0	2	1	1	.222

Year	Club	G	CG	W	L	IP	H	R	BB	SO	ERA
1950	Rockingham	20	5	8	7	109	91	69	125	101	4.79

Other teams played for: Satesboro (D)

Gibson, Samuel Braxton

Year	Club	G	CG	W	L	IP	H	R	BB	SO	ERA
1948	Warsaw	5	—	0	2	20	28	12	2	—	—

Other teams played for: Danville, Va. (C), Asheville (B), Toronto (AA), Detroit (ML), San Francisco (AA), New York Giants (ML), Portland (AA), Oakland (AA), Bremerton (B), Radford (D), Reidsville (B), Griffin (D)

Gibson, Samuel Clay Jr. "Gabby"

Year	Club	POS	G	AB	R	H	2B	3B	HR	BB	SB	RBI	BA
1947	Smith.-Selma	p	16	42	7	13	1	0	0	0	4	1	.310
1949	Sanford	1b/p	87	287	31	75	19	2	10	7	7	65	.261

Year	Club	G	CG	W	L	IP	H	R	BB	SO	ERA
1947	Smith.-Selma	13	6	2	6	82	90	65	49	34	4.28
1949	Sanford	32	23	17	9	241	219	127	131	157	3.17

Other teams played for: Leaksville (C), North Wilkesboro (D), Greensboro (C), New Iberia (C)

Gingerella, James L. Jr.

Year	Club	POS	G	AB	R	H	2B	3B	HR	BB	SB	RBI	BA
1950	Sanford	c	22	48	4	9	4	0	1	8	1	7	.188

Other teams played for: Big Stone Gap (D), St. Petersburg (B)

Giordanengo, Irvin R. "Beans"

Year	Club	POS	G	AB	R	H	2B	3B	HR	BB	SB	RBI	BA
1949	Wilmington	c	<10	—	—	—	—	—	—	—	—	—	—

Other teams played for: Goldsboro (D), New Castle (C), Rocky Mount (D), Meridian (C)

Giuliano, Thomas "Tom"

Year	Club	POS	G	AB	R	H	2B	3B	HR	BB	SB	RBI	BA
1949	Red Springs	ss	126	423	97	103	10	6	1	116	24	57	.243
1950	Red Springs	2b	124	473	110	125	19	9	2	127	35	51	.264

Other teams played for: Welch (D), Williamsport (A), Lancaster (B)

Glose, Gordan N.

Year	Club	POS	G	AB	R	H	2B	3B	HR	BB	SB	RBI	BA
1949	Clinton	3b	35										
	Wilmington	3b	3										
	totals:	3b	38	96	12	26	3	0	1	15	1	12	.271

Other teams played for: None

Gloser, Francis Joseph

Year	Club	POS	G	AB	R	H	2B	3B	HR	BB	SB	RBI	BA
1947	Red Springs	util	15	33	1	6	0	0	0	6	0	2	.091

Other teams played for: Rehobeth Beach (D)

12. Player Register—Godfrey

Godfrey, Philip Lee "Phil"

Year	Club	POS	G	AB	R	H	2B	3B	HR	BB	SB	RBI	BA
1949	Dunn-Erwin	ss	64	265	44	76	17	5	0	24	8	36	.287

Other teams played for: Union City (D), Nazareth (D), Troy (D), Greenville, NC (D), Rome (C)

Godwin, W. Troy

Year	Club	POS	G	AB	R	H	2B	3B	HR	BB	SB	RBI	BA
1947	Dunn-Erwin	2b	13	49	9	16	2	1	1	5	2	9	.327
1948	Dunn-Erwin	2b	38	144	28	46	5	3	0	14	13	12	.319
1950	Whiteville	of	82	316	73	79	16	2	1	56	13	29	.250

Other teams played for: Fitzgerald (D)

Golding, Fred James

Year	Club	POS	G	AB	R	H	2B	3B	HR	BB	SB	RBI	BA
1950	Wilmington	c	57	148	22	30	6	1	0	24	2	15	.203

Other teams played for: None

Gonzales, Rigoberto

Year	Club	POS	G	AB	R	H	2B	3B	HR	BB	SB	RBI	BA
1949	Smith.-Selma	c	7										
	Sanford	c	14										
	totals:	c	21	71	10	17	3	1	0	7	5	11	.239

Other teams played for: Palatka (D), New Castle (D)

Gonzalez, Rogelio "Chango"

Year	Club	POS	G	AB	R	H	2B	3B	HR	BB	SB	RBI	BA
1950	Whiteville	p	21	47	10	14	1	1	2	9	0	13	.298

Other teams played for: Lakeland (C), Tampa (C), Palatka (D), Laredo (C), Monterrey (Ind), Sherman-Denison (D), Veracruz (Ind), Cananea (C

Good, William L. "Bill"

Year	Club	G	CG	W	L	IP	H	R	BB	SO	ERA
1950	Rockingham	<10	—	—	—	—	—	—	—	—	—

Other teams played for: Lincolnton (D), Gastonia (D), Morganton (D), Statesville (D), Granite Falls (D)

Goodwin, Harold

Year	Club	G	CG	W	L	IP	H	R	BB	SO	ERA
1946	Smithfield	3	0	0	1	12	21	14	5	3	—

Other teams played for: None

12. Player Register—Gregory

Goodwin, William Frederick

Year	Club	POS	G	AB	R	H	2B	3B	HR	BB	SB	RBI	BA
1948	Lumberton	p	24	47	7	14	1	1	0	3	1	3	.234

Year	Club	G	CG	W	L	IP	H	R	BB	SO	ERA
1948	Lumberton	17	3	4	7	85	107	83	36	36	6.78

Other teams played for: Paducah (D), Belleville (D), Centralia (D)

Graham, Walter Odell

Year	Club	POS	G	AB	R	H	2B	3B	HR	BB	SB	RBI	BA
1950	Rockingham	p	36	102	7	20	4	2	0	2	0	13	.196

Year	Club	G	CG	W	L	IP	H	R	BB	SO	ERA
1950	Rockingham	27	19	13	11	206	176	103	103	88	3.06

Other teams played for: Greensboro (C), Schenectady (C), Wilmington, Del. (B), Newport News (B), Statesville (D), Mobile (AA), Bridgeport (B), Kingston (B)

Green, Andrew H.

Year	Club	POS	G	AB	R	H	2B	3B	HR	BB	SB	RBI	BA
1946	Smithfield	p	20	37	8	8	1	0	0	—	0	6	.216

Year	Club	G	CG	W	L	IP	H	R	BB	SO	ERA
1946	Smithfield	20	6	6	10	111	125	81	55	42	—

Other teams played for: La Crosse (D), Eau Claire (C), Jackson (B), Evansville (B)

Greene, Leonard Word "Doc"

Year	Club	POS	G	AB	R	H	2B	3B	HR	BB	SB	RBI	BA
1949	Sanford	of	46										
	Fayetteville	of	41										
	totals:	of	87	329	66	99	14	6	12	53	17	69	.301

Other teams played for: Charleston (B), Leaksville (D), Portsmouth (B), Los Angeles (AA), Tulsa (AA), Nashville (AA), Shreveport (AA), Houston (AA), Richmond (B), Macon (A), Greensboro (B), Jacksonville (A)

Gregory, Joseph

Year	Club	POS	G	AB	R	H	2B	3B	HR	BB	SB	RBI	BA
1946	Dunn-Erwin	ss	54										
	Wilmington	ss	35										
	totals:	ss	89	322	67	73	10	1	2	—	9	27	.227

Other teams played for: None

12. Player Register—Griffy

Griffy, James Norton

Year	Club	POS	G	AB	R	H	2B	3B	HR	BB	SB	RBI	BA
1950	Lumberton	3b	22	34	8	10	1	1	1	4	0	8	.294

Other teams played for: New Iberia (C), Griffin (D), Valdosta (D), Greenville, Miss. (C), Terre Haute (B)

Grimm, Robert Eugene

Year	Club	POS	G	AB	R	H	2B	3B	HR	BB	SB	RBI	BA
1950	Red Springs	p	28	49	3	6	0	0	0	2	0	0	.122

Year	Club	G	CG	W	L	IP	H	R	BB	SO	ERA
1950	Red Springs	28	10	10	10	166	142	73	104	75	3.25

Other teams played for: None

Grubb, James Kenneth "Jim"

Year	Club	POS	G	AB	R	H	2B	3B	HR	BB	SB	RBI	BA
1948	Lumberton	p	10	14	0	2	1	0	0	0	0	2	.143

Year	Club	G	CG	W	L	IP	H	R	BB	SO	ERA
1948	Lumberton	10	3	1	5	45	46	28	44	28	5.20

Other teams played for: Paris (D0

Grubbs, Frank

Year	Club	G	CG	W	L	IP	H	R	BB	SO	ERA
1946	Angier-Fuquay	1	—	0	0	5	—	—	—	—	—

Other teams played for: Greeneville, Tenn. (D), Mount Airy (D), Mooresville (D)

Guidice, Michael Joseph "Joe"

Year	Club	POS	G	AB	R	H	2B	3B	HR	BB	SB	RBI	BA
1950	Lumberton	of	16	65	13	19	0	3	1	8	4	13	.292

Other teams played for: Emporia (D), Greenville, NC (D), Suffolk (D), Wilson (D), Meridian (C), Hannibal (D)

Guinn, James K. "Jimmy"

Year	Club	POS	G	AB	R	H	2B	3B	HR	BB	SB	RBI	BA
1946	Dunn-Erwin	2b	52										
	Sanford	2b	59										
	totals:	2b	111	430	107	130	26	8	3	—	7	59	.302
1947	Sanford	2b	121	533	131	178	31	5	2	66	42	64	.334
1948	Sanford	2b	42	166	35	61	9	0	1	14	6	25	.367
1949	Lumberton	2b	132	504	116	145	16	5	0	11	12	48	.288

12. Player Register—Hardee

Other teams played for: Americus (D), Shelby (D), Charlottte (B), Greenville, SC (B), Enterprise (D)

Hager, Richard "Dick"

Year	Club	POS	G	AB	R	H	2B	3B	HR	BB	SB	RBI	BA
1948	Dunn-Erwin	ss	15	44	7	10	2	0	0	6	0	3	.227

Other teams played for: None

Haidet, Wilford Lawence

Year	Club	G	CG	W	L	IP	R	BB	SO	ERA
1946	Wilmington	3								
	Dunn-Erwin	2								
	totals:	5	1	0	3	15	16	23	20	11	—

Other teams played for: Hickory (D)

Haithcock, Claude

Year	Club	POS	G	AB	R	H	2B	3B	HR	BB	SB	RBI	BA
1949	Dunn-Erwin	of	123	536	95	175	41	10	0	60	21	69	.326

Other teams played for: None

Halkard, Robert Nicholas "Bob"

Year	Club	POS	G	AB	R	H	2B	3B	HR	BB	SB	RBI	BA
1949	Sanford	3b	18	67	11	12	2	1	0	4	1	9	.179

Other teams played for: Marion (D), New Bern (D), Shelby (D), Hot Springs (C)

Ham, Charles L.

Year	Club	POS	G	AB	R	H	2B	3B	HR	BB	SB	RBI	BA
1948	Sanford	c	56	104	14	23	3	0	0	14	1	6	.221

Other teams played for: Statesville (D), Dothan (D)

Hamson,

Year	Club	POS	G	AB	R	H	2B	3B	HR	BB	SB	RBI	BA
1946	Smith.-Selma	—	<10	—	—	—	—	—	—	—	—	—	—

Other teams played for: Unknown

Hardee, George Dewey, Jr. "Buck"

Year	Club	POS	G	AB	R	H	2B	3B	HR	BB	SB	RBI	BA
1950	Whiteville	c	24	59	6	20	3	0	0	8	0	5	.339

Other teams played for: None

12. Player Register—Hardee

Hardee, Raymond E. "Ray"

Year	Club	POS	G	AB	R	H	2B	3B	HR	BB	SB	RBI	BA
1946	Angier-Fuquay	p	24	56	13	16	1	0	1	—	0	6	.286

Year	Club	G	CG	W	L	IP	H	R	BB	SO	ERA
1946	Angier-Fuquay	17	13	9	8	130	149	95	73	94	—

Other teams played for: Newport News (C). Wilmington, Del. (B), Memphis (AA), Raleigh (C), Danville (C), San Diego (AAA), Reidsville (B), Danville (B)

Hardisky, Edward Joseph

Year	Club	POS	G	AB	R	H	2B	3B	HR	BB	SB	RBI	BA
1947	Wilmington	2b	117	456	88	113	16	5	0	61	24	53	.248
1948	Wilmington	2b	138	544	131	146	24	4	4	103	29	54	.268

Other teams played for: None

Hardy,

Year	Club	POS	G	AB	R	H	2B	3B	HR	BB	SB	RBI	BA
1946	Dunn-Erwin	—	<10	—	—	—	—	—	—	—	—	—	—

Other teams played for: Unknown

Harrell, Boney

Year	Club	POS	G	AB	R	H	2B	3B	HR	BB	SB	RBI	BA
1949	Clinton	of	5	17	3	7	1	0	0	—	0	3	.411

Other teams played for: None

Harrington, Thomas Hayes

Year	Club	POS	G	AB	R	H	2B	3B	HR	BB	SB	RBI	BA
1946	Sanford	util	15	25	8	6	2	0	0	—	1	2	.240

Year	Club	G	CG	W	L	IP	H	R	BB	SO	ERA
1946	Sanford	3	—	0	0	4	—	—	—	—	—

Other teams played for: Albany, Ga. (D), Asheville (B), Leaksville (D)

Harrington, William Womble "Bill"

Year	Club	POS	G	AB	R	H	2B	3B	HR	BB	SB	RBI	BA
1949	Red Springs	p	41	88	7	13	0	1	0	8	0	10	.148

Year	Club	G	CG	W	L	IP	H	R	BB	SO	ERA
1949	Red Springs	38	20	17	11	234	250	120	94	170	3.85

Other teams played for: Fayetteville (B), Savannah (A), Ottawa (AAA), Philadelphia Athletics (ML), Kansas City (ML), San Diego (AAA), Columbus (AAA),

12. Player Register—Hash

Birmingham (AA), Charleston, W.V. (AAA), Dallas (AAA), Shreveport (AA), Wilson (B)

Harrington, Zeb Strickland

Year	Club	POS	G	AB	R	H	2B	3B	HR	BB	SB	RBI	BA
1948	Sanford	p	27	42	5	9	0	0	0	4	0	1	.214

Year	Club	G	CG	W	L	IP	H	R	BB	SO	ERA
1948	Sanford	23	2	4	3	91	115	54	26	32	3.66

Other teams played for: None

Harris, James Emmet "Jimmy"

Year	Club	POS	G	AB	R	H	2B	3B	HR	BB	SB	RBI	BA
1949	Fayetteville	2b	71	276	56	65	4	3	1	36	18	24	.236

Other teams played for: Zanesville (D), Fort Smith (C), Cedar Rapids (B), Spartanburg (B), Peoria (B), Wilkes-Barre (A), Hagerstown (B), Charleston, W.V. (AAA)

Harrison, William J.

Year	Club	POS	G	AB	R	H	2B	3B	HR	BB	SB	RBI	BA
1946	Wilmington	3b	4										
	Smith.-Selma	3b	46										
	Dunn-Erwin	3b	43										
	totals:	3b	93	367	69	104	21	7	1	—	12	47	.283

Other teams played for: Palatka (D), Leesburg (D), Valley (D)

Harvey, William E.

Year	Club	POS	G	AB	R	H	2B	3B	HR	BB	SB	RBI	BA
1949	Red Springs	p	32	73	6	9	0	0	0	4	0	2	.123

Year	Club	G	CG	W	L	IP	H	R	BB	SO	ERA
1949	Red Springs	31	13	12	10	175	183	111	118	83	3.96

Other teams played for: Youngstown (C)

Hash, Joseph C.

Year	Club	POS	G	AB	R	H	2B	3B	HR	BB	SB	RBI	BA
1946	Clinton	p	14	27	3	9	12	0	0	—	0	1	.333

Year	Club	G	CG	W	L	IP	H	R	BB	SO	ERA
1946	Clinton	13	4	3	5	67	77	61	35	50	—

Other teams played for: Hickory (D), Danville, Va. (C), Suffolk (D), Petersburg (D)

Haswell, Jesse Lee

Year	Club	POS	G	AB	R	H	2B	3B	HR	BB	SB	RBI	BA
1948	Clinton	util	14	37	6	9	2	0	0	12	0	5	.243
1949	Clinton	c	72	210	32	51	5	0	2	36	2	27	.243

Other teams played for: Greensboro (C), Mooresville (D), Emporia (D), Statesville (D), Wilson (B)

Hatsfield, William

Year	Club	POS	G	AB	R	H	2B	3B	HR	BB	SB	RBI	BA
1946	Wilmington	2b	15	50	9	11	1	0	1	—	0	8	.220

Other teams played for: None

Haynes, Barney Smith Jr.

Year	Club	POS	G	AB	R	H	2B	3B	HR	BB	SB	RBI	BA
1947	Clinton	of	59	200	28	48	5	2	2	19	0	26	.240

Other teams played for: None

Hayward, Richard C.

Year	Club	POS	G	AB	R	H	2B	3B	HR	BB	SB	RBI	BA
1947	Dunn-Erwin	c	55	178	24	47	9	1	0	34	3	25	.264

Other teams played for: Kinston (D), Marion (D), Meridian (B)

Healey, John D. "Jack"

Year	Club	POS	G	AB	R	H	2B	3B	HR	BB	SB	RBI	BA
1948	Lumberton	ss	31	110	14	25	3	0	0	15	4	9	.227

Other teams played for: Janesville (D), Sioux Falls (C) St. Petersburg (D)

Heath, (Norman Wade "Bud"?)

Year	Club	G	CG	W	L	IP	H	R	BB	SO	ERA
1946	Smith.-Selma	3	—	0	0	10	—	—	—	—	—

Other teams played for: *Leaksville (C), Newnan (D), Morganton (D)*?

Hedrick, Bruce B.

Year	Club	POS	G	AB	R	H	2B	3B	HR	BB	SB	RBI	BA
1946	Angier-Fuquay	c	88										
	Sanford	c	18										
	totals:		106	399	63	132	31	5	8	—	1	87	.331
1947	Sanford	c	120	448	80	138	25	4	13	48	15	111	.308
1948	Sanford	c	129	454	61	131	19	3	11	46	1	99	.289
1949	Sanford	c	39	137	20	37	12	0	3	20	2	31	.270

Other teams played for: Wilmington, Del. (B), Spatanburg (B), Charleston, SC (B), Savannah (B), Elizabethton (B), Burlington, NC (B), Goldsboro (D), Kinston (D), Abbeville (C), Houma (C)

Heffner, Arthur S. "Art"

Year	Club	POS	G	AB	R	H	2B	3B	HR	BB	SB	RBI	BA
1946	Angier-Fuquay	of	12										
	Smith.-Selma	of	1										
	totals:	of	13	26	9	7	1	0	0	—	0	3	.269

Other teams played for: Pocomoke City (D), Goldsboro (D), New Bern (D)

Heitner, Bernard W.

Year	Club	POS	G	AB	R	H	2B	3B	HR	BB	SB	RBI	BA
1950	Clinton	p	13	25	3	5	1	0	0	3	0	1	.200

Year	Club	G	CG	W	L	IP	H	R	BB	SO	ERA
1950	Clinton	13	2	4	3	65	75	39	32	19	4.15

Other teams played for: Auburn (C), Amarillo (C), El Paso (C), Carlsbad (C)

Helms, John R.

Year	Club	POS	G	AB	R	H	2B	3B	HR	BB	SB	RBI	BA
1949	Fayetteville	of	122	452	71	126	22	0	15	75	3	79	.279
1950	Clinton	c	38	122	15	24	4	0	0	25	1	15	.197

Other teams played for: Spartanburg (B), Mobile (A), Nashville (A), West Palm Beach (C), Trois-Rivieres (C)

Helton, William "Bill"

Year	Club	POS	G	AB	R	H	2B	3B	HR	BB	SB	RBI	BA
1950	Wimington	of	28	88	21	21	2	0	0	17	5	14	.239

Other teams played for: None

Henson,

Year	Club	POS	G	AB	R	H	2B	3B	HR	BB	SB	RBI	BA
1946	Dunn-Erwin	—	<10	—	—	—	—	—	—	—	—	—	—

Other teams played for: Unknown

Hepler, Claude L.

Year	Club	POS	G	AB	R	H	2B	3B	HR	BB	SB	RBI	BA
1948	Warsaw	p	15	16	1	1	1	0	0	3	0	0	.063

12. Player Register—Hergert

Year	Club	G	CG	W	L	IP	H	R	BB	SO	ERA
1948	Warsaw	15	2	1	4	50	53	44	45	44	6.12

Other teams played for: None

Hergert, Walter

Year	Club	POS	G	AB	R	H	2B	3B	HR	BB	SB	RBI	BA
1946	Dunn-Erwin	p	9										
	Smith.-Selma	p	1										
	totals:	p	10	13	2	1	0	0	0	—	0	0	.077

Year	Club	G	CG	W	L	IP	H	R	BB	SO	ERA
1946	Dunn-Erwin	9									
	Smith.-Selma	1									
	totals:	10	1	0	5	43	46	36	30	18	—

Other teams played for: None

Hermann, Fred A. G.

Year	Club	POS	G	AB	R	H	2B	3B	HR	BB	SB	RBI	BA
1950	Sanford	2b	96	344	70	99	17	3	1	77	9	47	.283

Other teams played for: None

Herrick, Wayne T.

Year	Club	POS	G	AB	R	H	2B	3B	HR	BB	SB	RBI	BA
1949	Wilmington	p	28	35	7	9	1	2	1	1	0	5	.257

Year	Club	G	CG	W	L	IP	H	R	BB	SO	ERA
1949	Wilmington	21	3	3	7	78	99	102	81	42	9.06

Other teams played for: None

Herring,

Year	Club	POS	G	AB	R	H	2B	3B	HR	BB	SB	RBI	BA
1946	Smith.-Selma	—	<10	—	—	—	—	—	—	—	—	—	—

Other teams played for: Unknown

Hester, Ben

Year	Club	POS	G	AB	R	H	2B	3B	HR	BB	SB	RBI	BA
1949	Wilmington	3b	39	138	31	44	4	1	0	43	5	10	.319

Other teams played for: None

Hewlett, Emory Lee "Lefty"

Year	Club	POS	G	AB	R	H	2B	3B	HR	BB	SB	RBI	BA
1947	Wilmington	p	23	57	2	11	2	0	0	2	0	3	.193

12. Player Register—Holder

Year	Club	G	CG	W	L	IP	H	R	BB	SO	ERA
1947	Wilmington	23	9	4	13	144	182	135	100	87	7.32

Other teams played for: Jackson (B), Baton Rouge (C)

Hines, Joseph

Year	Club	POS	G	AB	R	H	2B	3B	HR	BB	SB	RBI	BA
1948	Warsaw	p	30	60	12	19	1	1	0	13	0	7	.317

Year	Club	G	CG	W	L	IP	H	R	BB	SO	ERA
1948	Warsaw	28	13	11	8	170	175	97	54	50	3.39

Other teams played for: Kinston (D)

Hinton,

Year	Club	G	CG	W	L	IP	H	R	BB	SO	ERA
1946	Smith.-Selma	2	0	0	1	14	23	16	3	3	—

Other teams played for: Unknown

Hlava, Julius P.

Year	Club	POS	G	AB	R	H	2B	3B	HR	BB	SB	RBI	BA
1947	Red Springs	p	15	14	1	2	0	0	0	3	0	0	.143

Year	Club	G	CG	W	L	IP	H	R	BB	SO	ERA
1947	Red Springs	14	2	0	7	45	69	57	33	20	8.80

Other teams played for: Nyack (D), West Palm Beach (B)

Hocke, Robert L.

Year	Club	POS	G	AB	R	H	2B	3B	HR	BB	SB	RBI	BA
1948	Clinton	2b	12	42	9	4	0	0	0	16	0	5	.095

Other teams played for: None

Hockenbury, Thomas J. "Tom"

Year	Club	POS	G	AB	R	H	2B	3B	HR	B	SB	RBI	BA
1947	Red Springs	c	44	108	11	19	3	1	0	9	3	11	.176

Other teams played for: Lexington, NC (D), Lansdale (D), Portsmouth, Ohio (D), Peekskill (D), Stamford (B), Concord (D), Jesup (D)

Holder, Hugh T.

Year	Club	POS	G	AB	R	H	2B	3B	HR	BB	SB	RBI	BA
1949	Red Springs	p	14	13	1	2	1	1	0	2	0	1	.154
1950	Red Springs	p	40	82	12	16	2	0	0	14	0	3	.195

12. Player Register—Holland

Year	Club	G	CG	W	L	IP	H	R	BB	SO	ERA
1949	Red Springs	14	—	—	—	<45	—	—	—	—	—
1950	Red Springs	29	15	10	11	200	177	127	176	124	4.50

Other teams played for: Savannah (A), Abilene (B), Columbia (A), Columbus, Ohio (AAA)

Holland, M. (probably R. McKinley)

Year	Club	POS	G	AB	R	H	2B	3B	HR	BB	SB	RBI	BA
1946	Clinton	of	10	34	4	6	1	1	1	—	0	5	.176

Holland, Robert F. "Bob"

Year	Club	G	CG	W	L	IP	H	R	BB	SO	ERA
1946	Wilmington	4									
	Angier-Fuquay	3									
	totals:	7	1	1	2	29	41	24	13	24	—

Other teams played for: Scranton (A)

Holland, Rufus McKinley "Mack"

Year	Club	POS	G	AB	R	H	2B	3B	HR	BB	SB	RBI	BA
1946	Clinton	—	<10	—	—	—	—	—	—	—	—	—	—
1947	Clinton	of	10	33	8	11	2	0	0	4	0	7	.333
1948	Clinton	of	99	332	52	95	12	7	5	37	0	66	.286
1949	Smith.-Selma	of	59	230	53	61	14	3	2	51	2	42	.265
1950	Smith.-Selma	of	9										
	Clinton	of	25										
	totals:	of	34	105	13	21	7	1	0	32	1	22	.200

Other teams played for: Rome (C), Norton (D)

Holliday, Andrew J. "Zero"

Year	Club	POS	G	AB	R	H	2B	3B	HR	BB	SB	RBI	BA
1946	Dunn-Erwin	of	95	255	48	86	13	9	4	—	5	48	.242
1947	Sanford	of	53	178	36	42	5	1	2	25	8	18	.236

Other teams played for: Raleigh (C), Wilson (D)

Hollis, Nesbit Odell

Year	Club	POS	G	AB	R	H	2B	3B	HR	BB	SB	RBI	BA
1950	Lumberton	of	125	505	111	165	16	16	2	93	14	79	.327

Other teams played for: Lansdale (D), Batavia (D), Kinston (D)

12. Player Register—Hornsby

Holmes, William O.

Year	Club	POS	G	AB	R	H	2B	3B	HR	BB	SB	RBI	BA
1946	Dunn-Erwin	1b	87	245	46	72	19	3	7	—	0	50	.294

Other teams played for: None

Holster,

Year	Club	G	CG	W	L	IP	H	R	BB	SO	ERA
1946	Smith.-Selma	1	0	0	0	1/3	—	—	—	—	—

Other teams played for: Unknown

Holt, Carlton "Buddy"

Year	Club	POS	G	AB	R	H	2B	3B	HR	BB	SB	RBI	BA
1946	Wilmington	p	12	18	1	2	0	0	0	—	0	1	.111
1949	Wilmington	p	11	16	2	2	0	0	0	0	0	0	.125

Year	Club	G	CG	W	L	IP	H	R	BB	SO	ERA
1946	Wilmington	12	4	2	6	58	61	49	38	36	—
1949	Wilmington	11	2	2	5	45	64	54	50	19	7.20

Other teams played for: Concord (D)

Honeycutt,

Year	Club	POS	G	AB	R	H	2B	3B	HR	BB	SB	RBI	BA
1946	Smith.-Selma	—	<10	—	—	—	—	—	—	—	—	—	—

Other teams played for: Unknown

Hooks, David

Year	Club	POS	G	AB	R	H	2B	3B	HR	BB	SB	RBI	BA
1950	Whiteville	of	34	110	13	22	2	0	0	20	0	8	.200

Other teams played for: Newnan (D), Morganton (D)

Hopper, James McDaniel "Jim"

Year	Club	G	CG	W	L	IP	H	R	BB	SO	ERA
1950	Rockingham	4	—	1	3	—	—	—	—	—	—

Other teams played for: Landis (D), Toronto (AA), Birmingham (AA), Columbus, Ohio (AAA), Pittsburgh (ML), Augusta (A), Chattanooga (AA), Seattle (AAA), Mooresville (D), Landis (D)

Hornsby, Leonard George "Lenny"

Year	Club	POS	G	AB	R	H	2B	3B	HR	BB	SB	RBI	BA
1946	Clinton	p	10	14	5	2	1	0	0	—	0	1	.143

12. Player Register—Horton

Year	Club	G	CG	W	L	IP	H	R	BB	SO	ERA
1946	Clinton	10	4	3	4	48	63	40	31	19	—

Other teams played for: Jackson (D), Anniston (B), Tallasee (D), Leaksville (C)

Horton, Harold

Year	Club	POS	G	AB	R	H	2B	3B	HR	BB	SB	RBI	BA
1946	Wilmington	—	<10	—	—	—	—	—	—	—	—	—	—

Other teams played for: None

Horvath, Joseph F.

Year	Club	POS	G	AB	R	H	2B	3B	HR	BB	SB	RBI	BA
1948	Lumberton	p	12	23	0	4	1	0	0	1	0	0	.174

Year	Club	G	CG	W	L	IP	H	R	BB	SO	ERA
1948	Lumberton	12	5	3	4	54	53	30	19	20	4.00

Other teams played for: Erie (D), Bluefield (D), Alexandria (C)

House, James F. "Jim"

Year	Club	POS	G	AB	R	H	2B	3B	HR	BB	SB	RBI	BA
1946	Angier-Fuquay	p	29	61	8	9	0	0	0	—	0	6	.148
1947	Sanford	p	22	58	5	11	1	0	0	8	0	7	.190

Year	Club	G	CG	W	L	IP	H	R	BB	SO	ERA
1946	Angier-Fuquay	27	11	11	10	179	198	121	75	117	—
1947	Sanford	21	8	9	8	138	147	95	66	76	5.15

Other teams played for: LEaksville (D)

Howard, St. Pierre Jr. "Pete"

Year	Club	POS	G	AB	R	H	2B	3B	HR	BB	SB	RBI	BA
1946	Smithfield	ss	90	363	85	99	13	12	0	—	14	46	.273
1947	Smith.-Selma	ss	120	483	110	147	17	7	6	91	59	50	.304

Other teams played for: Augusta (B), Richmond (B), Danville, Va. (C), Greensboro (C), Burlington, NC (C), Elizabeth City (D), Greenville, SC (B)

Hudson, James Terrence

Year	Club	POS	G	AB	R	H	2B	3B	HR	BB	SB	RBI	BA
1949	Sanford	2b	53										
	Wilmington	2b	77										
	totals:	2b	130	511	90	132	20	7	6	71	8	57	.258

Other teams played for: Fond du Lac (D), Chanute (D), Independence (D), High Point-Thomasville (D), Greensboro (D), Hickory (D)

12. Player Register—Israel

Hughes, Edward R.

Year	Club	G	CG	W	L	IP	H	R	BB	SO	ERA
1946	Dunn-Erwin	1	0	0	0	1	—	—	—	—	—

Other teams played for: Jonesboro (D), Newport (D), Portsmouth, Va. (B), Salina (C), Saginaw (C), Waterloo (B), Petersburg (C)

Hunt, Paul V.

Year	Club	POS	G	AB	R	H	2B	3B	HR	BB	SB	RBI	BA
1946	Angier-Fuquay	ss	109	396	69	116	19	3	7	—	0	61	.293

Other teams played for: None

Hutchins, Charles Ben "Charlie"

Year	Club	POS	G	AB	R	H	2B	3B	HR	BB	SB	RBI	BA
1947	Dunn-Erwin	3b	23	92	14	23	8	1	3	5	2	15	.250
1948	Warsaw	2b	105	428	57	132	21	4	10	7	2	86	.308
1949	Fayetteville	util	14	59	4	11	1	0	0	2	0	7	.186

Other teams played for: Shelby (D)

Ingle, Randolph M.

Year	Club	POS	G	AB	R	H	2B	3B	HR	BB	SB	RBI	BA
1946	Angier-F.	p	14										
	Wilmington	p	12										
	totals:	p	26	60	6	10	2	0	1	—	0	8	.167

Year	Club	G	CG	W	L	IP	H	R	BB	SO	ERA
1946	Angier.-Fuquay	9									
	Wilmington	7									
	totals:	16	2	4	4	83	99	81	91	71	—

Other teams played for: Erie (D), Danville, Va. (C), Raleigh (C)

Ingram, Ralph

Year	Club	G	CG	W	L	IP	H	R	BB	SO	ERA
1946	Smith.-Selma	8	4	1	5	47	68	53	33	19	—

Other teams played for: None

Israel,

Year	Club	G	CG	W	L	IP	H	R	BB	SO	ERA
1949	Sanford	<10	—	—	—	—	—	—	—	—	—

Other teams played for: Unknown

12. Player Register—Jackson

Jackson, Edward H.

Year	Club	POS	G	AB	R	H	2B	3B	HR	BB	SB	RBI	BA
1946	Dunn-Erwin	ss	31	108	20	13	3	1	1	—	2	14	.120
1948	Smith.-Selma	ss	85	306	59	72	7	13	1	81	8	35	.235
1949	Fayetteville	ss	64	220	59	50	11	1	4	67	10	28	.227

Other teams played for: Raleigh (C), Goldsboro (D), Greensboro (C), Roanoke Rapids (D)

Jackson, Elton Stanley

Year	Club	POS	G	AB	R	H	2B	3B	HR	BB	SB	RBI	BA
1947	Red Springs	ss	53	165	16	44	7	2	0	17	2	17	.267

Other teams played for: Martinsville (C), Moline (C), Kewanee (C), Tarboro (D), Savannah (A), Salisbury (B)

Jackson, Kenneth B.

Year	Club	POS	G	AB	R	H	2B	3B	HR	BB	SB	RBI	BA
1946	Angier-Fuquay	of	107	370	76	108	25	0	11	—	3	64	.292
1947	Dunn-Erwin	of	124	439	104	139	26	3	12	113	26	103	.317

Other teams played for: Johnstown (D), Olean (D)

Jacobson, Irving S. "Rabbit"

Year	Club	POS	G	AB	R	H	2B	3B	HR	BB	SB	RBI	BA
1949	Wilmington	of	102										
	Clinton	of	2										
	totals:	of	104	356	75	100	20	5	6	101	5	54	.281

Other teams played for: Dover (D), Federalsburg (D), New Castle (C), Stamford (B), Providence (B), North Wilkesboro (D)

Jacoby, Warren W.

Year	Club	G	CG	W	L	IP	H	R	BB	SO	ERA
1946	Clinton	3	1	0	2	12	20	13	5	7	—

Other teams played for: Opelousas (D), New Iberia (D), Rayne (D), Augusta (B), Joplin (C)

Jamin, Charles Frances "Charlie"

Year	Club	POS	G	AB	R	H	2B	3B	HR	BB	SB	RBI	BA
1947	Lumberton	of	122	494	105	151	17	14	16	63	3	117	.306
1948	Lumberton	of	74	263	42	74	2	6	1	39	10	56	.281
1950	Rockingham	of	55	218	30	52	2	8	0	37	2	34	.239

Other teams played for: Butler (D), Akron (C), Amsterdam (C), Statesville (D), Fayetteville (D)

12. Player Register—Johnson

Janik, Edmund

Year	Club	POS	G	AB	R	H	2B	3B	HR	BB	SB	RBI	BA
1946	Dunn-Erwin	c	75	248	39	52	3	4	0	—	3	23	.210

Other teams played for: None

Jenkins, John Thayer

Year	Club	POS	G	AB	R	H	2B	3B	HR	BB	SB	RBI	BA
1946	Wilmington	p	21	43	3	8	2	0	1	—	0	5	.186

Year	Club	G	CG	W	L	IP	H	R	BB	SO	ERA
1946	Wilmington	21	4	5	8	103	101	72	80	45	—

Other teams played for: Galax (D), Palatka (D)

John, Angelo Patsy

Year	Club	G	CG	W	L	IP	H	R	BB	SO	ERA
1946	Clinton	2	0	0	1	1	7	8	1	1	—

Other teams played for: Welch (D)

Johnson, Carl "Cyclone"

Year	Club	POS	G	AB	R	H	2B	3B	HR	BB	SB	RBI	BA
1947	Warsaw	p	35	89	10	20	0	0	0	8	0	8	.225

Year	Club	G	CG	W	L	IP	H	R	BB	SO	ERA
1947	Warsaw	32	19	13	10	216	219	123	74	225	4.29

Other teams played for: Cooleemee (D), Thomasville (D), Miami Beach (D), Sanford (D), Burlington (D), Dothan (D), Cairo (D), Kinston (D), Montgomery (A)

Johnson, Charles "Charlie"

Year	Club	POS	G	AB	R	H	2B	3B	HR	BB	SB	RBI	BA
1946	Dunn-Erwin	—	<10	—	—	—	—	—	—	—	—	—	—

Other teams played for: Unknown

Johnson, Harry T.

Year	Club	POS	G	AB	R	H	2B	3B	HR	BB	SB	RBI	BA
1946	Clinton	—	<10	—	—	—	—	—	—	—	—	—	—

Other teams played for: Bristol (D)

Johnson, Henry L.

Year	Club	POS	G	AB	R	H	2B	3B	HR	BB	SB	RBI	BA
1948	Smith.-Selma	p	13	16	2	3	0	0	0	2	0	1	.188

12. Player Register—Johnson

Year	Club	G	CG	W	L	IP	H	R	BB	SO	ERA
1948	Smith-Selma	13	1	1	6	46	55	49	41	16	7.43

Other teams played for: None

Johnson, Rivers Dunn Jr.

Year	Club	POS	G	AB	R	H	2B	3B	HR	BB	SB	RBI	BA
1948	Warsaw	util	11	22	3	4	1	0	0	0	1	4	.182

Other teams played for: None

Jones, "Buck"

Year	Club	G	CG	W	L	IP	H	R	BB	SO	ERA
1946	Angier-Fuquay	2	—	0	0	3	—	—	—	—	—

Other teams played for: Unknown

Jones, John Purcell

Year	Club	POS	G	AB	R	H	2B	3B	HR	BB	SB	RBI	BA
1948	Dunn-Erwin	1b	21	76	5	20	4	1	1	6	0	9	.263

Other teams played for: Kinston (D)

Jones, Raymond D.

Year	Club	G	CG	W	L	IP	H	R	BB	SO	ERA
1946	Clinton	2	—	0	0	2	—	—	—	—	—

Other teams played for: None

Jones, Theodore Debonchard Jr. "T.D."

Year	Club	POS	G	AB	R	H	2B	3B	HR	BB	SB	RBI	BA
1947	Warsaw	c	92	314	49	99	20	12	4	28	4	51	.315

Other teams played for: South Boston (D), Mount Airy (D), Goldsboro (D), Hopewell (D)

Jones, Thomas J. "Tom"

Year	Club	POS	G	AB	R	H	2B	3B	HR	BB	SB	RBI	BA
1949	Clinton	p	28	63	9	15	1	1	0	4	0	5	.238
1950	Clinton	p	33	76	10	22	2	0	0	4	0	17	.289

Year	Club	G	CG	W	L	IP	H	R	BB	SO	ERA
1949	Clinton	26	10	7	11	144	144	78	83	71	3.88
1950	Clinton	22	11	8	8	132	134	87	83	74	4.30

Other teams played for: Burlington (B), Asheville (B)

12. Player Register—Kaires

Jones, William Clifton "Bill"

Year	Club	POS	G	AB	R	H	2B	3B	HR	BB	SB	RBI	BA
1947	Dunn-Erwin	1b	31	125	22	25	1	3	3	10	5	16	.200

Other teams played for: Roanoke (B), Birmingham (A), Tallassee (D), Anniston (B), Vicksburg (B), El Paso (C), Natchez (C), Meridian (C)

Jordan, Ford

Year	Club	POS	G	AB	R	H	2B	3B	HR	BB	SB	RBI	BA
1947	Warsaw	ss	124	540	116	180	26	3	2	62	24	67	.333

Other teams played for: Raleigh (C), Evansville (B), Hartford (A), Hagerstown (B)

Jordan, John Bill James Jr.

Year	Club	POS	G	AB	R	H	2B	3B	HR	BB	SB	RBI	BA
1949	Red Springs	p	24	47	7	9	0	1	0	0	0	5	.191
1950	Red Springs	c/p	25	65	4	10	3	0	0	5	0	3	.154

Year	Club	G	CG	W	L	IP	H	R	BB	SO	ERA
1949	Red Springs	17	4	4	8	105	107	67	52	55	3.94
1950	Red Springs	10	1	4	2	48	44	30	41	37	4.50

Other teams played for: Mooresville (D), Martinsville (D), Miami (C), Moline (C), Kewanee (C)

Jordan, Robert A.

Year	Club	POS	G	AB	R	H	2B	3B	HR	BB	SB	RBI	BA
1950	Whiteville	ss	15	52	3	9	3	0	0	7	0	1	.173

Other teams played for: Unknown

Junker,

Year	Club	POS	G	AB	R	H	2B	3B	HR	BB	SB	RBI	BA
1948	Dunn-Ewin	p	8	—	—	—	—	—	—	—	—	—	—

Year	Club	G	CG	W	L	IP	H	R	BB	SO	ERA
1948	Dunn-Erwin	8	5	2	5	50	50	33	2	26	4.14

Other teams played for: Unknown

Kaires, William Robert

Year	Club	POS	G	AB	R	H	2B	3B	HR	BB	SB	RBI	BA
1947	Clinton	p	34	77	5	11	3	3	0	4	0	7	.143

Year	Club	G	CG	W	L	IP	H	R	BB	SO	ERA
1947	Clinton	32	18	11	13	200	213	151	85	144	4.28

Other teams played for: Goldsboro (D)

12. Player Register—Kallas

Kallas, William Thomas Jr. "Bill"

Year	Club	POS	G	AB	R	H	2B	3B	HR	BB	SB	RBI	BA
1948	Lumberton	2b	63	233	40	71	14	1	2	32	14	30	.305

Other teams played for: Visalia (C), Rock Hill (B), Keokuk (B), Greenville, SC (B), Spartanbug (B), Fayetteville (B), Kinston (B), Wilson (B)

Katkaveck, Leo Frank

Year	Club	POS	G	AB	R	H	2B	3B	HR	BB	SB	RBI	BA
1948	Warsaw	3b	19	71	12	23	3	2	0	5	0	16	.324

Other teams played for: Raleigh (C), Goldsboro (D), Roanoke Rapids (D)

Katkaveck, Stanley P. "Mickey"

Year	Club	POS	G	AB	R	H	2B	3B	HR	BB	SB	RBI	BA
1946	Wilmington	c	26	89	16	20	3	0	1	—	2	11	.225

Other teams played for: Columbus, Ga. (B), Union City (D), Monessen (D), Jacksonville (C), Portsmouth, Ohio (C), Asheville (B), Sacramento (AA), Mobile (B), Hartford (A), Albany, Ga. (D), Waycross (D)

Katz, Harry

Year	Club	POS	G	AB	R	H	2B	3B	HR	BB	SB	RBI	BA
1948	Clinton	1b	11										
	Dunn-Erwin	1b	114										
	totals:	1b	125	442	72	137	27	7	8	56	24	69	.310
1949	Dunn-Erwin	1b	75	285	51	66	8	2	0	47	28	32	.232

Other teams played for: None

Kavek,

Year	Club	G	CG	W	L	IP	H	R	BB	SO	ERA
1946	Dunn-Erwin	1	0	0	1	2	1	3	5	3	—

Other teams played for: Unknown

Kay, William M. "Bill"

Year	Club	POS	G	AB	R	H	2B	3B	HR	BB	SB	RBI	BA
1949	Clinton	of	61	188	47	51	7	2	0	43	18	15	.271
1950	Clinton	of	123	411	131	113	14	8	1	180	57	43	.275

Year	Club	G	CG	W	L	IP	H	R	BB	SO	ERA
1949	Clinton	10	9	2	10	130	138	91	97	43	4.50
1950	Clinton	13	4	4	5	80	94	58	61	26	4.73

Other teams played for: Fall River (B)

12. Player Register—Kivett

Keane, Robert Thomas "Bobby"

Year	Club	POS	G	AB	R	H	2B	3B	HR	BB	SB	RBI	BA
1946	Clinton	2b	61	171	33	45	5	1	0	—	1	17	.263
1947	Sanford	ss	72	226	28	47	9	2	2	27	11	25	.208
1948	Sanford	ss	127	495	98	150	19	4	1	64	13	58	.303

Other teams played for: Leaksville (C)

Kelly,

Year	Club	POS	G	AB	R	H	2B	3B	HR	BB	SB	RBI	BA
1946	Smith.-Selma	of	21	70	15	14	4	0	1	—	0	12	.200

Other teams played for: Unknown

King, Claude Jr.

Year	Club	POS	G	AB	R	H	2B	3B	HR	BB	SB	RBI	BA
1948	Warsaw	p	11	25	2	2	0	0	0	3	0	0	.080

Year	Club	G	CG	W	L	IP	H	R	BB	SO	ERA
1948	Warsaw	11	6	4	4	68	76	27	21	17	2.91

Other teams played for: Kingsport (D), Goldsboro (D), Griffin (D)

King, Culmer Lawrence

Year	Club	POS	G	AB	R	H	2B	3B	HR	BB	SB	RBI	BA
1948	Sanford	1b	140	533	94	161	26	4	2	40	12	75	.302
1949	Sanford	1b	18	76	9	12	4	1	0	8	3	6	.171

Other teams played for: None

Kittrell, Julian U. "Kit"

Year	Club	POS	G	AB	R	H	2B	3B	HR	BB	SB	RBI	BA
1949	Fayetteville	1b	107	351	63	100	22	3	8	98	7	82	.285

Other teams played for: Gainesville (D), Roanoke Rapids (D), Elizabeth City (D)

Kivett, Charles E.

Year	Club	POS	G	AB	R	H	2B	3B	HR	BB	SB	RBI	BA
1949	Smith.-Selma	p	17	25	1	2	0	0	0	3	0	1	.080

Year	Club	G	CG	W	L	IP	H	R	BB	SO	ERA
1949	Smith.-Selma	17	1	3	4	61	68	41	38	24	4.72

Other teams played for: None

Kivett, William Everett "Bill"

Year	Club	POS	G	AB	R	H	2B	3B	HR	BB	SB	RBI	BA
1947	Lumberton	c	59	211	38	64	10	7	4	21	0	39	.303

12. Player Register—Kluk

Other teams played for: Leaksville (C), Moultrie (D), Fayetteville (D), Ottawa (C), Selma (B), Rome (C)

Kluk, Paul Peter

Year	Club	POS	G	AB	R	H	2B	3B	HR	BB	SB	RBI	BA
1949	Smith.-Selma	c	54	148	32	61	7	2	3	38	0	50	.412

Other teams played for: Owensboro (D), Scranton (A), Greensboro (B), Newport News (B)

Kluttz, Alvin Clifton

Year	Club	POS	G	AB	R	H	2B	3B	HR	BB	SB	RBI	BA
1950	Clinton	c	61	185	41	69	17	4	4	25	0	35	.373

Other teams played for: Springfield (C), Asheville (B), Lynchburg (B), Carthage (D), Omaha (A), Houston (AA), Kingsport (D), Richmond (B), High Point-Thomasville (D)

Knight, Charles A.

Year	Club	POS	G	AB	R	H	2B	3B	HR	BB	SB	RBI	BA
1946	Smith.-Selma	1b	14	50	9	13	1	0	0	—	0	5	.260

Other teams played for: Hickory (D), Goldsboro (D), Danville (C), Mooresville (D), Anderson (B), Reidsville (B), Statesville (D), Lincolnton (D)

Knisely, Gordon Louis

Year	Club	POS	G	AB	R	H	2B	3B	HR	BB	SB	RBI	BA
1947	Lumberton	c	52	170	25	48	6	1	0	22	2	18	.282

Other teams played for: Statesville (D), Franklin (D), St. Augustine (D), New Castle (C)

Koch, Henry F.

Year	Club	POS	G	AB	R	H	2B	3B	HR	BB	SB	RBI	BA
1947	Smith.-Selma	p	14	21	2	2	0	0	0	3	0	2	.095

Year	Club	G	CG	W	L	IP	H	R	BB	SO	ERA
1947	Smith.-Selma	14	5	7	3	63	64	33	18	31	3.14

Other teams played for: Washington, Pa. (D), Johnson City (D), Cooleemee (D), Lynchburg (B), Wimington, Del. (B), Allentown (B), Birmingham (A), Rochester (AA), Columbus, Ohio (AA), Houston (AA)

Kohut, Joseph Jr.

Year	Club	POS	G	AB	R	H	2B	3B	HR	BB	SB	RBI	BA
1948	Red Springs	3b	12	34	2	6	0	0	0	3	0	5	.176

12. Player Register—Kunkle

Year	Club	POS	G	AB	R	H	2B	3B	HR	BB	SB	RBI	BA
1949	Red Springs	3b	97	299	37	56	16	2	2	38	8	42	.187

Other teams played for: Brewton (D), Tarboro (D)

Komar, John

Year	Club	POS	G	AB	R	H	2B	3B	HR	BB	SB	RBI	BA
1947	Dunn-Erwin	p	21	44	6	10	0	1	0	4	0	2	.227

Year	Club	G	CG	W	L	IP	H	R	BB	SO	ERA
1947	Dunn-Erwin	19	8	10	5	116	110	51	27	68	1.86

Other teams played for: Butler (C), Sunbury (B)

Konkol, Robert

Year	Club	POS	G	AB	R	H	2B	3B	HR	BB	SB	RBI	BA
1947	Red Springs	of	14	29	6	7	0	0	0	5	1	0	.241

Other teams played for: None

Kotchli, John

Year	Club	POS	G	AB	R	H	2B	3B	HR	BB	SB	RBI	BA
1947	Dunn-Erwin	p	15	26	6	3	0	0	0	9	0	3	.115

Year	Club	G	CG	W	L	IP	H	R	BB	SO	ERA
1947	Dunn-Erwin	15	6	7	4	81	99	61	25	19	3.44

Other teams played for: None

Kucharski, Louis A.

Year	Club	POS	G	AB	R	H	2B	3B	HR	BB	SB	RBI	BA
1950	Lumberton	of	18	66	10	16	3	1	0	11	2	11	.242

Other teams played for: New Iberia (C)

Kukulka, Edmund F.

Year	Club	POS	G	AB	R	H	2B	3B	HR	BB	SB	RBI	BA
1946	Smith.-Selma	3b	32	113	26	45	14	7	0	—	1	31	.398
1947	Smith.-Selma	3b	47										
	Clinton	3b	75										
	totals:	3b	122	471	107	163	24	18	9	81	7	90	.346

Other teams played for: Greensburg (D), Monessen (D), Butler (D), Orlando (D), Sumbury (C), Goldsboro (D)

Kunkle, Gerald David "Jerry"

Year	Club	POS	G	AB	R	H	2B	3B	HR	BB	SB	RBI	BA
1948	Sanford	ss	114	446	80	112	16	4	2	18	14	61	.251

Other teams played for: None

12. Player Register—Kurplewski

Kurplewski, Edward John

Year	Club	POS	G	AB	R	H	2B	3B	HR	BB	SB	RBI	BA
1949	Dunn-Erwin	p	28	42	6	8	1	1	0	4	0	4	.190

Year	Club	G	CG	W	L	IP	H	R	BB	SO	ERA
1949	Dunn-Erwin	26	3	6	3	88	108	79	71	39	6.34

Other teams played for: None

Lacey, Jesse

Year	Club	POS	G	AB	R	H	2B	3B	HR	BB	SB	RBI	BA
1949	Lumberton	1b	31	119	15	32	6	1	0	11	0	11	.269

Other teams played for: Roanoke Rapids (D)

Lagan, John Edwin "Lefty"

Year	Club	POS	G	AB	R	H	2B	3B	HR	BB	SB	RBI	BA
1950	Lumberton	p	33	85	13	11	2	0	0	10	0	3	.129

Year	Club	G	CG	W	L	IP	H	R	BB	SO	ERA
1950	Lumberton	33	20	21	3	229	205	87	113	140	3.10

Other teams played for: Americus (D), New Iberia (C), Odessa (C), Harlingen (B), Greenville, SC (B)

Lail, Robert Earl

Year	Club	POS	G	AB	R	H	2B	3B	HR	BB	SB	RBI	BA
1947	Warsaw	c	75	237	28	61	5	1	0	16	5	25	.257
1948	Warsaw	c	102	344	50	98	5	0	0	30	6	24	.285

Other teams played for: None

LaMantia, Benedict

Year	Club	POS	G	AB	R	H	2B	3B	HR	BB	SB	RBI	BA
1949	Wilmington	ss	12	48	6	12	2	0	0	10	0	5	.250

Other teams played for: Lincolnton (D)

Lamb, John LeRoy "Roy"

Year	Club	POS	G	AB	R	H	2B	3B	HR	BB	SB	RBI	BA
1946	Wilmington	1b/p	105	375	61	102	13	4	8	—	11	71	.272
1947	Wilmington	p	63	187	31	59	12	3	2	13	0	17	.316
1948	Wilmington	p	67	156	26	47	5	3	0	18	4	27	.301
1950	Whiteville	1b	26	88	11	21	4	1	0	14	1	13	.239

Year	Club	G	CG	W	L	IP	H	R	BB	SO	ERA
1946	Wilmington	18	4	2	8	89	103	92	52	45	—

12. Player Register—Langston

Year	Club	G	CG	W	L	IP	H	R	BB	SO	ERA
1947	Wilmington	26	16	14	8	181	73	167	91	103	2.53
1948	Wilmington	29	19	14	9	209	211	115	104	110	3.70

Other teams played for: Danville-Schoolfield (D), Rutherford County (D), Hendersonville (D)

Lambeth, Harold Adams "Red"

Year	Club	POS	G	AB	R	H	2B	3B	HR	BB	SB	RBI	BA
1949	Lumberton	of	51	134	21	41	5	1	0	13	1	17	.306
1950	Whiteville	of	50	192	24	51	10	3	0	19	7	24	.266

Other teams played for: Rutherford County (D), New River (D), Hickory (D), Marion (D)

Lance, Robert Merritt

Year	Club	POS	G	AB	R	H	2B	3B	HR	BB	SB	RBI	BA
1950	Smith.-Selma	ss	84	289	38	64	6	4	0	44	2	28	.221

Other teams played for: Sheboygan (D)

Lancester, Clarence W. "Tex"

Year	Club	POS	G	AB	R	H	2B	3B	HR	BB	SB	RBI	BA
1946	Wilmington	of	14	44	4	7	0	0	0	—	0	2	.159

Other teams played for: None

Landay, Harry W.

Year	Club	POS	G	AB	R	H	2B	3B	HR	BB	SB	RBI	BA
1946	Angier-Fuquay	—	<10	—	—	—	—	—	—	—	—	—	—

Other teams played for: Lexington, NC (D), Durham (C), Martinsville (C), Tarboro (D), Hendersonville (D), Marion, NC (D), New Bern (D)

Lane, Wilmer Pitman "Red"

Year	Club	POS	G	AB	R	H	2B	3B	HR	BB	SB	RBI	BA
1949	Lumberton	c	34	107	11	26	3	0	1	13	0	20	.243

Other teams played for: Savannah (B), Jacksonville (B), Chattanooga (A), Sanford, Fla. (D), Selma (B), Montgomery (A), Mooresville (D), Charlotte (B),

Langston, James D. "Buck"

Year	Club	POS	G	AB	R	H	2B	3B	HR	BB	SB	RBI	BA
1949	Clinton	p	33	85	6	16	5	0	0	6	1	4	.188

Year	Club	G	CG	W	L	IP	H	R	BB	SO	ERA
1949	Clinton	22	9	5	9	125	162	89	68	42	4.61

Other teams played for: Rome (D)

12. Player Register—LaPorta

LaPorta, John J.

Year	Club	POS	G	AB	R	H	2B	3B	HR	BB	SB	RBI	BA
1947	Lumberton	ss	10	26	3	3	0	0	0	7	0	1	.115

Other teams played for: St. Augustine (D), Carthage (D), Rock Hill (B)

Larrieu, John D.

Year	Club	POS	G	AB	R	H	2B	3B	HR	BB	SB	RBI	BA
1946	Clinton	1b	88	366	85	117	27	5	9	—	5	92	.320

Other teams played for: Tucson (D), Salt Lake City (C), Pine Bluff (C), Texarkana (C), Oklahoma City (A), Merced (C), Goldsboro (D)

Latta, William

Year	Club	POS	G	AB	R	H	2B	3B	HR	BB	SB	RBI	BA
1947	Clinton	ss	21	71	10	15	3	0	0	11	0	7	.211

Other teams played for: None

Lauffer, Robert G. "Bob"

Year	Club	POS	G	AB	R	H	2B	3B	HR	BB	SB	RBI	BA
1946	Wilmington	1b	21	77	13	17	4	1	0	—	1	9	.221

Other teams played for: Galax (D), Salem/Lenoir (D)

Leach, Riley T.

Year	Club	POS	G	AB	R	H	2B	3B	HR	BB	SB	RBI	BA
1946	Dunn-Erwin	1b	77	283	55	80	12	2	0	—	14	28	.283

Veteran catcher Wilmer "Red" Lane, seen here in the uniform of Mooresville in the North Carolina State League in 1948, wrapped up his long career with Lumberton in 1949. He played for several high-level minor league clubs, including Savannah and Chattanooga, in the years before the war (courtesy the late Norman Small).

12. Player Register—Lento

Year	Club	POS	G	AB	R	H	2B	3B	HR	BB	SB	RBI	BA
1947	Dunn-Erwin	1b	86	325	66	84	7	4	1	49	19	39	.258

Other teams played for: Goldsboro

LeBlanc, Robert Joseph

Year	Club	POS	G	AB	R	H	2B	3B	HR	BB	SB	RBI	BA
1947	Lum./Wilm.	2b	84	301	40	62	12	2	1	39	13	32	.206

Other teams played for: Chanute (D)

Lee, Stanley Scott

Year	Club	POS	G	AB	R	H	2B	3B	HR	BB	SB	RBI	BA
1950	Clinton	p	25	50	6	5	0	2	0	3	0	3	.100

Year	Club	G	CG	W	L	IP	H	R	BB	SO	ERA
1950	Clinton	25	5	5	10	143	146	96	101	71	5.35

Other teams played for: None

Lefler, Neil Graham

Year	Club	G	CG	W	L	IP	H	R	BB	SO	ERA
1946	Angier-Fuquay	2	—	0	0	9	—	—	—	—	—

Other teams played for: Greensboro (C), Wilson (D), New Bern (D)

Lehman, George F.

Year	Club	POS	G	AB	R	H	2B	3B	HR	BB	SB	RBI	BA
1950	Red Springs	p	16	37	2	6	0	0	0	3	0	3	.162

Year	Club	G	CG	W	L	IP	H	R	BB	SO	ERA
1950	Red Springs	15	5	4	5	86	96	75	97	53	6.80

Other teams played for: None

Lento, Alfred A.

Year	Club	POS	G	AB	R	H	2B	3B	HR	BB	SB	RBI	BA
1947	Wilmington	p	10										
	Smith.-Selma	p	12										
	totals:	p	22	41	5	4	0	0	0	7	1	0	.098
1948	Smith.-Selma	p	17	23	2	6	0	1	0	1	0	2	.261

Year	Club	G	CG	W	L	IP	H	R	BB	SO	ERA
1947	Wilmington	9									
	Smith.-Selma	10									
	totals:	19	4	2	8	89	109	74	34	59	6.27
1948	Smith.-Selma	15	2	3	6	57	59	32	31	32	3.16

Other teams played for: None

12. Player Register—Linder

Linder, Raymond R.

Year	Club	POS	G	AB	R	H	2B	3B	HR	BB	SB	RBI	BA
1947	Clinton	c	28	89	12	26	1	1	1	8	1	17	.292

Other teams played for: Charleston, W.V. (C), Thomasville (D), Spatanburg (B)

Lindsey, Haskell

Year	Club	POS	G	AB	R	H	2B	3B	HR	BB	SB	RBI	BA
1950	Whiteville	ss	11	38	5	6	0	0	0	4	1	3	.158

Other teams played for: New River (D)

Liner, Henry "Buck"

Year	Club	POS	G	AB	R	H	2B	3B	HR	BB	SB	RBI	BA
1950	Wilmington	p	55	109	12	27	3	1	0	9	0	16	.248

Year	Club	G	CG	W	L	IP	H	R	BB	SO	ERA
1950	Wilmington	31	1	7	6	109	126	99	96	92	6.69

Other teams played for: Welch (D), Ogden (C), Durham (B)

Litinski, Stanley A.

Year	Club	POS	G	AB	R	H	2B	3B	HR	BB	SB	RBI	BA
1948	Clinton	p	16										
	Dunn-Erwin	p	2										
	totals:	p	18	32	4	3	0	0	0	4	0	2	.094

Year	Club	G	CG	W	L	IP	H	R	BB	SO	ERA
1948	Clinton	16									
	Dunn-Erwin	2									
	totals:	18	2	5	6	91	121	77	39	35	6.13

Other teams played for: None

Lloyd, William H. "Bill"

Year	Club	POS	G	AB	R	H	2B	3B	HR	BB	SB	RBI	BA
1948	Smith.-Selma	p	26	56	4	12	2	0	0	9	0	2	.214
1949	Smith.-Selma	p	5										
	Fayetteville	p	27										
	totals: p		32	71	9	17	1	0	0	8	0	8	.239

Year	Club	G	CG	W	L	IP	H	R	BB	SO	ERA
1948	Smith.-Selma	25	10	7	10	158	162	72	30	48	2.39
1949	Smith.-Selma	5									
	Fayetteville	24									
	totals:	29	9	8	13	155	187	111	52	58	3.77

Other teams played for: Wilson (D)

12. Player Register—Luchetta

Lorenz, Marvin Peter

Year	Club	POS	G	AB	R	H	2B	3B	HR	BB	SB	RBI	BA
1946	Angier-Fuquay	1b	103	426	87	144	33	2	15	—	4	86	.338
1948	Clinton	1b/p	134	555	127	185	13	42	6	54	9	103	.333
1949	Clinton	1b	130	531	68	152	19	3	2	36	5	89	.286
1950	Smith.-Selma	1b/p	111										
	Clinton	1b/p	15										
	totals:	1b	126	501	77	151	29	4	2	57	6	91	.301

Year	Club	G	CG	W	L	IP	H	R	BB	SO	ERA
1946	Angier-Fuquay	2	0	0	0	3	—	—	—	—	—
1948	Clinton	10	_	3	1	52	70	38	17	—	5.19
1950	Smith.-Selma	6									
	Clinton	2									
	totals:	8	5	2	3	56	66	24	23	22	3.38

Other teams played for: Clinton, Iowa (B), Tallahassee (D), Bluefield (D), Raleigh (C)

Lorman, Douglas George

Year	Club	POS	G	AB	R	H	2B	3B	HR	BB	SB	RBI	BA
1947	Lumberton	p	23	71	3	13	4	0	0	3	0	4	.183

Year	Club	G	CG	W	L	IP	H	R	BB	SO	ERA
1947	Lumberton	23	18	16	6	189	185	81	66	82	3.00

Other teams played for: Decatur, Ill. (B)

Lowenstein, Donald

Year	Club	POS	G	AB	R	H	2B	3B	HR	BB	SB	RBI	BA
1949	Wilmington	p	30	59	6	9	3	0	0	2	0	2	.153

Year	Club	G	CG	W	L	IP	H	R	BB	SO	ERA
1949	Wilmington	26	4	6	8	108	124	92	91	45	5.17

Other teams played for: Hopewell (D), Petersburg (D)

Lowry, Curtis Grayson

Year	Club	POS	G	AB	R	H	2B	3B	HR	BB	SB	RBI	BA
1948	Clinton	3b	138	522	93	141	28	6	4	90	12	81	.270

Other teams played for: New Bern (D), Goldsboro (D)

Luchetta, Frank A.

Year	Club	POS	G	AB	R	H	2B	3B	HR	BB	SB	RBI	BA
1950	Sanford	of	36	135	38	36	5	2	0	37	6	13	.267

Other teams played for: Waycross (D)

12. Player Register—Lynch

Lynch, Charles Wright "Charley"

Year	Club	POS	G	AB	R	H	2B	3B	HR	BB	SB	RBI	BA
1948	Lumberton	p	21	51	3	4	1	0	0	7	0	4	.078
1949	Lumberton	p	29	60	8	13	2	0	0	9	0	3	.217

Year	Club	G	CG	W	L	IP	H	R	BB	SO	ERA
1948	Lumberton	21	11	7	6	133	152	73	35	106	4.40
1949	Lumberton	27	12	10	11	152	146	85	59	108	3.61

Other teams played for: None

Lynch, Robert "Bob"

Year	Club	G	CG	W	L	IP	H	R	BB	SO	ERA
1946	Angier-Fuquay	2	0	0	1	8	14	15	1	3	—

Other teams played for: Unknown

Maas, Duane Frederick "Duke"

Year	Club	POS	G	AB	R	H	2B	3B	HR	BB	SB	RBI	BA
1949	Dunn-Erwin	p	14	23	6	8	0	0	0	3	0	4	.348

Year	Club	G	CG	W	L	IP	H	R	BB	SO	ERA
1949	Dunn-Erwin	12	2	3	2	48	47	38	37	39	5.25

Other teams played for: Roanoke Rapids (D), Jamestown (D), Durham (B), Wilkes-Barre (A), Buffalo (AAA), Charleston, W.V. (AAA), Detroit (ML), Kansas City (ML), New York Yankees (ML), Richmond (AAA)

MacLean, Donald Hector

Year	Club	POS	G	AB	R	H	2B	3B	HR	BB	SB	RBI	BA
1947	Clinton	of	63	247	37	75	7	8	2	20	7	33	.304
1948	Clinton	of	131	495	91	177	25	12	10	75	19	115	.358

Other teams played for: Landis (D), Burlington (B), Raleigh (B)

Magliolo, John A.

Year	Club	POS	G	AB	R	H	2B	3B	HR	BB	SB	RBI	BA
1948	Dunn-Erwin	p	27	67	7	12	1	1	0	2	1	2	.179
1949	Dunn-Erwin	1b	99	338	100	114	13	14	6	69	19	54	.337

Year	Club	G	CG	W	L	IP	H	R	BB	SO	ERA
1948	Dunn-Erwin	9	6	4	3	58	66	43	28	47	4.50

Other teams played for: Youngstown (C), Sunbury (B), Lincoln (A), Des Moines (A)

12. Player Register—Marko

Malloy, John Thomas "Jack"

Year	Club	POS	G	AB	R	H	2B	3B	HR	BB	SB	RBI	BA
1949	Lumberton	p	35	84	9	20	1	0	1	2	1	5	.238

Year	Club	G	CG	W	L	IP	H	R	BB	SO	ERA
1949	Lumberton	34	17	14	11	205	178	110	157	178	4.08

Other teams played for: Elizabethton (D), Lincoln (A), Fond du Lac (D)

Maloney, Lloyd T.

Year	Club	POS	G	AB	R	H	2B	3B	HR	BB	SB	RBI	BA
1948	Warsaw	2b	24	93	15	25	5	1	1	14	0	15	.269

Other teams played for: Jackson, Tenn. (D), Sanford (D), Rocky Mount (D), New Bern (D), Hendersonville (d)

Manara, Thomas

Year	Club	POS	G	AB	R	H	2B	3B	HR	BB	SB	RBI	BA
1949	Smith.-Selma	3b	64	187	24	25	3	0	0	30	2	15	.137

Other teams played for: None

Mangini, Joseph Louis "Joe"

Year	Club	POS	G	AB	R	H	2B	3B	HR	BB	SB	RBI	BA
1947	Red Springs	1b	102	404	64	121	14	14	4	38	30	63	.300
1948	Red Springs	1b	139	583	127	176	38	24	6	54	44	113	.303

Other teams played for: Martinsville (B), Savannah (A), Lincoln (A), Williamsport (A), Ottawa (AAA)

Mann, Robert H. "Bob"

Year	Club	POS	G	AB	R	H	2B	3B	HR	BB	SB	RBI	BA
1946	Angier-Fuquay	util	12	37	8	14	2	0	0	—	0	7	.378

Other teams played for: Anaheim (C), Riverside (C)

Marino, Emil John

Year	Club	POS	G	AB	R	H	2B	3B	HR	BB	SB	RBI	BA
1950	Red Springs	of	16	52	7	10	0	0	1	12	0	6	.192

Other teams played for: Federalsburg (D), Cordele (D), Orlando (D), Lockport (C)

Marko, Stephen J.

Year	Club	POS	G	AB	R	H	2B	3B	HR	BB	SB	RBI	BA
1949	Dunn-Erwin	c	129	503	93	164	20	10	5	57	18	98	.326

Other teams played for: Tarboro (D), Roanoke Rapids (D), Bristol (B)

12. Player Register—Marsh

Marsh, Frederick Dallas

Year	Club	POS	G	AB	R	H	2B	3B	HR	BB	SB	RBI	BA
1947	Clinton	of	85	397	57	119	24	5	4	7	12	55	.300

Other teams played for: Newport (D), Erwin (D), Miami (D), Fort Pierce (D), Bluefield (D), Lancaster (B), Rochester (AA), Knoxville (B), Big Stone Gap (D), Sumter (B), Anderson (B), Columbia (A), Augusta (A)

Martin, Odell W.

Year	Club	POS	G	AB	R	H	2B	3B	HR	BB	SB	RBI	BA
1950	Wilmington	p	19	36	3	3	2	0	0	4	0	4	.083

Year	Club	G	CG	W	L	IP	H	R	BB	SO	ERA
1950	Wilmington	17	6	5	6	92	68	45	75	70	3.62

Other teams played for: Columbia (A), Colonial Heights-Petersburg (D), Sunbury (B)

Marx, Elzer Ino "Slats"

Year	Club	POS	G	AB	R	H	2B	3B	HR	BB	SB	RBI	BA
1947	Lumberton	1b	121	489	122	154	20	9	19	79	3	100	.315

Other teams played for: Fayetteville (D), Clinton, Iowa (C), Grand Rapids (A), Macon (A)

Masinick, Julius "Bud"

Year	Club	POS	G	AB	R	H	2B	3B	HR	BB	SB	RBI	BA
1950	Lumberton	p	13	26	5	6	0	0	0	3	0	2	.231

Year	Club	G	CG	W	L	IP	H	R	BB	SO	ERA
1950	Lumberton	12	5	6	2	71	69	41	33	31	4.56

Other teams played for: Galax (D)

Mason, Charles G.

Year	Club	POS	G	AB	R	H	2B	3B	HR	BB	SB	RBI	BA
1947	Smith.-Selma	of	70	201	22	62	4	2	0	13	0	28	.308

Other teams played for: *Scranton (A)* ?

Mason, Herman Buel

Year	Club	POS	G	AB	R	H	2B	3B	HR	BB	SB	RBI	BA
1949	Smith.-Selma	ss	77										
	Fayetteville	ss	55										
	totals:	ss	132	457	77	110	24	2	3	83	9	62	.241

Other teams played for: Andalusia (D), Morganton (D), Hickory (D), Burlignton (B), New Bern (D), Greenville (D), Rock Hill (B)

12. Player Register—McBane

Matthews, Roy Lee

Year	Club	POS	G	AB	R	H	2B	3B	HR	BB	SB	RBI	BA
1950	Whiteville	p	8										
	Rockingham	p	15										
	totals:	p	23	41	11	12	3	0	0	8	0	2	.293

Year	Club	G	CG	W	L	IP	H	R	BB	SO	ERA
1950	Whiteville	8									
	Rockingham	15									
	totals:	23	8	5	6	110	126	84	54	26	5.73

Other teams played for: Salisbury (D)

Matthews, Wesley Norton

Year	Club	POS	G	AB	R	H	2B	3B	HR	BB	SB	RBI	BA
1949	Smith.-Selma	of	50	174	39	52	8	3	1	27	3	14	.290

Other teams played for: Bartlesville (D)

May, Herbert A.

Year	Club	POS	G	AB	R	H	2B	3B	HR	BB	SB	RBI	BA
1949	Sanford	of	53	194	34	61	14	0	3	32	3	50	.314
1950	Sanford	of	117	423	86	144	29	2	10	101	11	93	.340

Other teams played for: Kingsport (D), Salisbury (D), Wellsville (D), Norfolk (B), Rocky Mount (D), Roanoke Rapids (D), Greensboro (C), Augusta (A), Greensboro (B), Muncie (D), Rock Hill (B), Greenville, SC (B)

Mazzei, Amerigo E. "Mego"

Year	Club	POS	G	AB	R	H	2B	3B	HR	BB	SB	RBI	BA
1949	Clinton	ss	130	466	75	114	16	5	2	95	17	54	.245
1950	Clinton	ss	53	184	28	45	2	0	0	33	0	17	.245

Other teams played for: None

McBane, George L.

Year	Club	POS	G	AB	R	H	2B	3B	HR	BB	SB	RBI	BA
1950	Wilmington	p	12										
	Clinton	p	1										
	Whiteville	p	3										
	totals:	p	16	19	2	0	0	0	0	4	0	0	.000

Year	Club	G	CG	W	L	IP	H	R	BB	SO	ERA
1950	Wilmington	12									
	Clinton	1									

12. Player Register—McBride

Year	Club	G	CG	W	L	IP	H	R	BB	SO	ERA
	Whiteville	1									
	totals:	14	1	3	4	52	90	48	18	12	7.10

Other teams played for: High Point –Thomasville (D)

McBride, Stanley

Year	Club	POS	G	AB	R	H	2B	3B	HR	BB	SB	RBI	BA
1946	Sanford	p	22	51	12	13	2	0	0	—	0	5	.255

Year	Club	G	CG	W	L	IP	H	R	BB	SO	ERA
1946	Sanford	19	3	5	4	84	110	68	56	46	—

Other teams played for: None

McBryde, Myron Homer

Year	Club	POS	G	AB	R	H	2B	3B	HR	BB	SB	RBI	BA
1950	Rockingham	c	42	150	23	38	3	1	0	25	0	27	.253

Other teams played for: None

McCarty, Edward Joseph

Year	Club	POS	G	AB	R	H	2B	3B	HR	BB	SB	RBI	BA
1947	Warsaw	3b	75	250	36	65	7	0	2	47	4	22	.260
1948	Warsaw	3b	53										
	Smith.-Selma	3b	29										
	totals:	3b	82	276	51	78	14	1	5	71	0	43	.283

Other teams played for: St. Augustine (D), Gainesville (D), Palatka (D)

McClintock, James H.

Year	Club	POS	G	AB	R	H	2B	3B	HR	BB	SB	RBI	BA
1946	Clinton	ss	37	151	45	55	12	4	3	—	9	31	.364

Other teams played for: Leaksville (C), Durham (C)

McCormick, Lenwood

Year	Club	POS	G	AB	R	H	2B	3B	HR	BB	SB	RBI	BA
1950	Whiteville	p	24	52	9	11	0	0	0	4	0	1	.212

Year	Club	G	CG	W	L	IP	H	R	BB	SO	ERA
1950	Whiteville	22	5	4	8	126	122	69	67	58	4.00

Other teams played for: Kinston (D)

McCrary, James Ernest

Year	Club	POS	G	AB	R	H	2B	3B	HR	BB	SB	RBI	BA
1948	Red Springs	ss	44	130	16	27	2	2	0	16	2	21	.208

12. Player Register—McGhee

Other teams played for: Moultrie (D), Lexington (D), Cordele (D), Cocoa (D), Middlesboro (C)

McDonald, Gordon C.

Year	Club	POS	G	AB	R	H	2B	3B	HR	BB	SB	RBI	BA
1949	Lumberton	p	31	55	11	8	1	0	0	21	0	5	.145

Year	Club	G	CG	W	L	IP	H	R	BB	SO	ERA
1949	Lumberton	28	8	15	6	180	169	75	74	66	2.95

Other teams played for: Rutherford County (D), Morristown (D)

McDuffie, Glenn

Year	Club	POS	G	AB	R	H	2B	3B	HR	BB	SB	RBI	BA
1950	Whiteville	util	10	43	9	12	1	2	0	3	0	9	.279

Other teams played for: Emporia (D), Concord (D)

McElroy, Royce E.

Year	Club	POS	G	AB	R	H	2B	3B	HR	BB	SB	RBI	BA
1950	Lumberton	c	<10	3*	2*	1*	—	—	—	—	—	1*	—

Other teams played for: New Iberia (C), Lafayette (C)

McFadden, John A.

Year	Club	POS	G	AB	R	H	2B	3B	HR	BB	SB	RBI	BA
1947	Sanford	p	37	81	6	12	0	0	0	1	0	9	.148
1948	Sanford	p	34	101	11	24	6	0	1	4	0	14	.238

Year	Club	G	CG	W	L	IP	H	R	BB	SO	ERA
1947	Sanford	36	11	15	5	192	147	67	47	170	2.44
1948	Sanford	34	22	20	9	241	221	96	61	187	3.02

Other teams played for: Newnan (D)

McGhee, Thomas Fred "Tommy"

Year	Club	POS	G	AB	R	H	2B	3B	HR	BB	SB	RBI	BA
1948	Warsaw	of	134	547	104	139	21	9	17	79	30	72	.254

Other teams played for: Muncie (D), Tallahassee (D), Burlington-Graham (B)

* Incomplete stats

12. Player Register—McIntosh

McIntosh, Joseph Pitt "Joe"

Year	Club	POS	G	AB	R	H	2B	3B	HR	BB	SB	RBI	BA
1950	Clinton	p	5										
	Wilmington	p	21										
	totals:	p	26	44	4	5	1	0	0	7	0	1	.114

Year	Club	G	CG	W	L	IP	H	R	BB	SO	ERA
1950	Clinton	5									
	Wilmington	19									
	totals:	24	8	7	12	124	116	81	106	71	4.43

Other teams played for: Shelby (D), Marion (D), Hendersonville (D), Gastonia (D), Norton (D)

McIntosh, "Tootsie"

Year	Club	POS	G	AB	R	H	2B	3B	HR	BB	SB	RBI	BA
1949	Dunn-Erwin	ss	5	19	2	4	0	0	0	—	0	1	.210

Other teams played for: Unknown

McKeithen, Ernest Harlan

Year	Club	POS	G	AB	R	H	2B	3B	HR	BB	SB	RBI	BA
1946	Wilmington	c	<10	—	—	—	—	—	—	—	—	—	—

Other teams played for:

McLaughlin, James T. "Jim"

Year	Club	POS	G	AB	R	H	2B	3B	HR	BB	SB	RBI	BA
1949	Clinton	c	28	96	17	24	3	2	0	18	4	14	.250

Other teams played for: Franklin (D), Hopewell (D), Petersburg (D)

McQuillen, Joseph Carl

Year	Club	POS	G	AB	R	H	2B	3B	HR	BB	SB	RBI	BA
1947	Dunn-Erwin	of	128	538	103	178	36	11	19	48	21	121	.331
1948	Dunn-Erwin	of	54	194	28	52	12	2	1	24	10	37	.268

Other teams played for: Sanford, Fla. (D), Orlando (D), Mooresville (D), Augusta (B), Norfolk (B), Binghamton (A), Montgomery (B), Dallas (AA), Greenville, NC (D), Federalsburg (D), Pulaski (D), Oil City (D), Franklin (D), Hannibal (D), St. Hyacinthe (C)

McVicker, Frank Blair

Year	Club	POS	G	AB	R	H	2B	3B	HR	BB	SB	RBI	BA
1948	Warsaw	p	33	86	7	16	1	1	0	8	0	14	.186
1949	Fayetteville	p	—	—	—	—	—	—	—	—	—	—	—

12. Player Register—Melvin

Year	Club	G	CG	W	L	IP	H	R	BB	SO	ERA
1948	Warsaw	23	17	15	14	220	232	143	98	124	3.97
1949	Fayetteville	7	5	4	2	55	56	28	23	26	3.44

Other teams played for: None

McWhorter, Guy L.

Year	Club	POS	G	AB	R	H	2B	3B	HR	BB	SB	RBI	BA
1950	Rockingham	p	20	17	1	3	0	0	0	4	0	1	.176

Year	Club	G	CG	W	L	IP	H	R	BB	SO	ERA
1950	Rockingham	20	2	2	5	68	78	59	54	27	6.22

Other teams played for: Reidsville (D)

Meador,

Year	Club	G	CG	W	L	IP	H	R	BB	SO	ERA
1946	Angier-Fuquay	2	0	0	0	4	—	—	—	—	—

Other teams played for: Unknown

Mehlhorn, Robert C. "Bob"

Year	Club	POS	G	AB	R	H	2B	3B	HR	BB	SB	RBI	BA
1948	Smith.-Selma	p	26	50	5	10	0	0	0	1	0	5	.200
1949	Clinton	p	28	49	6	14	3	0	0	4	1	4	.286

Year	Club	G	CG	W	L	IP	H	R	BB	SO	ERA
1948	Smith.-Selma	26	5	9	3	126	136	77	59	47	4.21
1949	Clinton	25	9	8	9	120	128	69	64	54	4.20

Other teams played for: None

Mejido, Juan

Year	Club	POS	G	AB	R	H	2B	3B	HR	BB	SB	RBI	BA
1946	Dunn-Erwin	1b	18	63	4	17	1	1	0	—	0	7	.270

Other teams played for: Del Rio (D), Abbeville (C), Laredo (C), Roanoke Rapids (D), Geneva (C), Havana (A), Abilene (C), Big Spring (C)

Melvin, Donald M.

Year	Club	POS	G	AB	R	H	2B	3B	HR	BB	SB	RBI	BA
1947	Dunn-Erwin	p	33	72	9	15	1	1	0	6	2	9	.208
1948	Dunn-Erwin	1b	43	172	20	37	7	2	0	18	4	13	.215

Year	Club	G	CG	W	L	IP	H	R	BB	SO	ERA
1946	Dunn-Erwin	7	3	2	4	31	43	26	19	15	—
1947	Lumberton	14	6	4	5	71	93	66	36	32	5.70

Other teams played for: Fayetteville (D)

12. Player Register—Merica

Merica, Frank Edward

Year	Club	POS	G	AB	R	H	2B	3B	HR	BB	SB	RBI	BA
1949	Smith.-Selma	p	7										
	Wilmington	p	10										
	totals:	p	17	26	3	4	0	0	0	7	0	1	.154

Year	Club	G	CG	W	L	IP	H	R	BB	SO	ERA
1949	S.-S./Wilm.	10	—	—	—	<45	—	—	—	—	—

Other teams played for: None

Merrion, Donald J.

Year	Club	POS	G	AB	R	H	2B	3B	HR	BB	SB	RBI	BA
1948	Dunn-Erwin	p	13	27	3	1	0	0	0	5	0	0	.037

Year	Club	G	CG	W	L	IP	H	R	BB	SO	ERA
1948	Dunn-Erwin	13	4	4	6	77	109	77	41	40	5.38

Other teams played for: Trois-Rivieres (C)

Mesmer, Edward James

Year	Club	POS	G	AB	R	H	2B	3B	HR	BB	SB	RBI	BA
1950	Red Springs	util	10	14	2	1	0	1	0	6	0	1	.071

Other teams played for: Federalsburg (D), Portsmouth, Ohio (D)

Meyer, James F.

Year	Club	POS	G	AB	R	H	2B	3B	HR	BB	SB	RBI	BA
1946	Clinton	of	103	384	81	115	19	9	11	—	5	59	.299

Other teams played for: Roanoke Rapids (D), Lawrenceville (D)

Micham, Jerry Marcus

Year	Club	POS	G	AB	R	H	2B	3B	HR	BB	SB	RBI	BA
1950	Wilmington	of	89	343	54	92	10	6	1	44	8	29	.268

Other teams played for: Muncie (D), Daytona Beach (D), Douglas (D)

Miller, Gail Malcolm "Mick"

Year	Club	POS	G	AB	R	H	2B	3B	HR	BB	SB	RBI	BA
1950	Wilmington	p	28	50	3	4	1	0	0	5	0	3	.080

Year	Club	G	CG	W	L	IP	H	R	BB	SO	ERA
1950	Wilmington	27	4	9	9	129	105	86	154	108	5.30

Other teams played for: Matoon (D)

12. Player Register—Milner

Miller, Henry Loftin "Hoggie"

Year	Club	POS	G	AB	R	H	2B	3B	HR	BB	SB	RBI	BA
1946	Dunn-Erwin	2b	15	46	5	7	0	1	0	—	0	4	.152
1947	Dunn-Erwin	3b	117	499	93	145	16	10	3	37	28	75	.291
1948	Dunn-Erwin	3b	139	553	93	165	33	13	7	62	25	89	.298
1949	Dunn-Erwin	3b	135	567	114	177	33	11	8	41	42	107	.312
1950	Whiteville	3b	126	502	76	151	24	10	3	46	12	80	.321

Other teams played for: Hopkinsvile (D), Cairo (D) Shelby (D), Rocky Mount (D), Fayetteville (B), Augusta (A).

Miller, James W. "Jim"

Year	Club	POS	G	AB	R	H	2B	3B	HR	BB	SB	RBI	BA
1947	Red Springs	p	33	73	12	18	1	0	0	5	2	3	.247

Year	Club	G	CG	W	L	IP	H	R	BB	SO	ERA
1947	Red Springs	27	12	11	10	179	188	119	90	92	3.51

Other teams played for: Appleton (D), Martinsville (C), Kewanee (C), Sunbury (B), Williamsport (A), Savannah (A), Columbus (AAA), Little Rock (AA), Knoxville (A), Amarillo (AA), Albany (A), Lancaster (A).

Miller, Ronald Keith

Year	Club	POS	G	AB	R	H	2B	3B	HR	BB	SB	RBI	BA
1950	Rockingham	2b	118	435	70	121	9	2	0	86	39	40	.278

Other teams played for: None

Miller, Robert F.

Year	Club	POS	G	AB	R	H	2B	3B	HR	BB	SB	RBI	BA
1949	Smith.-Selma	p	17	29	2	6	0	2	0	2	0	3	.207

Year	Club	G	CG	W	L	IP	H	R	BB	SO	ERA
1949	Smith.-Selma	12	3	3	6	57	60	53	54	27	4.58

Other teams played for: Olean (D).

Mills, Joseph Doughton

Year	Club	POS	G	AB	R	H	2B	3B	HR	BB	SB	RBI	BA
1946	Angier-Fuquay	3b	103	445	94	136	21	5	4	—	20	60	.306

Other teams played for: Raleigh (C), Petersburg (D), Goldsboro (D), Concord (D), Hopewell (D), Leesburg (D), Emporia (D), Suffolk (D), Palatka (D), Mooresville (D).

Milner, James Richard "Jim" or "Punch"

Year	Club	POS	G	AB	R	H	2B	3B	HR	BB	SB	RBI	BA
1947	Warsaw	1b	126	531	82	168	31	3	2	29	11	101	.316

12. Player Register—Milo

Other teams played for: Mooresville (D), Leaksville (D), Fort Pierce (D), Miami Beach (D), Dothan (D), Richmond (B), Lexington (D), Concord (D)

Milo,

Year	Club	POS	G	AB	R	H	2B	3B	HR	BB	SB	RBI	BA
1946	Smith.-Selma	—	<10	—		—	—	—	—	—	—	—	—	—

Other teams played for: Unknown

Milosevich, Michael "Mike"

Year	Club	POS	G	AB	R	H	2B	3B	HR	BB	SB	RBI	BA
1950	Lumberton	ss	128	497	100	156	36	2	14	81	5	121	.314

Other teams played for: Washington, Penn. (D), Joplin (C), Akron (C), Binghamton (A), Norfolk (B), Kansas City (AA), Newark (AAA), New York Yankees (ML), New Orleans (AA), Atlanta (AA), Hazlehurst-Baxley (D), Americus (D)

Milwood, Grady Lee

Year	Club	POS	G	AB	R	H	2B	3B	HR	BB	SB	RBI	BA
1948	Lumberton	3b	20	60	11	15	2	0	0	7	3	4	.250

Other teams played for: Rutherford County (D)

Mitchell, Robert Ernest

Year	Club	POS	G	AB	R	H	2B	3B	HR	BB	SB	RBI	BA
1948	Dunn-Erwin	of	40	103	12	21	2	0	0	9	2	20	.204
1949	Dunn-Erwin	p	25	56	9	12	0	0	1	3	2	6	.214

Mike Milosevich, a.k.a. Mike Milo, played parts of the 1944 and '45 seasons with the New York Yankees. In 1950, at age 35, he signed with Lumberton, hit .314 and was named a league all-star. He retired from baseball after spending the 1951 season as player-manager for the Americus Rebels of the Class D Georgia-Florida League (courtesy Frank Dennison).

12. Player Register—Montsinger

Year	Club	G	CG	W	L	IP	H	R	BB	SO	ERA
1948	Dunn-Erwin	21	—	6	9	110	105	73	62	—	—
1949	Dunn-Erwin	23	11	10	8	132	134	123	124	94	6.34

Other teams played for: None

Mitchell, Robert Lincoln

Year	Club	POS	G	AB	R	H	2B	3B	HR	BB	SB	RBI	BA
1949	Fayetteville	1b	12	46	2	8	2	0	0	4	0	3	.174

Other teams played for: Greensboro (C), Leaksville (C), Reidsville (C), Raleigh (C), Wilson (D)

Mitchell, Thomas E.

Year	Club	POS	G	AB	R	H	2B	3B	HR	BB	SB	RBI	BA
1950	Whiteville	of	28	85	4	22	4	3	0	3	4	15	.259

Other teams played for: Wytheville/Bassett (D)

Moir, Charles Robert "Charlie"

Year	Club	POS	G	AB	R	H	2B	3B	HR	BB	SB	RBI	BA
1950	Wilmington	of	102	388	61	108	14	6	9	43	4	73	.278

Other teams played for: Mooresville (D)

Monterose, Dominick

Year	Club	POS	G	AB	R	H	2B	3B	HR	BB	SB	RBI	BA
1946	Dunn-Erwin	p	18										
	Angier-Fuquay	p	4										
	totals:	p	22	37	3	2	1	0	0	—	0	3	.054

Year	Club	G	CG	W	L	IP	H	R	BB	SO	ERA
1946	Dunn-Erwin	19									
	Angier-Fuquay	3									
	totals:	22	2	5	9	103	110	94	87	52	—

Other teams played for: Salisbury (D)

Montgomery, Robert W.

Year	Club	G	CG	W	L	IP	H	R	BB	SO	ERA
1950	Lumberton	<10	—	—	—	—	—	—	—	—	—

Other teams played for: Mooresville (D)

Montsinger, R. M.

Year	Club	POS	G	AB	R	H	2B	3B	HR	BB	SB	RBI	BA
1946	A-F/Clinton	—	<10	—	—	—	—	—	—	—	—	—	—

Other teams played for: None

12. Player Register—Mooney

Mooney, James W.

Year	Club	POS	G	AB	R	H	2B	3B	HR	BB	SB	RBI	BA
1949	Fayetteville	c	62	213	19	57	13	0	0	3	1	33	.268

Other teams played for: Reidsville (D), Raleigh (D), Rocky Mount (D)

Moore, A.

Year	Club	POS	G	AB	R	H	2B	3B	HR	BB	SB	RBI	BA
1946	Smith.-Selma	p	13	13	0	0	0	0	0	—	0	1	.000

Year	Club	G	CG	W	L	IP	H	R	BB	SO	ERA
1946	Smith.-Selma	11	1	1	5	38	44	42	15	15	—

Other teams played for: Unknown

Moore, John Jack

Year	Club	POS	G	AB	R	H	2B	3B	HR	BB	SB	RBI	BA
1949	Sanford	ss	35	104	28	24	5	0	1	29	1	15	.231

Other teams played for: Welch (D), Keokuk (D), Portsmouth (D), Moline/Kewanee (C), Hendersonville (D), Dublin (D), Auburn (C), Pittsfield (C)

Morris, Noah C.

Year	Club	POS	G	AB	R	H	2B	3B	HR	BB	SB	RBI	BA
1946	Smith.-Selma	1b	48										
	Clinton	1b	31										
	totals:	1b	79	313	47	91	8	2	3	—	3	50	.291
1947	Smith.-Selma	1b	26	89	17	20	1	0	0	13	1	11	.225

Other teams played for: None

Morris, Phil

Year	Club	POS	G	AB	R	H	2B	3B	HR	BB	SB	RBI	BA
1946	Clinton	—	<10	—	—	—	—	—	—	—	—	—	—

Other teams played for: Ayden (D), Martinsville (D), Wilson (D), Mount Airy (D), Topeka (C), Lexington (D), Kinston (D)

Moser, Floyd Pierce Sr.

Year	Club	POS	G	AB	R	H	2B	3B	HR	BB	SB	RBI	BA
1950	Red Springs	of	106	377	50	112	16	6	5	48	8	58	.271

Other teams played for: Oshkosh (D), Lenoir (D), Tarboro (D)

Mossor, Earl Dalton

Year	Club	POS	G	AB	R	H	2B	3B	HR	BB	SB	RBI	BA
1946	Clinton	p	52	133	15	40	4	2	3	—	0	17	.301

12. Player Register—Murray

Year	Club	G	CG	W	L	IP	H	R	BB	SO	ERA
1946	Clinton	34	21	21	8	239	224	120	109	166	—

Other teams played for: Portsmouth (B), St. Paul (AAA), Brooklyn (ML), Montreal (AAA), Mobile (AA), Portland (Open), Forth Worth (AA), Atlanta (AA), Louisville (AA), Tulsa (AA), Miami (AAA), Dallas (AA), Tulsa (AA), New Orleans (AA)

Mottler, Ernest H.

Year	Club	POS	G	AB	R	H	2B	3B	HR	BB	SB	RBI	BA
1949	Fayetteville	c	45	128	21	26	5	0	3	34	2	20	.203

Other teams played for: Sanford, Fla. (D), Orlando (D), Vidalia-Lyons (D), Dublin (D), New River (D), Kingsport (D)

Mueger, George H.

Year	Club	POS	G	AB	R	H	2B	3B	HR	BB	SB	RBI	BA
1949	Wilmington	ss	14	57	11	8	1	0	0	7	2	5	.140

Other teams played for: None

Mullarky, Armand J.

Year	Club	G	CG	W	L	IP	H	R	BB	SO	ERA
1946	Dunn-Erwin	7	1	0	1	26	42	28	23	9	—

Other teams played for: Fayetteville (D)

Mungo, Van Lingle

Year	Club	POS	G	AB	R	H	2B	3B	HR	BB	SB	RBI	BA
1946	Clinton	p/1b	17	51	10	24	3	2	1	—	0	13	.471
1947	Clinton	1b	33	127	24	46	14	1	3	11	0	28	.362

Year	Club	G	CG	W	L	IP	H	R	BB	SO	ERA
1946	Clinton	5	0	1	1	18	16	10	3	25	—

Other teams played for: Fayetteville (D), Charlotte (B), Winston-Salem (C), Hartford (A), Brooklyn (ML), New York Giants (ML), Montreal (AA), Minneapolis (AA)

Murray, Harlan

Year	Club	POS	G	AB	R	H	2B	3B	HR	BB	SB	RBI	BA
1950	Rockingham	ss	122	448	68	110	21	8	1	76	2	54	.246

Other teams played for: None

12. Player Register—Murray

Murray, John

Year	Club	POS	G	AB	R	H	2B	3B	HR	BB	SB	RBI	BA
1946	Clinton	—	<10	—	—	—	—	—	—	—	—	—	—

Other teams played for: New Bern (D), Selma, Ala, (B)

Muscovitch, John J. Jr. "Ducky"

Year	Club	POS	G	AB	R	H	2B	3B	HR	BB	SB	RBI	BA
1947	Wilmington	of	34	135	20	39	7	2	0	6	10	13	.289
1948	Wilmington	of	69	261	63	78	12	4	0	40	21	43	.299

Other teams played for: None

Mustian, Vernon Martin "Preacher"

Year	Club	POS	G	AB	R	H	2B	3B	HR	BB	SB	RBI	BA
1950	Lumberton	p	30	64	5	11	1	0	0	4	0	12	.172

Year	Club	G	CG	W	L	IP	H	R	BB	SO	ERA
1950	Lumberton	24	13	11	6	148	131	76	48	61	4.01

Other teams played for: Greenville, NC (D), Edenton (D)

Musumeci, Fred

Year	Club	POS	G	AB	R	H	2B	3B	HR	BB	SB	RBI	BA
1947	Wilmington	ss	109	438	92	117	12	5	3	66	38	40	.267

Other teams played for: Reidsville (C)

Musumeci, John

Year	Club	POS	G	AB	R	H	2B	3B	HR	BB	SB	RBI	BA
1949	Fayetteville	3b	127	479	73	126	26	5	1	42	13	72	.263
1950	Lumberton	3b	107	433	71	139	18	19	1	50	7	76	.321

Other teams played for: Americus (D), New Iberia (C), Abbeville (C), St. Hyacinthe (C), Trois-Rivieres (C), Lubbock (C)

Nagle, Thomas J.

Year	Club	POS	G	AB	R	H	2B	3B	HR	BB	SB	RBI	BA
1948	Clinton	p	22	57	8	16	1	0	0	2	0	0	.281

Year	Club	G	CG	W	L	IP	H	R	BB	SO	ERA
1948	Clinton	21	13	10	8	135	144	85	80	76	4.40

Other teams played for: Hagerstown (B), Quebec (C), Martinsville (C), Youngstown (C), Salisbury, Md. (B)

12. Player Register—Niezgoda

Napier, Richard Payne

Year	Club	POS	G	AB	R	H	2B	3B	HR	BB	SB	RBI	BA
1950	Smith.-Selma	p	20	41	4	7	1	0	0	5	0	2	.171

Year	Club	G	CG	W	L	IP	H	R	BB	SO	ERA
1950	Smith.-Selma	18	11	5	9	113	109	66	81	81	4.46

Other teams played for: Baton Rouge (C), Thibodaux (C), Rocky Mount (D)

Narleski, William Edward Jr.

Year	Club	POS	G	AB	R	H	2B	3B	HR	BB	SB	RBI	BA
1949	Fayetteville	p	31	60	8	17	2	0	0	3	0	4	.283

Year	Club	G	CG	W	L	IP	H	R	BB	SO	ERA
1949	Fayetteville	30	9	8	11	144	157	108	105	74	4.69

Other teams played for: Reidsville (C)

Narron, Samuel Woody "Sam"

Year	Club	POS	G	AB	R	H	2B	3B	HR	BB	SB	RBI	BA
1947	Smith.-Selma	c	27	91	23	35	9	2	7	12	1	33	.385
1948	Smith.-Selma	c	49	126	16	40	8	0	2	17	2	33	.317

Other teams played for: Martinsville (D), Albany (D), Sacramento (AA), Asheville (B), Rochester (AA), St. Louis Cardinals (ML), Houston (A1), St. Paul (AA), Mobile (AA), Montreal (AAA)

Nesselrode, Orville Burlin "Hank"

Year	Club	POS	G	AB	R	H	2B	3B	HR	BB	SB	RBI	BA
1946	Sanford	of	114	449	95	159	28	9	30	-5		150	.354
1947	Sanford	of	121	477	121	168	32	3	32	76	22	166	.352
1948	Sanford	of	141	549	119	199	46	4	27	103	17	159	.362

Other teams played for: South Boston (D), Winston-Salem (D), Oklahoma City (A1), Salina (C), Charleston, SC (B)

Nessing, Joseph Charles

Year	Club	POS	G	AB	R	H	2B	3B	HR	BB	SB	RBI	BA
1946	Sanford	ss	119	436	92	137	15	5	6	—	12	67	.318
1947	Sanford	3b	119	496	119	150	31	3	3	53	56	74	.302
1949	Sanford	1b	19	69	10	20	3	0	0	13	3	10	.290

Other teams played for: Knoxville (B), Greenville, NC (D), Goldsboro (D)

Niezgoda, Leo

Year	Club	POS	G	AB	R	H	2B	3B	HR	BB	SB	RBI	BA
1946	Smith.-Selma	1b	116	519	107	173	23	8	6	—	12	71	.333

Other teams played for: Trenton (B), Jacksonville (A), Knoxville (B)

12. Player Register—Niven

Niven, William Edward

Year	Club	POS	G	AB	R	H	2B	3B	H	BB	SB	RBI	BA
1948	Wilmington	p	32	63	13	16	2	0	0	9	0	5	.254
1949	Wilmington	p	44	67	8	12	5	2	0	5	0	9	.179
1950	Wilmington	p	21	48	4	11	2	0	0	6	0	2	.229

Year	Club	G	CG	W	L	IP	H	R	BB	SO	ERA
1948	Wilmington	29	10	11	6	170	176	113	77	82	4.18
1949	Wilmington	34	2	6	12	124	173	144	88	72	7.48
1950	Wilmington	17	6	5	5	101	104	64	72	48	3.83

Other teams played for: None

Norman, Rown

Year	Club	POS	G	AB	R	H	2B	3B	HR	BB	SB	RBI	BA
1947	Dunn-Erwin	3b	21	91	8	21	5	1	0	6	0	9	.231

Other teams played for: None

Northrop, Robert

Year	Club	G	CG	W	L	IP	H	R	BB	SO	ERA
1946	Clinton	1	0	0	0	4	—	—	—	—	—

Other teams played for: Mooresville (D)

Novack, Ernest W. "Ernie"

Year	Club	POS	G	AB	R	H	2B	3B	HR	BB	SB	RBI	BA
1949	Lumberton	p	15	23	1	2	0	0	0	1	0	1	.087
1950	Whiteville	p	33	80	5	15	1	1	0	3	0	4	.188

Year	Club	G	CG	W	L	IP	H	R	BB	SO	ERA
1949	Lumberton	15	2	3	3	62	65	26	23	28	3.34
1950	Whiteville	19	10	7	7	117	112	49	47	57	2.85

Other teams played for: Rutherford County (D), Elizabeth City (D), Mooresville (D)

Novak, Walter

Year	Club	POS	G	AB	R	H	2B	3B	HR	BB	SB	RBI	BA
1950	Clinton	ss	33	129	19	38	8	2	2	24	0	22	.295

Other teams played for: New River (D), Rocky Mount (D)

O'Brien,

Year	Club	G	CG	W	L	IP	H	R	BB	SO	ERA
1948	Red Springs	8	4	4	2	47	39	21	27	23	3.64

Other teams played for: Unknown

12. Player Register—Olbert

O'Coine, Marshall Joseph

Year	Club	POS	G	AB	R	H	2B	3B	HR	BB	SB	RBI	BA
1948	Clinton	p	25	58	6	7	1	0	0	3	0	4	.121
1949	Clinton	p	10	20	4	6	2	0	0	2	0	1	.300

Year	Club	G	CG	W	L	IP	H	R	BB	SO	ERA
1948	Clinton	24	11	9	6	144	175	96	62	53	4.56
1949	Clinton	10	2	3	4	57	74	47	25	32	6.16

Other teams played for: Waycross (D), Thibodaux (C), Miami Beach (B), Augusta (A), St. Petersburg (B)

Odom, David Everett "Dave"

Year	Club	POS	G	AB	R	H	2B	3B	HR	BB	SB	RBI	BA
1946	Wilmington	p	7										
	Angier-Fuquy	p	7										
	Sanford	p	5										
	totals:	p	19	45	3	9	1	0	1	—	0	8	.200

Year	Club	G	CG	W	L	IP	H	R	BB	SO	ERA
1946	Wilmington	7									
	Angier-Fuquay	7									
	Sanford	4									
	totals:	18	10	8	6	113	122	90	64	41	—

Other teams played for: Mitchell (D), Jamestown (D), Albuquerque (D), Bassett (D), Beaumont (A1), South Boston (D), Mayodan (D), Sanford (D), Boston Braves (ML), Hartford (A), Indianapolis (AA), Nashville (A1), Greensboro (C)

Oehler, Edward

Year	Club	POS	G	AB	R	H	2B	3B	HR	BB	SB	RBI	BA
1947	Clinton	1b	3										
	Smith.-Selma	1b	84										
	totals:	1b	87	322	48	99	8	6	0	47	1	49	.307
1948	Smith.-Selma	1b	62										
	Warsaw	1b	36										
	totals:	1b	98	316	45	81	9	3	0	69	3	33	.256
1949	Smith.-Selma	1b	75	251	49	61	7	2	0	68	2	36	.243

Other teams played for: Lawrenceville (D)

Olbert, Zigmond Stanley "Ziggy"

Year	Club	POS	G	AB	R	H	2B	3B	HR	BB	SB	RBI	BA
1946	Wilmington	p	18	28	4	6	2	0	0	—	1	4	.214

12. Player Register—Olsen

Year	Club	G	CG	W	L	IP	H	R	BB	SO	ERA
1946	Wilmington	16	5	3	5	71	91	67	40	38	—

Other teams played for: None

Olsen, Norman

Year	Club	POS	G	AB	R	H	2B	3B	HR	BB	SB	RBI	BA
1946	Clinton	2b	41										
	Wilmington	2b	36										
	totals:	2b	67	263	43	61	10	0	0	—	3	20	.232

Other teams played for: Miami Beach (C)

Osgood, Charles Benjamin "Charlie"

Year	Club	POS	G	AB	R	H	2B	3B	HR	BB	SB	RBI	BA
1947	Lumberton	p	11	20	1	6	1	0	0	0	0	1	.300

Year	Club	G	CG	W	L	IP	H	R	BB	SO	ERA
1947	Lumberton	9	2	2	3	46	64	45	28	18	7.82

Other teams played for: Trenton (B), Newport News (B), Montreal (AA), Brooklyn Dodgers (ML), Shelby (B), Macon (A), Fayetteville (B), Selma (B)

O'Shields, Garland Lee

Year	Club	POS	G	AB	R	H	2B	3B	HR	BB	SB	RBI	BA
1947	Clinton	1b	56	212	32	54	10	0	3	24	2	30	.255

Other teams played for: Knoxville (B)

Osofsky, Aaron M.

Year	Club	POS	G	AB	R	H	2B	3B	HR	BB	SB	RBI	BA
1947	Smith.-Selma	p	46	78	10	14	0	0	0	10	0	11	.179
1948	Smith.-Selma	p	42	87	12	20	3	0	0	18	0	16	.230

Year	Club	G	CG	W	L	IP	H	R	BB	SO	ERA
1947	Smith.-Selma	38	9	8	11	186	190	120	110	120	3.77
1948	Smith.-Selma	41	22	24	5	271	233	122	114	208	2.76

Other teams played for: Hagerstown (B), New Bern (D), Kinston (D), St. Jean (C), Portsmouth (B), Trois-Rivieres (C)

Owens, Edward M. "Peg"

Year	Club	POS	G	AB	R	H	2B	3B	HR	BB	SB	RBI	BA
1948	Sanford	of	128	464	71	114	16	4	8	70	6	73	.246
1949	Sanford	of	34										
	Wilmington	of	7										
	totals:	of	41	125	16	27	7	0	3	30	3	17	.216

12. Player Register—Parker

Year	Club	POS	G	AB	R	H	2B	3B	HR	BB	SB	RBI	BA
1950	Wilmington	of	17	57	18	15	2	3	0	17	2	15	.263

Other teams played for: None

Padgett, Dean Edward "Spec"

Year	Club	POS	G	AB	R	H	2B	3B	HR	BB	SB	RBI	BA
1948	Lumberton	1b	137	549	105	170	18	9	16	45	29	115	.310

Other teams played for: Rutherford County (D), Lockport (D), Rock Hill (B), Des Moines (A), Macon (A), Augusta (A), Charlotte(A)

Palmer, Dennis A.

Year	Club	POS	G	AB	R	H	2B	3B	HR	BB	SB	RBI	BA
1948	Dunn-Erwin	ss	20	60	10	13	1	0	2	10	0	9	.217

Other teams played for: None

Papa, Alfonso P.

Year	Club	POS	G	AB	R	H	2B	3B	HR	BB	SB	RBI	BA
1947	Red Springs	c	47	145	18	31	5	0	0	13	4	12	.214

Other teams played for: None

Parise, Joseph M.

Year	Club	POS	G	AB	R	H	2B	3B	HR	BB	SB	RBI	BA
1948	Smith.-Selma	of	94	336	65	96	18	6	4	60	22	46	.286
1949	Smith.-Selma	of	76	101	26	42	7	2	3	12	3	25	.416

Other teams played for: Burlington, NC (C), Farnham (C), Sanford, Fla. (D)

Parker, Eugene R.

Year	Club	G	CG	W	L	IP	H	R	BB	SO	ERA
1946	Dunn-Erwin	6	2	2	1	28	20	17	22	30	—

Other teams played for: Leaksville (D), Raleigh (C)

Parker, Lloyd Benjamin

Year	Club	POS	G	AB	R	H	2B	3B	HR	BB	SB	RBI	BA
1948	Lumberton	p	18	47	3	4	0	1	0	3	0	6	.085

Year	Club	G	CG	W	L	IP	H	R	BB	SO	ERA
1948	Lumberton	17	9	6	8	120	122	74	45	56	4.73

Other teams played for: Clinton, Iowa (C), Rutherford County (D)

12. Player Register—Parnell

Parnell, Albert

Year	Club	POS	G	AB	R	H	2B	3B	HR	BB	SB	RBI	BA
1947	Red Springs	of	118	444	60	127	21	8	3	50	24	59	.286
1948	Red Springs	of	138	528	89	144	27	9	5	68	15	89	.273
1949	Red Springs	of	90	328	67	95	19	7	6	73	24	75	.290
1950	Red Springs	of	118	424	83	132	17	7	9	100	17	80	.311

Other teams played for: Martinsville (B), Savannah (A), Fayetteville (B)

Parness, Leon S.

Year	Club	POS	G	AB	R	H	2B	3B	HR	BB	SB	RBI	BA
1950	Red Springs	ss	118	444	62	112	19	4	0	59	3	41	.252

Other teams played for: None

Parrish, Clyde

Year	Club	POS	G	AB	R	H	2B	3B	HR	BB	SB	RBI	BA
1948	Red Springs	c	76	183	22	31	1	0	0	21	5	13	.169
1949	Red Springs	c	17	24	2	2	0	0	0	6	0	1	.083

Other teams played for: Augusta (A)

Parrish, Dennis

Year	Club	POS	G	AB	R	H	2B	3B	HR	BB	SB	RBI	BA
1950	Whiteville	p	22	34	2	2	1	0	0	4	0	2	.059

Year	Club	G	CG	W	L	IP	H	R	BB	SO	ERA
1950	Whiteville	21	3	6	8	91	101	68	65	32	5.54

Other teams played for: None

Pascal, Robert Michael

Year	Club	POS	G	AB	R	H	2B	3B	HR	BB	SB	RBI	BA
1949	Smith.-Selma	1b	43	159	37	53	17	0	2	33	2	44	.333

Other teams played for: Lawrenceville (D), Oshkosh (D), St. Cloud (C), Abilene (B), Magic Valley (C), Fort Worth (AA), Des Moines (A), Sioux City (A), Albany (A), Holdredge (D)

Pasteris, Emile John

Year	Club	POS	G	AB	R	H	2B	3B	HR	BB	SB	RBI	BA
1948	Wilmington	of	82	303	39	70	10	3	0	39	7	38	.231
1949	Wilmington	of	131	503	87	129	24	5	0	76	9	51	.256
1950	Wilmington	of	26	102	22	26	2	1	0	20	0	11	.255

Other teams played for: Wellsville (D), Greenville, NC (D)

12. Player Register—Pearce

Payne, Banks A.

Year	Club	POS	G	AB	R	H	2B	3B	HR	BB	SB	RBI	BA
1948	Warsaw	of/p	57	154	13	34	1	1	0	2	0	11	.221

Year	Club	G	CG	W	L	IP	H	R	BB	SO	ERA
1948	Warsaw	17	5	3	4	86	112	60	41	14	5.02

Other teams played for: None

Payne, Horace Virgil

Year	Club	POS	G	AB	R	H	2B	3B	HR	BB	SB	RBI	BA
1948	Smith.-Selma	2b	131	505	75	152	21	10	1	51	10	71	.301
1950	Smith.-Selma	2b	33	115	14	26	6	1	0	21	0	11	.226

Other teams played for: Elizabethton (D), Pennington Gap (D), Superior (C), Greenville, NC (D), Goldsboro (D)

Payne, James Cecil "Zip"

Year	Club	POS	G	AB	R	H	2B	3B	HR	BB	SB	RBI	BA
1949	Fayetteville	of	14	37	3	8	1	1	0	7	0	4	.216

Other teams played for: Goldsboro (D), Columbia (B), Henderson (C), Wichita (A), Mayodan (D), Bassett (D), Leaksville (D), Portsmouth (B), Lynchburg (B), Rochester (AA), Winston-Salem (C)

Payonk, Andrew J. Jr.

Year	Club	POS	G	AB	R	H	2B	3B	HR	BB	SB	RBI	BA
1948	Lumberton	c	16	40	6	7	0	0	0	5	0	1	.175

Other teams played for: Janesville (D)

Paz, Louis Raymond

Year	Club	POS	G	AB	R	H	2B	3B	HR	BB	SB	RBI	BA
1950	Clinton	p	23	37	6	3	0	0	0	8	0	2	.081

Year	Club	G	CG	W	L	IP	H	R	BB	SO	ERA
1950	Clinton	22	3	4	5	96	105	80	67	62	6.75

Other teams played for: Amsterdam (C)

Pearce, Jacob A. "Jake"

Year	Club	G	CG	W	L	IP	H	R	BB	SO	ERA
1946	Dunn-Erwin	5	2	1	3	37	47	20	8	17	—

Other teams played for: Raleigh (C), Petersburg (D)

12. Player Register—Pearsall

Pearsall, Wallace A. "Wally"

Year	Club	POS	G	AB	R	H	2B	3B	HR	BB	SB	RBI	BA
1947	Lumberton	of	122	456	93	124	21	12	11	77	3	84	.272

Other teams played for: Fayetteville (D, B), Macon (A), Des Moines (A)

Pellegrino, Michael

Year	Club	G	CG	W	L	IP	H	R	BB	SO	ERA
1946	Clinton	2	0	0	0	3	—	—	—	—	—

Other teams played for: None

Pepio, Nicholas J. "Nick"

Year	Club	POS	G	AB	R	H	2B	3B	HR	BB	SB	RBI	BA
1948	Warsaw	ss	121	425	62	161	14	7	0	70	12	58	.238

Other teams played for: Concord (D), Landis (D), Salisbury (D), Lexington (D), Goldsboro (D), Raleigh (C), Kingston (B)

Perini, Edward Paul "Eddie"

Year	Club	POS	G	AB	R	H	2B	3B	HR	BB	SB	RBI	BA
1948	Dunn-Erwin	of	95	381	78	108	13	6	1	43	22	34	.283

Other teams played for: None

Perry, Benjamin Franklin Jr.

Year	Club	POS	G	AB	R	H	2B	3B	HR	BB	SB	RBI	BA
1949	Wilmington	1b	21	62	5	14	1	0	0	6	0	10	.226

Other teams played for: Radford (D)

Perry, Edward Jr.

Year	Club	G	CG	W	L	IP	H	R	BB	SO	ERA
1946	Smith.-Selma	3	0	0	1	7	7	12	16	5	—

Other teams played for: None

Perry, Robert H.

Year	Club	POS	G	AB	R	H	2B	3B	HR	BB	SB	RBI	BA
1948	Wilmington	ss	82										
	Dunn-Erwin	ss	46										
	totals:	ss	128	494	67	113	20	5	1	35	3	60	.229
1949	Dunn-Erwin	ss	12										
	Sanford	ss	34										
	totals:	ss	46	181	27	45	6	4	1	19	3	20	.249

Other teams played for: Easton (D), Welch (D), Tarboro (D), Valley (D), Anniston (B)

12. Player Register—Piccin

Peterson, Lee Crandall

Year	Club	POS	G	AB	R	H	2B	3B	HR	BB	SB	RBI	BA
1946	Clinton	p	11	28	5	13	1	2	0	—	0	9	.464

Year	Club	G	CG	W	L	IP	H	R	BB	SO	ERA
1946	Clinton	9	6	6	1	69	53	20	35	74	—

Other teams played for: Decatur (B), Winston-Salem (C), Columbus, Ga. (A), Columbus, Ohio (AAA), Paducah (D), Johnson City (D)

Petti, Michael Anthony

Year	Club	POS	G	AB	R	H	2B	3B	HR	BB	SB	RBI	BA
1949	Smith.-Selma	3b	57	215	26	60	9	2	0	28	3	24	.279
1950	Smith.-Selma	3b	34	144	19	45	6	1	1	14	0	22	.313

Other teams played for: Easton (D), Amsterdam (C), Radford (D), Pulaski (D), Lima (D)

Pettit, James Ray "Jim"

Year	Club	POS	G	AB	R	H	2B	3B	HR	BB	SB	RBI	BA
1949	Wilmington	c	74	218	28	55	6	5	3	43	1	36	.252
1950	Sanford	c	123	409	64	124	23	3	2	85	2	75	.303

Other teams played for: Mooresville (D), Greensboro (B)

Pfeiffer, Allen W.

Year	Club	POS	G	AB	R	H	2B	3B	HR	BB	SB	RBI	BA
1949	Red Springs	p	26	66	6	10	0	0	0	8	2	5	.152

Year	Club	G	CG	W	L	IP	H	R	BB	SO	ERA
1949	Red Springs	23	17	12	8	189	178	80	64	94	2.38

Other teams played for: Galax (D), Youngstown (C)

Phillips, Buck

Year	Club	POS	G	AB	R	H	2B	3B	HR	BB	SB	RBI	BA
1947	Dunn-Erwin	2b	19	74	10	19	4	0	0	8	2	7	.257

Other teams played for: Kinston (D), Seminole (D), Concord (D)

Piccin, Frank J.

Year	Club	POS	G	AB	R	H	2B	3B	HR	BB	SB	RBI	BA
1950	Red Springs	c	85	270	37	64	10	4	1	49	3	44	.237

Other teams played for: None

12. Player Register—Piccone

Piccone, John

Year	Club	POS	G	AB	R	H	2B	3B	HR	BB	SB	RBI	BA
1948	Clinton	of	132	477	89	112	15	5	3	90	12	48	.235

Other teams played for: Iola (D)

Pickard, George Armand

Year	Club	POS	G	AB	R	H	2B	3B	HR	BB	SB	RBI	BA
1948	Warsaw	p	5										
	Clinton	p	5										
	totals:	p	10	14	0	0	0	0	0	0	0	1	.000

Other teams played for: Emporia (D)

Pierce, David Donald

Year	Club	POS	G	AB	R	H	2B	3B	HR	BB	SB	RBI	BA
1949	Lumberton	c	28	84	16	24	3	1	0	21	1	10	.286

Other teams played for: Statesville (D), Sumter (B), Erie (D), Hagerstown (B)

Pierre, Robert "Bob"

Year	Club	POS	G	AB	R	H	2B	3B	HR	BB	SB	RBI	BA
1947	Red Springs	2b	14	59	10	11	1	0	0	3	2	2	.186

Other teams played for: Federalsburg (D), Bluefield (D), Welch (D)

Pilkington, Lewis "Bingo"

Year	Club	POS	G	AB	R	H	2B	3B	HR	BB	SB	RBI	BA
1947	Smith.-Selma	of	20	75	15	19	3	1	0	14	6	9	.253

Other teams played for: Ardmore (D)

Pipak, Joseph R.

Year	Club	POS	G	AB	R	H	2B	3B	HR	BB	SB	RBI	BA
1950	Clinton	p	24	49	8	10	1	1	0	6	0	7	.204

Year	Club	G	CG	W	L	IP	H	R	BB	SO	ERA
1950	Clinton	24	11	9	10	143	131	74	84	93	3.59

Other teams played for: Richmond, Ind. (D), Srpingfield, Ohio (D), Lakeland (B), Longview (B), Greenville, Tex. (B), Bryan (B), Port Arthur (C), Knoxville (B), Wichita (A)

Plantz, Stephen Edward

Year	Club	POS	G	AB	R	H	2B	3B	HR	BB	SB	RBI	BA
1946	Smith.-Selma	c	73	192	37	41	4	2	4	—	3	41	.214
1947	Smith.-Selma	c	10	31	5	12	2	1	0	10	1	4	.387

Other teams played for: Butler (D), Syracuse (AA), Lynchburg (B), York (B), Allentown (B), Gainseville, Tex. (B)

Plosica, Robert R. "Bob"

Year	Club	POS	G	AB	R	H	2B	3B	HR	BB	SB	RBI	BA
1950	Whiteville	1b	21	72	5	12	2	0	1	10	0	8	.167

Other teams played for: None

Poklemba, Andrew E.

Year	Club	POS	G	AB	R	H	2B	3B	HR	BB	SB	RBI	BA
1946	Wilmington	1b	80	293	48	82	16	1	2	—	3	48	.280
1947	Wilmington	of	99	354	51	99	19	3	7	34	17	49	.280

Other teams played for: Hartford (A), Decatur (B)

Pollock, Terry G.

Year	Club	POS	G	AB	R	H	2B	3B	HR	BB	SB	RBI	BA
1948	Warsaw	p	23	62	5	7	2	0	0	7	0	2	.113

Year	Club	G	CG	W	L	IP	H	R	BB	SO	ERA
1948	Warsaw	23	12	12	8	178	168	88	64	100	3.44

Other teams played for: Goldsboro (D)

Pontbriand, Roger "Chip"

Year	Club	POS	G	AB	R	H	2B	3B	HR	BB	SB	RBI	BA
1947	Dunn-Erwin	p	17	41	5	6	1	1	0	5	0	1	.146

Year	Club	G	CG	W	L	IP	H	R	BB	SO	ERA
1947	Dunn-Erwin	15	9	5	6	104	126	56	34	50	3.04

Other teams played for: Norfolk (B), Blackstone (D)

Poole, James Ralph Jr.

Year	Club	POS	G	AB	R	H	2B	3B	HR	BB	SB	RBI	BA
1948	Sanford	2b	64	273	56	77	10	1	1	21	6	42	.282

Other teams played for: Fort Pierce (D), Greensboro (B), Roanoke (B), Moultrie (D), Statesville (D), Knoxville (B), Burlington (C)

Popelsky, Anthony

Year	Club	POS	G	AB	R	H	2B	3B	HR	BB	SB	RBI	BA
1947	Smith.-Selma	c	47	146	16	32	2	3	0	22	2	14	.219

Other teams played for: Welch (D)

12. Player Register—Posevac

Posevac, John

Year	Club	POS	G	AB	R	H	2B	3B	HR	BB	SB	RBI	BA
1947	Sanford	ss	12	46	5	13	1	0	0	2	2	3	.283

Other teams played for: None

Poteat, Parks H.

Year	Club	POS	G	AB	R	H	2B	3B	HR	BB	SB	RBI	BA
1946	Sanford	util	22	87	13	23	3	0	0	—	0	14	.264

Other teams played for: None

Powell, Carl M.

Year	Club	POS	G	AB	R	H	2B	3B	HR	BB	SB	RBI	BA
1946	Sanford	2b	59	227	33	67	5	2	0	—	5	19	.295

Other teams played for: Leaksville (D), Reidsville (D), South Boston (D), Mount Airy (D)

Powell, Richard

Year	Club	POS	G	AB	R	H	2B	3B	HR	BB	SB	RBI	BA
1948	Wilmington	c	35	116	21	23	5	0	0	12	3	10	.198

Other teams played for: None

Powers, Elmer

Year	Club	POS	G	AB	R	H	2B	3B	HR	BB	SB	RBI	BA
1950	Rockingham	p	12	22	6	6	1	0	0	6	0	2	.273

Year	Club	G	CG	W	L	IP	H	R	BB	SO	ERA
1950	Rockingham	11	4	2	5	52	46	32	40	29	3.98

Other teams played for: None

Praley, Albert Frank

Year	Club	POS	G	AB	R	H	2B	3B	HR	BB	SB	RBI	BA
1949	Wilmington	p	43	84	14	18	1	1	0	3	0	9	.214

Year	Club	G	CG	W	L	IP	H	R	BB	SO	ERA
1949	Wilmington	34	8	7	11	166	190	144	123	86	5.04

Other teams played for: None

Price, Eldridge C.

Year	Club	POS	G	AB	R	H	2B	3B	HR	BB	SB	RBI	BA
1950	Smith.-Selma	3b	47	177	21	38	7	4	0	17	1	21	.215

Other teams played for: Roanoke Rapids (D)

Price, Leslie Beecham "Billy"

Year	Club	POS	G	AB	R	H	2B	3B	HR	BB	SB	RBI	BA
1949	Clinton	p	22	62	3	6	0	0	0	0	0	2	.097

Year	Club	G	CG	W	L	IP	H	R	BB	SO	ERA
1949	Clinton	22	14	12	5	152	130	65	85	99	2.19

Other teams played for: Leaksville (C), Fayetteville (D), Shelby (B), Durham (D), New Bern (D), Tarboro (D).

Pritchard, Thomas Marion

Year	Club	G	CG	W	L	IP	H	R	BB	SO	ERA
1946	Clinton	5	0	0	1	13	25	16	11	8	—

Other teams played for: Durham (C), Tarboro (D), Roanoke Rapids (D), Butler (C), Davenport (D).

Privette, John B.

Year	Club	POS	G	AB	R	H	2B	3B	HR	BB	SB	RBI	BA
1946	Angier-Fuquay	of	15	63	10	18	2	0	1	—	0	3	.286

Other teams played for: None

Prowell, Dean G.

Year	Club	POS	G	AB	R	H	2B	3B	HR	BB	SB	RBI	BA
1949	Dunn-Erwin	2b	101	409	50	58	7	3	1	71	5	39	.142
1950	Whiteville	2b	119	382	86	93	21	2	2	152	12	40	.243

Other teams played for: None

Pryor, John Paul

Year	Club	G	CG	W	L	IP	H	R	BB	SO	ERA
1946	Smith.-Sel./San.	5	0	1	0	17	18	13	10	5	—

Other teams played for: Johnson City (D), Allentown (B), Galax (D), Bloomingdale (D), Portland, Maine (B), Greensboro (C), Leaksville (C), North Wilkesboro (D).

Pugh, Robert Thomas "Bob"

Year	Club	POS	G	AB	R	H	2B	3B	HR	BB	SB	RBI	BA
1946	Sanford	of	106	392	75	108	21	2	13	—	0	95	.276
1947	Sanford	of	82	316	50	93	20	7	5	26	7	67	.294
1950	Rockingham	of/p	110	311	53	79	15	8	5	57	3	63	.253

Year	Club	G	CG	W	L	IP	H	R	BB	SO	ERA
1946	Sanford	12	—	4	1	58	89	47	31	—	—
1950	Rockingham	40	12	11	11	196	210	103	79	47	3.99

Other teams played for: Granite Falls (D), Lexington (D).

12. Player Register—Purchia

Purchia, Nicholas

Year	Club	POS	G	AB	R	H	2B	3B	HR	BB	SB	RBI	BA
1949	Clinton	2b	136	542	118	150	29	1	0	89	7	54	.279
1950	Clinton	2b	124	452	91	127	24	4	0	104	9	89	.281

Other teams played for: Richmond (B)

Quigley, Albert

Year	Club	POS	G	AB	R	H	2B	3B	HR	BB	SB	RBI	BA
1946	Wilmington	p	12	21	2	2	1	0	0	—	0	2	.095

Year	Club	G	CG	W	L	IP	H	R	BB	SO	ERA
1946	Wilmington	12	3	2	3	55	50	53	61	28	—

Other teams played for: None

Rapp (Rzepczynski), Walter M.

Year	Club	POS	G	AB	R	H	2B	3B	HR	BB	SB	RBI	BA
1949	Sanford	util	10	10	1	1	0	0	0	1	0	0	.100

Other teams played for: Pennington Gap (D)

Ratteree, William L. "Bill"

Year	Club	POS	G	AB	R	H	2B	3B	HR	BB	SB	RBI	BA
1946	Angier-Fuquay	c	71	226	42	66	12	0	7	—	3	38	.292
1947	Dunn-Erwin	c	21	71	19	20	3	2	2	12	3	13	.282

Other teams played for: Newport News (C), Wilmington, Del. (B), Greensboro (C), Fayetteville (B)

Ray, Daniel C. "Dan"

Year	Club	POS	G	AB	R	H	2B	3B	HR	BB	SB	RBI	BA
1946	Angier-Fuquay	1b	4										
	Smithfield	1b	38										
	totals:	1b	42	147	19	33	7	2	0	—	0	12	.224

Other teams played for: Durham (C)

Reardon, John

Year	Club	G	CG	W	L	IP	H	R	BB	SO	ERA
1946	Dunn-Erwin	5	1	0	3	21	25	18	22	11	—

Other teams played for: Leaksville (D)

Reaves,

Year	Club	POS	G	AB	R	H	2B	3B	HR	BB	SB	RBI	BA
1946	Angier-Fuquay	—	<10	—	—	—	—	—	—	—	—	—	—

Other teams played for: Unknown

12. Player Register—Rhabe

Reese, Kenneth E. "Kenny"

Year	Club	POS	G	AB	R	H	2B	3B	HR	BB	SB	RBI	BA
1949	Fayetteville	3b	6	21	6	5	2	1	0	—	2	3	.238

Other teams played for: El Dorado (C), Texarkana (B)

Reges, James Clinton "Jim"

Year	Club	POS	G	AB	R	H	2B	3B	HR	BB	SB	RBI	BA
1948	Lumberton	of	76	244	37	75	7	3	3	44	9	42	.307
1949	Lumberton	of	22	76	12	20	0	1	2	12	0	11	.263

Other teams played for: Rocky Mount (D)

Reiter, James Edward

Year	Club	POS	G	AB	R	H	2B	3B	HR	BB	SB	RBI	BA
1950	Smith.-Selma	c	61	254	39	69	15	1	5	17	3	37	.272

Other teams played for: Albany, Ga. (D), Geneva, Al. (D), Goldsboro (D), Grand Rapids (A), Des Moines (A)

Reside, Neal M.

Year	Club	POS	G	AB	R	H	2B	3B	HR	BB	SB	RBI	BA
1946	Smithfield	—	<10	—	—	—	—	—	—	—	—	—	—

Other teams played for: Lima (D), Lynchburg (B), Columbus, Ga. (A)

Reynolds, Robert Arthur

Year	Club	POS	G	AB	R	H	2B	3B	HR	BB	SB	RBI	BA
1950	Wilmington	of	3										
	Clinton	of	27										
	totals:	of	30	104	14	19	2	0	1	12	2	15	.183

Other teams played for: Appleton (D), Owensboro (D), Wilson (D)

Rhabe, Nicholas James

Year	Club	POS	G	AB	R	H	2B	3B	HR	BB	SB	RBI	BA
1949	Fayetteville	of	18	77	14	29	6	1	0	6	1	13	.377
1950	Clinton	of	58	239	30	77	14	2	1	15	2	57	.322

Other teams played for: Mayodan (D), Leaksville (D), Cooleemee (D), Durham (B), Lynchburg (D), Harrisonburg (D), Salem-Roanoke (D), Williamston (D), Richmond (B), Petersburg (C), Pulaski (C), Elmira (A), Winston-Salem (B), Charlotte (B), Utica (A), Hartford (A), Newark (AA), Indianapolis (AA), Los Angeles (AA), Portland (AA), Leaksville (C), Tarboro (D), Charlotte (B), Concord (D), Pensacola (B), Gadsden (B), Hickory (D), Statesville (D)

12. Player Register—Richards

Richards, Donald L.

Year	Club	POS	G	AB	R	H	2B	3B	HR	BB	SB	RBI	BA
1950	Sanford	of	33	124	23	42	10	2	1	24	4	20	.339

Other teams played for: Providence (B), Marion (D), Greensboro (B), St. Petersburg (B), Blackwell (C), Iola (C), Greenville, Miss. (C)

Richards, John Edward

Year	Club	POS	G	AB	R	H	2B	3B	HR	BB	SB	RBI	BA
1949	Dunn-Erwin	of	127	513	107	180	30	6	12	67	13	105	.351

Other teams played for: Fort Lauderdale (C), Tarboro (D), Richmond, Ind. (D)

Richards, Robert W.

Year	Club	POS	G	AB	R	H	2B	3B	HR	BB	SB	RBI	BA
1950	Smith.-Selma	p	16	26	4	3	0	0	0	4	0	1	.115

Year	Club	G	CG	W	L	IP	H	R	BB	SO	ERA
1950	Smith.-Selma	15	3	3	4	69	69	46	37	31	3.78

Other teams played for: New River (D)

Rickard, Charles Robert

Year	Club	POS	G	AB	R	H	2B	3B	HR	BB	SB	RBI	BA
1949	Lumberton	ss	31	125	17	26	4	4	0	14	2	6	.208

Other teams played for: Nazareth (D), St. Augustine (D), Saginanw (A)

Ridings, Brannon W.

Year	Club	POS	G	AB	R	H	2B	3B	HR	BB	SB	RBI	BA
1950	Smith.-Selma	c	42	143	19	31	12	0	0	23	0	22	.217

Other teams played for:

Riley, Gaither William

Year	Club	POS	G	AB	R	H	2B	3B	HR	BB	SB	RBI	BA
1946	Sanford	of	29										
	Angier-F.	of	7										
	Smith.-Selma	of	12										
	Dunn-Erwin	of	3										
	totals:	of	51	177	31	48	5	0	5	—	3	32	.271

Other teams played for: Williamson (D), Ayden (D), Wilson (D), New Bern (D), South Boston (D)

12. Player Register—Robinson

Riley, Raymond D.

Year	Club	POS	G	AB	R	H	2B	3B	HR	BB	SB	RBI	BA
1946	Clinton	of	90	363	68	99	17	5	4	—	13	65	.273

Other teams played for: Tarboro (D), Jackson, Tenn. (D), Trois-Rivieres (C), Leaksville (C)

Ripple, Charles Dawson "Charlie"

Year	Club	G	CG	W	L	IP	H	R	BB	SO	ERA
1950	Whiteville	8	6	1	6	59	63	41	25	40	5.49

Other teams played for: Wilmington (B), Utica (A), Memphis (AA), Philadelphia Phillies (ML), Seattle (AAA), Sacramento (AAA), Dallas (AA), Columbia (A)

Ritter, Robert J.

Year	Club	POS	G	AB	R	H	2B	3B	HR	BB	SB	RBI	BA
1950	Sanford	3b	106	398	69	99	17	5	1	54	17	53	.249

Other teams played for: Kingsport (D), Leesburg (D), Lakeland (B)

Roberson, Aaron

Year	Club	G	CG	W	L	IP	H	R	BB	SO	ERA
1946	Clinton	3	0	0	0	4	—	—	—	—	—

Other teams played for: None

Roberts, David

Year	Club	POS	G	AB	R	H	2B	3B	HR	BB	SB	RBI	BA
1946	Sanford	2b	37	137	40	5	12	1	1	—	5	21	.255

Other teams played for: Unknown

Roberts, Donald Vance

Year	Club	POS	G	AB	R	H	2B	3B	HR	BB	SB	RBI	BA
1950	Wilmington	of	127	493	78	146	25	11	3	62	12	75	.296

Other teams played for: None

Robertson, William M.

Year	Club	POS	G	AB	R	H	2B	3B	HR	BB	SB	RBI	BA
1948	Warsaw	1b	52	195	38	44	6	2	0	26	1	19	.226

Other teams played for: None

Robinson, Hearn James

Year	Club	POS	G	AB	R	H	2B	3B	HR	BB	SB	RBI	BA
1946	Smith.-Selma	p	28	69	8	16	1	1	0	—	0	14	.232

12. Player Register—Rodriguez

Year	Club	G	CG	W	L	IP	H	R	BB	SO	ERA
1946	Smith.-Selma	24	14	14	9	165	198	122	77	88	—

Other teams played for: Washington, Penn. (D), Springfield, Mo. (C), Greenville, NC (D)

Rodriguez, Virgil

Year	Club	POS	G	AB	R	H	2B	3B	HR	BB	SB	RBI	BA
1950	Rockingham	of	29	86	19	21	4	3	1	25	0	14	.244

Other teams played for: None

Roebuck, Garland Lee

Year	Club	G	CG	W	L	IP	H	R	BB	SO	ERA
1946	Dunn-Erwin	3	—	0	0	10	—	—	—	—	—

Other teams played for: None

Roedel, Robert L.

Year	Club	POS	G	AB	R	H	2B	3B	HR	BB	SB	RBI	BA
1950	Whiteville	c	115	370	48	86	14	4	0	74	3	49	.232

Year	Club	G	CG	W	L	IP	H	R	BB	SO	ERA
1950	Whiteville	10	0	0	1	49	67	41	28	32	6.98

Other teams played for: Carrollton (Ga.), Lawrenceville (D), Kinston (D), Superior (C)

Rogers, Angus W. "Gus"

Year	Club	POS	G	AB	R	H	2B	3B	HR	BB	SB	RBI	BA
1946	Angier-Fuquay	ss	47	137	24	32	5	0	2	—	3	18	.234
1947	Red Springs	ss	103	420	84	126	21	4	0	43	19	41	.300
1948	Red Springs	2b	127	518	107	133	19	6	1	78	15	53	.257

Other teams played for:

Rogers, Marion Eugene "Tinky"

Year	Club	POS	G	AB	R	H	2B	3B	HR	BB	SB	RBI	BA
1948	Wilmington	ss	30	118	14	28	6	0	0	12	2	10	.237
1949	Wilmington	2b	94	368	52	109	18	4	1	30	5	43	.296
1950	Wilmington	2b	27	90	22	24	6	0	0	26	0	17	.267

Other teams played for: Leaksville/Abingdon (D)

Rose, James Harold

Year	Club	POS	G	AB	R	H	2B	3B	HR	BB	SB	RBI	BA
1950	Smith.-Selma	p	12	23	4	3	0	0	0	2	0	1	.130

12. Player Register—Rowland

Year	Club	G	CG	W	L	IP	H	R	BB	SO	ERA
1950	Smith.-Selma	12	6	4	5	67	89	44	28	30	4.84

Other teams played for: Rocky Mount (D), Wilson (D)

Roseberry, Joseph Carl "Joe"

Year	Club	POS	G	AB	R	H	2B	3B	HR	BB	SB	RBI	BA
1949	Fayetteville	of	125	416	97	170	37	3	6	88	19	78	.408

Year	Club	G	CG	W	L	IP	H	R	BB	SO	ERA
1949	Fayetteville	25	8	7	7	125	141	91	63	69	4.03

Other teams played for: Marion, Ohio (D), Winston-Salem (C), Mount Airy (D)

Rosenwinkel, Raymond L.

Year	Club	POS	G	AB	R	H	2B	3B	HR	BB	SB	RBI	BA
1948	Warsaw	of	85	289	50	80	16	3	7	33	15	38	.277

Other teams played for: Goldsboro (D), Kinston (D), Fayetteville (B), Corning (D), St. Hyacinthe (C)

Rossi, Marion G. B.

Year	Club	POS	G	AB	R	H	2B	3B	HR	BB	SB	RBI	BA
1950	Smith.-Selma	2b	92										
	Wilmington	2b	27										
	totals:	2b	119	415	64	81	10	4	0	89	8	49	.195

Other teams played for: Cairo (D)

Rothermel, William "Bill"

Year	Club	POS	G	AB	R	H	2B	3B	HR	BB	SB	RBI	BA
1950	Lumberton	p	14	29	2	7	1	0	0	2	0	3	.241

Year	Club	G	CG	W	L	IP	H	R	BB	SO	ERA
1950	Lumberton	12	7	8	2	86	70	25	47	63	2.30

Other teams played for: Bristol (B)

Rowan, Linwood C.

Year	Club	POS	G	AB	R	H	2B	3B	HR	BB	SB	RBI	BA
1948	Wilmington	ss	12	32	7	13	1	0	1	4	1	4	.406

Other teams played for: None

Rowland, Charles H. "Buddy"

Year	Club	POS	G	AB	R	H	2B	3B	HR	BB	SB	RBI	BA
1947	Warsaw	c	44	136	24	27	6	3	0	17	1	13	.199

Other teams played for: Mount Airy (D), Goldsboro (D), Reidsville (B), Shelby (D)

12. Player Register—Rudden

Rudden, Matthew

Year	Club	POS	G	AB	R	H	2B	3B	HR	BB	SB	RBI	BA
1947	Clinton	ss	23	104	20	26	2	0	1	8	8	14	.250

Other teams played for: Middletown (D), Newark, Ohio (D), Roankoe Rapids (D), Concord (D)

Russell, Eugene C.

Year	Club	POS	G	AB	R	H	2B	3B	HR	BB	SB	RBI	BA
1950	Clinton	p	14	30	3	5	0	0	0	1	0	1	.167

Year	Club	G	CG	W	L	IP	H	R	BB	SO	ERA
1950	Clinton	13	3	4	5	65	68	57	48	32	4.85

Other teams played for: None

Russell, Norman L.

Year	Club	G	CG	W	L	IP	H	R	BB	SO	ERA
1946	Wilmington	3	0	0	1	13	6	7	12	8	—

Other teams played for: Greensburg (D), Hamilton (D), Mobile (B), Houston (A), Montgomery (B)

Ryan, Terence Aloysius "Terry"

Year	Club	POS	G	AB	R	H	2B	3B	HR	BB	SB	RBI	BA
1949	Clinton	c	82	258	29	54	7	2	0	32	2	24	.209

Other teams played for: None

Sack, James Edward

Year	Club	POS	G	AB	R	H	2B	3B	HR	BB	SB	RBI	BA
1949	Smith-Selma	2b	124	518	111	147	22	4	0	83	16	40	.287

Other teams played for: Greenville, SC (A), Radford (D), Pulaski (D)

Sailor, Rowland

Year	Club	POS	G	AB	R	H	2B	3B	HR	BB	SB	RBI	BA
1946	Dunn-Erwin	3b	15	45	9	12	2	0	0	—	2	9	.267

Other teams played for: None

Saladino, James "Jim"

Year	Club	POS	G	AB	R	H	2B	3B	HR	BB	SB	RBI	BA
1946	Clinton	—	<10	—	—	—	—	—	—	—	—	—	—

Other teams played for: St. Augustine (D)

12. Player Register—Sanders

Salmon, Homer

Year	Club	POS	G	AB	R	H	2B	3B	HR	BB	SB	RBI	BA
1946	Sanford	p	20	39	4	10	0	0	0	—	0	5	.256

Year	Club	G	CG	W	L	IP	H	R	BB	SO	ERA
1946	Sanford	20	1	4	2	89	95	70	55	51	—

Other teams played for: None

Salter, Clarence W.

Year	Club	POS	G	AB	R	H	2B	3B	HR	BB	SB	RBI	BA
1948	Sanford	p	36	94	11	13	1	0	0	9	0	7	.138

Year	Club	G	CG	W	L	IP	H	R	BB	SO	ERA
1948	Sanford	34	16	17	7	220	220	124	79	147	3.56

Other teams played for: None

Salyer, Curtis William

Year	Club	POS	G	AB	R	H	2B	3B	HR	BB	SB	RBI	BA
1947	Warsaw	2b	42	181	31	49	5	3	1	11	16	14	.271

Other teams played for: Goldsboro (D), Lawrenceville (D), Clarksdale (C), Pensacola (B), Rocky Mount (D)

Samson, Forrest LaVerne "Shine"

Year	Club	POS	G	AB	R	H	2B	3B	HR	BB	SB	RBI	BA
1948	Dunn-Erwin	of	76	282	41	87	11	9	14	19	6	51	.309

Other teams played for: Newark, Ohio (D), Easton (D), Rome (C), Asheville (B)

Sanders, Carol Victor "Pete"

Year	Club	POS	G	AB	R	H	2B	3B	HR	BB	SB	RBI	BA
1949	Smith.-Selma	c	91	297	28	76	5	2	0	32	2	43	.256

Other teams played for: None

Sanders, Paul David "Red"

Year	Club	POS	G	AB	R	H	2B	3B	HR	BB	SB	RBI	BA
1947	Clinton	c	64	201	21	44	8	0	0	26	1	23	.219
1948	Clinton	c	89	251	31	50	12	0	1	68	1	33	.199

Other teams played for: Hazard (D), Morristown (D)

Sanders, Vernon

Year	Club	POS	G	AB	R	H	2B	3B	HR	BB	SB	RBI	BA
1948	Dunn-Erwin	util	15	66	5	8	0	0	0	4	0	2	.121

Other teams played for: None

12. Player Register—Santomauro

Santomauro, Joseph L.

Year	Club	G	CG	W	L	IP	H	R	BB	SO	ERA
1946	Angier-Fuquay	8	1	1	2	35	43	36	12	13	—

Other teams played for: Fort Lauderdale (D), Welch (D), Greensboro (C), Raleigh (C), Hot Springs (C), Leaksville (D), Pennington Gap (D), Vidalia-Lyons (D)

Saunders, Dennis R.

Year	Club	POS	G	AB	R	H	2B	3B	HR	BB	SB	RBI	BA
1946	Angier-Fuquay	2b	34	0		12							.261
	Clinton	2b	3	0									
	Dunn-Erwin	2b	17	0									
	totals:	2b	54	194	30	45	4	0	0	—	1	19	.231

Other teams played for: Durham (C), Burlington (C), Bluefield (D), Pawtucket (B)

Scalli, Arthur R. "Art"

Year	Club	POS	G	AB	R	H	2B	3B	HR	BB	SB	RBI	BA
1946	Smith.-Selma	of	30	110	18	20	6	0	1	—	3	14	.182

Other teams played for: Cooleemee (D), Landis (D), Greenville, SC (B), Hickory (D), Hagerstown (B), Lancaster (B)

Schroeder, Warren Frederick "Wally"

Year	Club	POS	G	AB	R	H	2B	3B	HR	BB	SB	RBI	BA
1948	Warsaw	of	17	63	14	23	7	0	0	6	2	18	.365

Other teams played for: Goldsboro (D), Florence (B), Augusta (A), Texas City (B), Port Arthur (B), Corpus Christi (B)

Schubach, Frederick

Year	Club	POS	G	AB	R	H	2B	3B	HR	BB	SB	RBI	BA
1948	Red Springs	c	21	38	7	8	0	0	0	11	0	3	.211

Other teams played for: Federalsburg (D), Welch (D), Tarboro (D), Kewanee (C)

Schultz,

Year	Club	G	CG	W	L	IP	H	R	BB	SO	ERA
1947	Dunn-Erwin	8	2	2	6	59	61	83	27	42	6.55

Other teams played for: Unknown

Schumann, George R.

Year	Club	POS	G	AB	R	H	2B	3B	HR	BB	SB	RBI	BA
1949	Fayetteville	p	13	27	0	6	0	0	0	0	0	0	.222

12. Player Register—Sellers

Year	Club	G	CG	W	L	IP	H	R	BB	SO	ERA
1949	Fayetteville	12	5	5	4	65	57	45	66	42	5.54

Other teams played for: None

Schumann, Henry H. "Hank"

Year	Club	POS	G	AB	R	H	2B	3B	HR	BB	SB	RBI	BA
1949	Fayetteville	of	133	469	81	119	20	3	7	73	16	74	.254

Other teams played for: Hickory (D)

Scott, Edward Gregg

Year	Club	POS	G	AB	R	H	2B	3B	HR	BB	SB	RBI	BA
1947	Dunn-Erwin	of	48	202	50	75	13	6	6	16	7	35	.371

Other teams played for: Norfolk (B), Amsterdam (C), Quncy (B), Cedar Rapids (C), Farnham (C)

Scrobola, Andrew N. "Andy"

Year	Club	POS	G	AB	R	H	2B	3B	HR	BB	SB	RBI	BA
1946	Angier-Fuquay	of	105	451	89	135	34	2	11	—	5	88	.299
1947	Warsaw	of	118	480	83	142	28	2	8	85	24	70	.296
1948	Warsaw	of	123	463	84	142	29	6	4	56	16	73	.307
1949	Clinton	of	133	547	100	169	22	9	1	64	11	62	.315
1950	Wilmington	of	<10	—	—	—	—	—	—	—	—	—	—

Other teams played for: Leaksville (D)

Sebastian, Sherman

Year	Club	G	CG	W	L	IP	H	R	BB	SO	ERA
1946	Clinton	6	1	1	0	19	23	11	5	3	—

Other teams played for: None

Sellers, Samuel "Sam"

Year	Club	POS	G	AB	R	H	2B	3B	HR	BB	SB	RBI	BA
1946	Angier-Fuquay	p	—	—	—	—	—	—	—	—	—	—	—
1947	Red Springs	p	14	29	3	6	0	1	0	2	0	4	.207

Year	Club	G	CG	W	L	IP	H	R	BB	SO	ERA
1946	Angier-Fuquay	4	2	1	2	22	21	15	18	15	—
1947	Red Springs	11	4	4	5	67	83	58	32	34	5.37

Other teams played for: None

12. Player Register—Shelton

Shelton, Baldwin Edwin

Year	Club	G	CG	W	L	IP	H	R	BB	SO	ERA
1946	Dunn-Erwin	2	1	1	1	10	6	7	6	3	—

Other teams played for: Greenville, Miss. (C), Clarksdale (C)

Shimko, Robert A. "Bob"

Year	Club	POS	G	AB	R	H	2B	3B	HR	BB	SB	RBI	BA
1950	Red Springs	p	49	51	3	9	1	0	0	9	0	4	.176

Year	Club	G	CG	W	L	IP	H	R	BB	SO	ERA
1950	Red Springs	49	0	9	7	145	130	78	86	64	3.54

Other teams played for: Cordele (D)

Shoffner, Phalti Moody

Year	Club	POS	G	AB	R	H	2B	3B	HR	BB	SB	RBI	BA
1946	Sanford	1b	116	456	110	138	21	4	6	—	2	67	.303
1947	Sanford	1b	121	501	114	166	27	4	8	66	1	74	.331

Other teams played for: Portsmouth (C), Springfield (C), Dort Lauderdale (C)

Short, George A.

Year	Club	POS	G	AB	R	H	2B	3B	HR	BB	SB	RBI	BA
1949	Sanford	util	3										
	Fayetteville	util	10										
	totals:	util	13	31	3	3	0	0	0	6	0	2	.097

Other teams played for: None

Shrewsbury, Eugene Robert "Gene"

Year	Club	POS	G	AB	R	H	2B	3B	HR	BB	SB	RBI	BA
1949	Lumberton	c	79	217	28	49	2	0	0	45	1	18	.226

Other teams played for: Brsitol (D), Hagerstown (B)

Shubeck, Charles B.

Year	Club	POS	G	AB	R	H	2B	3B	HR	BB	SB	RBI	BA
1947	Clinton	p	39	85	8	16	0	0	0	6	0	5	.188

Year	Club	G	CG	W	L	IP	H	R	BB	SO	ERA
1947	Clinton	36	14	8	13	205	273	161	77	53	5.27

Other teams played for: None

Sidoruk, Walter P.

Year	Club	POS	G	AB	R	H	2B	3B	HR	BB	SB	RBI	BA
1949	Fayetteville	p	16										
	Dunn-Erwin	p	4										
	totals:	p	20	26	2	3	0	0	0	6	0	1	.115

Year	Club	G	CG	W	L	IP	H	R	BB	SO	ERA
1949	Fayetteville	16									
	Dunn-Erwin	4									
	totals:	20	0	2	3	76	94	67	46	27	6.39

Other teams played for: None

Sikorski, Alfred "Fred"

Year	Club	POS	G	AB	R	H	2B	3B	HR	BB	SB	RBI	BA
1950	Red Springs	p	24	46	3	8	0	0	0	4	0	4	.174

Year	Club	G	CG	W	L	IP	H	R	BB	SO	ERA
1950	Red Springs	22	3	6	4	99	109	78	85	31	5.73

Other teams played for: None

Siler, Calvin Kenneth "C.K."

Year	Club	POS	G	AB	R	H	2B	3B	HR	BB	SB	RBI	BA
1950	Sanford	p	26	60	8	13	2	1	0	1	0	7	.217

Year	Club	G	CG	W	L	IP	H	R	BB	SO	ERA
1950	Sanford	21	9	11	3	136	120	52	55	72	2.78

Other teams played for: None

Silvers, Lewis D.

Year	Club	POS	G	AB	R	H	2B	3B	HR	BB	SB	RBI	BA
1950	Smith.-Selma	of	103	378	69	96	9	13	3	60	4	40	.254

Other teams played for: None

Simmons, Charles Roland

Year	Club	POS	G	AB	R	H	2B	3B	HR	BB	SB	RBI	BA
1948	Red Springs	c	63	174	18	40	4	0	0	20	0	15	.230

Other teams played for: None

12. Player Register—Simmons

Simmons, Gerald

Year	Club	POS	G	AB	R	H	2B	3B	HR	BB	SB	RBI	BA
1950	Whiteville	c	33										
	Red Springs	c	11										
	totals:	c	44	127	8	31	5	1	0	10	2	15	.244

Other teams played for: None

Simmons, Raymond C.

Year	Club	G	CG	W	L	IP	H	R	BB	SO	ERA
1946	Sanford	3	1	0	3	14	22	16	6	4	—

Other teams played for: Burlington (D), Greensboro (C)

Singleton, Lee E.

Year	Club	POS	G	AB	R	H	2B	3B	HR	BB	SB	RBI	BA
1949	Sanford	1b	37	118	13	26	4	1	3	17	0	21	.220

Other teams played for: Pocatello (C), Fresno (C), Willows (D), Greensboro (B)

Skinner, Robert "Bob"

Year	Club	POS	G	AB	R	H	2B	3B	HR	BB	SB	RBI	BA
1946	Wilmington	of	67	251	28	61	9	3	2	—	3	31	.243

Other teams played for: Johnstown (C), Bridgeport (B), Tyler (C), Sherman (D)

Sklodowski, Sigmund "Ziggy"

Year	Club	POS	G	AB	R	H	2B	3B	HR	BB	SB	RBI	BA
1949	Sanford	of	96	370	77	113	27	8	0	55	11	53	.305
1950	Sanford	of	118	428	79	118	20	2	5	81	8	81	.276

Other teams played for: Fargo-Moorhead (C), Greenville, Miss. (C), Natchez (C)

Slater, Walter

Year	Club	POS	G	AB	R	H	2B	3B	HR	BB	SB	RBI	BA
1949	Smith.-Selma	of	35	113	28	26	3	0	2	38	1	17	.230

Other teams played for: Oak Ridge/Hazard (D)

Smith, Alfred E.

Year	Club	POS	G	AB	R	H	2B	3B	HR	BB	SB	RBI	BA
1950	Clinton	3b	33	113	20	31	7	3	0	23	2	18	.274

Other teams played for: None

12. Player Register—Smith

Smith, Edwin F. Jr.

Year	Club	POS	G	AB	R	H	2B	3B	HR	BB	SB	RBI	BA
1946	Clinton	p	8	—	—	—	—	—	—	—	—	—	—
1949	Dunn-Erwin	p	27	82	9	16	2	0	0	6	1	11	.195

Year	Club	G	CG	W	L	IP	H	R	BB	SO	ERA
1946	Clinton	8	0	0	2	22	23	22	23	21	—
1949	Dunn-Erwin	24	17	16	6	194	195	124	101	168	4.50

Other teams played for: Bristol (D), Roanoke Rapids (D), Tarboro (D)

Smith, Evert Weston Hjalmar

Year	Club	POS	G	AB	R	H	2B	3B	HR	BB	SB	RBI	BA
1948	Warsaw	ss	28	96	7	13	1	1	0	17	2	7	.167

Other teams played for: Goldsboro (D), Rome (C), Mooresville (D)

Smith, James W.

Year	Club	G	CG	W	L	IP	H	R	BB	SO	ERA
1946	Clinton	3	0	1	0	13	22	16	8	7	—

Other teams played for: None

Smith, Lonnie Harold

Year	Club	POS	G	AB	R	H	2B	3B	HR	BB	SB	RBI	BA
1946	Clinton	3b	116	460	117	140	15	9	21	—	19	92	.304

Other teams played for: Danville (C), Jacksonville (A), Rocky Mount (D), Lexington (D)

Smith, Milton R.

Year	Club	G	CG	W	L	IP	H	R	BB	SO	ERA
1946	Clinton	10	2	3	1	43	40	25	15	11	—

Other teams played for: None

Smith, Norman B.

Year	Club	POS	G	AB	R	H	2B	3B	HR	BB	SB	RBI	BA
1948	Clinton	p	16	26	1	1	0	0	0	1	0	0	.038

Year	Club	G	CG	W	L	IP	H	R	BB	SO	ERA
1948	Clinton	16	5	3	7	79	94	71	45	26	6.04

Other teams played for: None

12. Player Register—Smith

Smith, Paul R.

Year	Club	POS	G	AB	R	H	2B	3B	HR	BB	SB	RBI	BA
1946	Wilmington	of	80	280	61	95	20	3	4	—	5	60	.339

Other teams played for: Roanoke (B), Durham (C), Oneonta (C), Dayton (D)

Somers, George William

Year	Club	POS	G	AB	R	H	2B	3B	HR	BB	SB	RBI	BA
1949	Lumberton	p	15	11	2	4	0	0	0	0	0	1	.354

Year	Club	G	CG	W	L	IP	H	R	BB	SO	ERA
1949	Lumberton	12	—	—	—	<45	—	—	—	—	—

Other teams played for: None

Southerland, Douglas

Year	Club	POS	G	AB	R	H	2B	3B	HR	BB	SB	RBI	BA
1947	Red Springs	util	14	40	1	5	0	1	0	3	0	1	.125

Other teams played for: None

Spaine, Harry R.

Year	Club	POS	G	AB	R	H	2B	3B	HR	BB	SB	RBI	BA
1949	Clinton	of	110										
	Lumberton	of	23										
	totals:	of	133	519	88	155	20	5	13	60	3	118	.299

Other teams played for: Mooresville (D), Mount Vernon (D)

Spicer, Robert Oberton "Bob"

Year	Club	POS	G	AB	R	H	2B	3B	HR	BB	SB	RBI	BA
1947	Lumberton	p	34	90	11	28	5	1	1	4	0	10	.311

Year	Club	G	CG	W	L	IP	H	R	BB	SO	ERA
1947	Lumberton	24	20	16	7	198	182	87	55	83	3.18

Other teams played for: Fayetteville (B), Nashville (AA), Macon (A), Springfield (AAA), Savannah (A), Columbus, Ohio (AAA), Kansas City (MLB), Little Rock (AA), Shreveport (AA), Asheville (A), Chattanooga (AA), Des Moines (B)

Sprinker,

Year	Club	POS	G	AB	R	H	2B	3B	HR	BB	SB	RBI	BA
1946	Clinton	—	<10	—	—	—	—	—	—	—	—	—	—

Other teams played for: None

12. Player Register—Steele

Stamper, Clarence Watson "Snook"

Year	Club	POS	G	AB	R	H	2B	3B	HR	BB	SB	RBI	BA
1946	Dunn-Erwin	of	48	196	36	55	9	5	0	—	3	26	.281

Other teams played for: None

Stanley, Shelton S.

Year	Club	POS	G	AB	R	H	2B	3B	HR	BB	SB	RBI	BA
1947	Lumberton	3b	107	431	94	117	20	8	4	53	10	58	.271
1948	Lumberton	ss	55	201	43	58	6	2	0	41	10	16	.289

Other teams played for: Wellsville (D), Erwin, Tenn. (D), Leaksville (C), Forest City (D), Selma, Ala. (B), Rutherford County (D)

Staples, Griffin Lee Jr.

Year	Club	POS	G	AB	R	H	2B	3B	HR	BB	SB	RBI	BA
1946	Clinton	2b	52	208	34	53	7	1	0	—	7	20	.255

Other teams played for: None

Staton, James Clifford

Year	Club	POS	G	AB	R	H	2B	3B	HR	BB	SB	RBI	BA
1946	Wilmington	c	100	416	44	75	9	2	2	—	1	41	.180
1947	Wilmington	c	76	241	39	63	9	2	3	41	0	31	.261
1948	Wilmington	c	85	229	37	56	13	2	0	46	3	28	.246

Other teams played for: None

Steck, James T. Jr. "Jim"

Year	Club	POS	G	AB	R	H	2B	3B	HR	BB	SB	RBI	BA
1949	Wilmington	ss	35	148	24	40	2	3	0	5	3	10	.270

Other teams played for: Baltimore (AAA)

Steckel, Robert K. "Bob"

Year	Club	POS	G	AB	R	H	2B	3B	HR	BB	SB	RBI	BA
1947	Wilmington	3b	105	371	51	74	17	7	3	42	9	47	.199
1948	Wilmington	3b	118	426	63	93	21	12	2	40	7	51	.218
1949	Wilmington	3b	65	211	41	52	8	9	1	42	5	32	.246

Other teams played for: Valley (D)

Steele,

Year	Club	G	CG	W	L	IP	H	R	BB	SO	ERA
1946	Smithfield	1	—	0	0	6	—	—	—	—	—

Other teams played for: Unknown

12. Player Register—Stephens

Stephens, Otis Haley "Lobo"

Year	Club	POS	G	AB	R	H	2B	3B	HR	BB	SB	RBI	BA
1946	Angier-Fuquay	of	43	142	43	46	11	1	6	—	0	25	.324
1947	Warsaw	of	126	475	103	142	36	11	11	86	8	93	.299

Other teams played for: Hickory (D), Montgomery (B), Williamsport (A), Martinsville (B), Savannah (A), Macon (A)

Stephenson, Harry

Year	Club	POS	G	AB	R	H	2B	3B	HR	BB	SB	RBI	BA
1946	Clinton	util	12	39	11	7	0	0	2	—	0	7	.179

Other teams played for: Findlay (D), Springfield, Ill., (C), Rochester (AA), Winston-Salem (C)

Stephenson, James L.

Year	Club	POS	G	AB	R	H	2B	3B	HR	BB	SB	RBI	BA
1946	Dunn-Erwin	p	39	73	12	16	2	1	0	—	1	12	.219
1947	Wilmington	p	9	—	—	—	—	—	—	—	—	—	—

Year	Club	G	CG	W	L	IP	H	R	BB	SO	ERA
1946	Dunn-Erwin	35	9	12	8	181	227	119	33	46	—
1947	Wilmington	9	3	3	2	51	27	70	6	14	4.59

Other teams played for: Raleigh (C)

Stephenson, Louis Alton Sr.

Year	Club	POS	G	AB	R	H	2B	3B	HR	BB	SB	RBI	BA
1946	Dunn-Erwin	c	73	212	34	53	9	1	1	—	3	31	.250

Year	Club	G	CG	W	L	IP	H	R	BB	SO	ERA
1946	Dunn-Erwin	6	0	1	0	19	31	20	6	2	—

Other teams played for: Mayodan (D)

Stern, Joseph Michael "Joe"

Year	Club	POS	G	AB	R	H	2B	3B	HR	BB	SB	RBI	BA
1949	Clinton	of	94										
	Lumberton	of	24										
	totals:	of	118	443	72	129	16	6	15	40	13	93	.291

Other teams played for: Blackstone (D), Nazareth (D), Visalia (C), Danville, Il. (D), Hot Springs (C), Owensboro (D), Hickory (D)

Stevens, George

Year	Club	POS	G	AB	R	H	2B	3B	HR	BB	SB	RBI	BA
1946	Dunn-Erwin	p	10	23	8	8	1	0	0	—	0	2	.217

12. Player Register—Stone

Year	Club	G	CG	W	L	IP	H	R	BB	SO	ERA
1946	Dunn-Erwin	10	6	3	4	59	71	50	37	18	—

Other teams played for: None

Stevens, Malcolm Julius

Year	Club	POS	G	AB	R	H	2B	3B	HR	BB	SB	RBI	BA
1950	Clinton	of	31	112	24	29	4	0	8	33	1	33	.259

Other teams played for: Lubbock (D), Lamesa (D), Oklahoma City (A), Salina (C), Muskogee (C), Mobile (AA), Durham (C), Hendersonville (D), Richmond (B), Gastonia (D), Texas City (B)

Stewart, Frank

Year	Club	POS	G	AB	R	H	2B	3B	HR	BB	SB	RBI	BA
1946	Dunn-Erwin	—	<10	—	—	—	—	—	—	—	—	—	—

Other teams played for: Greenville, NC (D)

Stewart, Sherman Eugene

Year	Club	POS	G	AB	R	H	2B	3B	HR	BB	SB	RBI	BA
1950	Sanford	1b	88	340	75	121	28	5	3	52	8	60	.356

Other teams played for: New Bern (D), Lakeland (B), West Palm Beach (B), Fayetteville (B)

Stewart, Wayne J.

Year	Club	POS	G	AB	R	H	2B	3B	HR	BB	SB	RBI	BA
1950	Smith.-Selma	util	10	10	1	1	0	0	0	2	0	0	.100

Other teams played for: None

Stolte, William J.

Year	Club	POS	G	AB	R	H	2B	3B	HR	BB	SB	RBI	BA
1949	Fayetteville	p	13	29	1	5	1	0	0	0	0	5	.172

Year	Club	G	CG	W	L	IP	H	R	BB	SO	ERA
1949	Fayetteville	13	4	3	1	71	86	58	27	27	5.58

Other teams played for: Federalsburg (D), Suffolk (D), Hopewell (D), Griffin (D)

Stone, Boyce Henry

Year	Club	POS	G	AB	R	H	2B	3B	HR	BB	SB	RBI	BA
1947	Clinton	p	14	30	3	4	1	1	0	2	0	3	.133

Year	Club	G	CG	W	L	IP	H	R	BB	SO	ERA
1947	Clinton	14	3	3	4	74	102	96	62	82	8.87

Other teams played for: Concord (D), Shelby (D), Newton-Conover (D)

12. Player Register—Stone

Stone, William D.

Year	Club	POS	G	AB	R	H	2B	3B	HR	BB	SB	RBI	BA
1946	Sanford	p	32	77	6	15	2	0	0	—	0	9	.195
1947	Sanford	p	37	91	11	19	3	1	0	7	0	9	.209

Year	Club	G	CG	W	L	IP	H	R	BB	SO	ERA
1946	Sanford	30	15	16	8	188	182	109	80	184	—
1947	Sanford	27	18	18	7	189	155	74	78	176	2.81

Other teams played for: Burlington (D), Martinsville (C)

Storch, Harry P.

Year	Club	POS	G	AB	R	H	2B	3B	HR	BB	SB	RBI	BA
1950	Sanford	p	34	79	9	16	4	0	0	10	0	9	.203

Year	Club	G	CG	W	L	IP	H	R	BB	SO	ERA
1950	Sanford	34	18	15	10	204	197	97	78	99	3.22

Other teams played for: New Bern (D), Wilson (D), Rocky Mount (D)

Streza, John

Year	Club	POS	G	AB	R	H	2B	3B	HR	BB	SB	RBI	BA
1950	Lumberton	1b	127	469	113	150	43	4	8	108	4	111	.320

Other teams played for: Union Springs (D), Williamson (D), Houston (A), Mobile (B), Columbus, Ga. (B), Shreveport (AA), Durham (C), Miami Beach (C), Florence (B), Greenville, NC (D), Albany (A), Harlan (D), Fort Lauderdale (B), Key West (B), Centralia (D), Paris (B), Wilkes-Barre (A), Fort Walton Beach (D), Wausau (C)

Strickland, Sherrill Alonza

Year	Club	POS	G	AB	R	H	2B	3B	HR	BB	SB	RBI	BA
1946	Wilmington	of	36	156	21	44	10	3	0	—	5	14	.282

Other teams played for: None

Strickland, W.B. "Elliott"

Year	Club	POS	G	AB	R	H	2B	3B	HR	BB	SB	RBI	BA
1946	S-S/D-E	of	<10	—	—	—	—	—	—	—	—	—	—

Other teams played for: None

Stringfellow, Charles Sidney

Year	Club	POS	G	AB	R	H	2B	3B	HR	BB	SB	RBI	BA
1947	Dunn-Erwin	2b	29	80	5	17	2	2	0	13	2	8	.213

Other teams played for: None

12. Player Register—Taylor

Subbiondo, Joseph "Joe"

Year	Club	POS	G	AB	R	H	2B	3B	HR	BB	SB	RBI	BA
1950	Whiteville	util	10	24	2	6	0	0	0	6	1	4	.250

Other teams played for: DeLand (D), Newnan (D), North Wilkesboro (D), Radford (D), Wytheville/Bassett (D), Franklin (D), Butler (C), Quebec (C), Danville, Il. (D), Appleton (D)

Summerlin, Eugene A. "Gene"

Year	Club	POS	G	AB	R	H	2B	3B	HR	BB	SB	RBI	BA
1950	Smith.-Selma	p	10										
	Clinton	p	14										
	totals:	p	24	41	5	8	1	0	3	5	0	8	.195

Year	Club	G	CG	W	L	IP	H	R	BB	SO	ERA
1950	Smith.-Selma	10									
	Clinton	10									
	totals:	20	3	4	8	82	89	72	82	38	7.24

Other teams played for: Panama City (D), Monroe (C), Alexandria (C), Shreveport (AA), Carlsbad (B), Lubbock/Texas City (B), Amarillo (A), Pampa/San Angelo (B), Kinston/Wilson (B)

Tate, John Loy

Year	Club	POS	G	AB	R	H	2B	3B	HR	BB	SB	RBI	BA
1947	Dunn—Erwin	p	26	65	8	13	1	0	0	4	0	7	.200
1948	Dunn—Erwin	p	10	29	2	5	1	0	0	1	0	2	.172

Year	Club	G	CG	W	L	IP	H	R	BB	SO	ERA
1947	Dunn—Erwin	22	11	10	7	152	158	110	55	120	3.73
1948	Dunn—Erwin	9	6	1	7	69	91	55	35	49	4.83

Other teams played for: Statesville (D), Greenville, NC (D), Charleston, SC (A), Danville, Va. (B)

Taylor,

Year	Club	POS	G	AB	R	H	2B	3B	HR	BB	SB	RBI	BA
1947	Clinton	p	—	—	—	—	—	—	—	—	—	—	—

Year	Club	G	CG	W	L	IP	H	R	BB	SO	ERA
1947	Clinton	7	3	3	3	48	40	61	13	29	6.00

Other teams played for: Unknown

Taylor, James Leon "Jim"

Year	Club	POS	G	AB	R	H	2B	3B	HR	BB	SB	RBI	BA
1946	Angier—F.	p	26										

12. Player Register—Taylor

Year	Club	POS	G	AB	R	H	2B	3B	HR	BB	SB	RBI	BA
	Dunn—Erwin	p	10										
	totals:	p	36	61	7	14	6	1	0	—	0	3	.230

Year	Club	G	CG	W	L	IP	H	R	BB	SO	ERA
1946	Angier—Fuquay	23									
	Dunn—Erwin	9									
	totals:	32	5	5	9	138	156	120	109	80	—

Other teams played for: Danville—Schoolfield (D), New Bern (D), Burlington (D), Kinston (D), Roanoke Rapids (D), Lawrenceville (D)

Taylor, Roscoe E.

Year	Club	POS	G	AB	R	H	2B	3B	HR	BB	SB	RBI	BA
1949	Fayetteville	of/p	4	5*	—	3*	2	—	—	1*	—	—	—

Year	Club	G	CG	W	L	IP	H	R	BB	SO	ERA
1946	Fayetteville	1	0	0	0	2.2	2	0	0	0	0.00

Other teams played for: Rocky Mount (D), Pulaski (D), Greensboro (C), Burlington (C)

Teague, Dwight Eugene "Red"

Year	Club	POS	G	AB	R	H	2B	3B	HR	BB	SB	RBI	BA
1950	Wilmington	1b	119	459	88	150	30	9	6	61	4	94	.327

Other teams played for: Mount Airy (D), Lockport (D), Miami (B), Burlington—Graham (B)

Teater, Roland Dean "Rollie"

Year	Club	POS	G	AB	R	H	2B	3B	HR	BB	SB	RBI	BA
1950	Lumberton	c	74	228	34	72	11	0	1	62	2	38	.316

Other teams played for: Lawrenceville (D), Tallassee (D)

Teer, Harold A.

Year	Club	POS	G	AB	R	H	2B	3B	HR	BB	SB	RBI	BA
1949	Sanford	3b	64	220	37	59	9	2	1	58	6	29	.268
1950	Sanford	of	96	320	68	75	16	3	0	68	6	34	.234

Other teams played for: Mount Airy (D), Greensboro (B)

Thomas, Roland

Year	Club	POS	G	AB	R	H	2B	3B	HR	BB	SB	RBI	BA
1946	Clinton	—	<10	—	—	—	—	—	—	—	—	—	—

Other teams played for: Geneva (D), Goldsboro (D)

* Incomplete stats

12. Player Register—Toenes

Thomason, Curtis

Year	Club	POS	G	AB	R	H	2B	3B	HR	BB	SB	RBI	BA
1950	Clinton	p	13	8	2	1	0	0	0	3	0	1	.125

Year	Club	G	CG	W	L	IP	H	R	BB	SO	ERA
1950	Clinton	13									

Other teams played for: None

Thompson, Marvin Hubert "Tommy"

Year	Club	G	CG	W	L	IP	H	R	BB	SO	ERA
1946	Smith.—Selma	5	2	2	1	30	33	17	15	19	—

Other teams played for: Wilson (D), New Bern (D)

Thrush, John Orrin "Jack"

Year	Club	POS	G	AB	R	H	2B	3B	HR	BB	SB	RBI	BA
1948	Wilmington	1b	122	474	73	117	12	8	0	35	9	55	.247
1949	Wilmington	1b	20	76	9	12	1	1	0	6	1	11	.158

Other teams played for: None

Tiedemann, Albert F. "Ab"

Year	Club	POS	G	AB	R	H	2B	3B	HR	BB	SB	RBI	BA
1949	Wilmington	util	11	32	5	9	0	0	0	2	1	8	.281

Other teams played for: Baltimore (AA), Richmond (B)

Timm, Charles A.

Year	Club	POS	G	AB	R	H	2B	3B	HR	BB	SB	RBI	BA
1949	Smith.-Sema.	p	10	30	6	8	1	0	0	2	0	5	.266

Year	Club	G	CG	W	L	IP	H	R	BB	SO	ERA
1949	Smith.-Selma	10	7	6	2	72	86	44	16	48	3.75

Other teams played for: Alexandria (D), Beaumont (A), Sioux City (A), Charleston, W.V. (C), Portsmouth, Va. (B), Henderson (C), Bassett (D), Columbia (B), Durham (B), Raleigh (C), Kinston (D), Greensboro (C), Rutherford County (D), Reidsville (B)

Toenes, James

Year	Club	G	CG	W	L	IP	H	R	BB	SO	ERA
1946	Clinton	6	—	0	0	13	—	—	—	—	—

Other teams played for: None

12. Player Register—Townsend

Townsend, Thomas F. "Freddy"

Year	Club	POS	G	AB	R	H	2B	3B	HR	BB	SB	RBI	BA
1947	Wilmington	p	21	49	4	7	0	0	1	10	0	3	.143
1948	Wilmington	p	26	34	2	4	0	0	0	2	0	3	.129

Year	Club	G	CG	W	L	IP	H	R	BB	SO	ERA
1947	Wilmington	20	9	10	4	133	155	92	68	87	4.67
1948	Wilmington	26	1	3	8	77	113	86	54	51	7.13

Other teams played for: Bluefield (D)

Trabucco, Peter Ralph

Year	Club	POS	G	AB	R	H	2B	3B	HR	BB	SB	RBI	BA
1948	Lumberton	of	34	135	20	34	6	3	1	9	3	16	.252

Other teams played for: Marion, Ohio (D), Elizabethton (D), Clinton, Iowa (C), Clovis (C), Albuquerque (B)

Trent, Walter Edgar

Year	Club	POS	G	AB	R	H	2B	3B	HR	BB	SB	RBI	BA
1946	Dunn-Erwin	p	2										
	Smith-Selma	p	15										
	totals:	p	17	31	6	7	1	0	0	—	0	6	.226

Year	Club	G	CG	W	L	IP	H	R	BB	SO	ERA
1946	Dunn-Erwin	2									
	Smith.-Selma	15									
	totals:	17	4	4	4	76	86	74	66	65	—

Other teams played for: New Bern (D)

Trentalange, Joseph T.

Year	Club	POS	G	AB	R	H	2B	3B	HR	BB	SB	RBI	BA
1946	Sanford	ss	19	59	13	14	1	0	0	—	1	9	.237

Other teams played for: Roanoke Rapids (D)

Trombetta, John Joseph Jr.

Year	Club	POS	G	AB	R	H	2B	3B	HR	BB	SB	RBI	BA
1948	Dunn-Erwin	util	16	39	3	5	0	0	0	8	0	3	.128
1949	Wilmington	c	18	43	4	4	1	0	0	7	0	4	.093

Other teams played for: Mahoney (D), Port Chester (B), Maryville-Alcoa (D), Columbia (A)

12. Player Register—Tyson

Turnage, James Elmon

Year	Club	POS	G	AB	R	H	2B	3B	HR	BB	SB	RBI	BA
1946	Dunn-Erwin	p	19	51	5	10	3	1	0	—	1	5	.196
1947	Warsaw	p	9	—	—	—	—	—	—	—	—	—	—

Year	Club	G	CG	W	L	IP	H	R	BB	SO	ERA
1946	Dunn-Erwin	19	5	6	7	113	140	100	52	34	—
1947	Warsaw	9	2	2	5	48	39	61	34	25	5.64

Other teams played for: Kinston (D)

Turner, John Wesley "Jack"

Year	Club	POS	G	AB	R	H	2B	3B	HR	BB	SB	RBI	BA
1946	Sanford	ss	22	82	23	20	4	0	1	—	2	8	.244

Other teams played for: Thomasville (D)

Turowicz, Nicholas Francis "Nick"

Year	Club	POS	G	AB	R	H	2B	3B	HR	BB	SB	RBI	BA
1946	Clinton	p	<10	—	—	—	—	—	—	—	—	—	—
1949	Fayetteville	p	11	18	4	4	2	0	0	1	0	0	.222

Year	Club	G	CG	W	L	IP	H	R	BB	SO	ERA
1946	Clinton	6	1	3	2	34	38	36	29	17	—
1949	Fayetteville	10	3	3	3	46	38	37	37	32	4.50

Other teams played for: Springfield, Ohio (D), Erie (C), Trenton (B), Fayetteville (D), Greensboro (B), Burlington (B)

Turowski, Andrew

Year	Club	POS	G	AB	R	H	2B	3B	HR	BB	SB	RBI	BA
1950	Rockingham	ss	56	208	54	55	7	7	4	47	24	51	.264

Other teams played for: Bristol (D), Rocky Mount (D)

Tutterrow, Gerald M.

Year	Club	POS	G	AB	R	H	2B	3B	HR	BB	SB	RBI	BA
1948	Dunn-Erwin	util	18	59	8	12	1	0	0	10	0	1	.203

Other teams played for: Greenville, NC (D)

Tyson, Cecil Washington "Turkey"

Year	Club	POS	G	AB	R	H	2B	3B	HR	BB	SB	RBI	BA
1949	Lumberton	1b	93	314	62	100	9	2	0	94	2	62	.318
1950	Rockingham	1b	124	403	76	127	19	9	2	133	2	77	.315

Other teams played for: Tallahassee (D), Greenwood (C), Winston-Salem (B),

12. Player Register—Uhls

Martinsville (D), Hagerstown (B), Trenton (B), Utica (A), Philadelphia Phillies (MLB), Durham (C), Rocky Mount (D), Raleigh (B), Colonial Heights-Petersburg (D)

Uhls, William Joseph

Year	Club	POS	G	AB	R	H	2B	3B	HR	BB	SB	RBI	BA
1947	Clinton	of	40										
	Smith.-Selma	of	14										
	totals:	of	54	200	55	67	15	1	4	35	7	44	.335
1948	Smith.-Selma	of	43	159	27	45	9	1	0	25	2	24	.283

Other teams played for: Lakeland (C), Burlington (C)

Van Nordheim, Edward L.

Year	Club	POS	G	AB	R	H	2B	3B	HR	BB	SB	RBI	BA
1947	Lumberton	p	22	63	5	9	1	0	0	2	0	6	.302

Year	Club	G	CG	W	L	IP	H	R	BB	SO	ERA
1947	Lumberton	22	14	13	7	156	173	90	58	81	4.04

Other teams played for: Erwin (D), Sioux Falls (C)

Varlotta, Anthony M. "Tony" or "Rabbits"

Year	Club	G	CG	W	L	IP	H	R	BB	SO	ERA
1946	Sanford	1	0	0	0	2	—	—	—	—	—

Other teams played for: Hornell (D), Salisbury, NC (D), Lexington, NC (D)

Vazquez, Ralph

Year	Club	POS	G	AB	R	H	2B	3B	HR	BB	SB	RBI	BA
1950	Wilmington	p	20	35	6	11	3	0	1	5	0	8	.314

Year	Club	G	CG	W	L	IP	H	R	BB	SO	ERA
1950	Wilmington	10	4	3	4	48	61	33	25	29	4.31

Other teams played for: Sunbury (B), Columbia (A)

Vaughn, Raymond Morris

Year	Club	POS	G	AB	R	H	2B	3B	HR	BB	SB	RBI	BA
1947	Smith.-Selma	p	11										
	Clinton	p	6										
	totals:	p	17	30	2	5	1	0	0	3	0	5	.167

Year	Club	G	CG	W	L	IP	H	R	BB	SO	ERA
1946	Smith.-Selma	4	1	1	1	19	17	16	14	6	—
1947	Smith.-Selma	11									

12. Player Register—Viera

Year	Club	G	CG	W	L	IP	H	R	BB	SO	ERA
	Clinton	6									
	totals:	17	4	2	8	81	120	104	49	35	6.44

Other teams played for: Chanute (D)

Vaughn, Robert R.

Year	Club	POS	G	AB	R	H	2B	3B	HR	BB	SB	RBI	BA
1946	Smith.-Selma	p	21	58	8	16	0	0	0	—	0	10	.276

Year	Club	G	CG	W	L	IP	H	R	BB	SO	ERA
1946	Smith.-Selma	13	1	2	2	68	84	51	57	53	—

Other teams played for: None

Vendetta, Joseph P.

Year	Club	POS	G	AB	R	H	2B	3B	HR	BB	SB	RBI	BA
1946	Smith.-Selma	util	11	30	7	7	0	1	0	—	1	6	.233

Other teams played for: Pulaski (C), Hornell (D), Lancaster (B), Raleigh (C), Mount Airy (D), Galax (D), Leaksville (D), Wytheville (D)

Vereault, George H. "Lefty"

Year	Club	POS	G	AB	R	H	2B	3B	HR	BB	SB	RBI	BA
1950	Smith.-Selma	p	24										
	Red Springs	p	6										
	totals:	p	30	71	7	10	1	2	0	9	0	11	.155

Year	Club	G	CG	W	L	IP	H	R	BB	SO	ERA
1950	Smith.-Selma	24									
	Red Springs	5									
	totals:	29	15	13	8	196	160	89	140	102	2.66

Other teams played for: Cordele (D)

Verespy, George J.

Year	Club	POS	G	AB	R	H	2B	3B	HR	BB	SB	RBI	BA
1946	Smith.-Selma	—	<10	—	—	—	—	—	—	—	—	—	—

Other teams played for: Oil City (C), Waterloo (B), Hot Springs (C), Colorado Springs (A), Temple (B), Davenport (B), Keokuk (B)

Viera, August A. "Gus" (or Vierira)

Year	Club	POS	G	AB	R	H	2B	3B	HR	BB	SB	RBI	BA
1948	Lumberton	p	26	49	5	7	0	1	0	9	1	3	.143
1949	Lumberton	p	31	80	7	15	0	1	0	7	0	9	.188

12. Player Register—Vinajeras

Year	Club	G	CG	W	L	IP	H	R	BB	SO	ERA
1948	Lumberton	26	12	7	10	133	148	115	107	72	5.82
1949	Lumberton	30	16	14	7	196	172	107	136	120	3.49

Other teams played for: Sioux Falls (C), High Point-Thomasville (B)

Vinajeras, Efrain J.

Year	Club	POS	G	AB	R	H	2B	3B	HR	BB	SB	RBI	BA
1946	Dunn-Erwin	ss	52	188	46	44	2	1	0	—	7	14	.234
1947	Dunn-Erwin	p	23	52	12	14	1	0	0	6	1	4	.269

Year	Club	G	CG	W	L	IP	H	R	BB	SO	ERA
1947	Dunn-Erwin	22	8	4	8	109	124	69	28	84	3.96

Other teams played for: Havana (C)

Vojcsik, James Emerick "Jim" or "Snake Eyes"

Year	Club	POS	G	AB	R	H	2B	3B	HR	BB	SB	RBI	BA
1949	Red Springs	c	56	181	32	43	10	2	3	20	1	22	.238

Other teams played for: Lincoln (A), Moline/Kewanee (C), Savannah (A), West Palm Beach (B)

Vorell, Robert F. "Bob"

Year	Club	POS	G	AB	R	H	2B	3B	HR	BB	SB	RBI	BA
1946	Clinton	of	32	119	35	34	4	1	6	—	11	26	.286
1947	Clinton	of	92	313	82	93	12	8	12	72	16	67	.297

Other teams played for: Durham (C), Greensboro (C), Tarboro (D), Leaksville (C), Bridgeport (B), New Iberia (C), Greenville, Miss. (C), Gloversville (C), Kingston (C)

Voss, Charles William

Year	Club	POS	G	AB	R	H	2B	3B	HR	BB	SB	RBI	BA
1950	Red Springs	p	11	21	6	4	1	0	0	5	0	1	.190

Year	Club	G	CG	W	L	IP	H	R	BB	SO	ERA
1950	Red Springs	9	2	5	1	51	68	49	33	25	5.82

Other teams played for: Lima (D), Tarboro (D)

Wagner, Bruce C.

Year	Club	POS	G	AB	R	H	2B	3B	HR	BB	SB	RBI	BA
1950	Wilmington	c	81	228	42	55	14	1	2	61	3	35	.241

Other teams played for: None

12. Player Register—Walther

Walker, Stephen Edward

Year	Club	POS	G	AB	R	H	2B	3B	HR	BB	SB	RBI	BA
1950	Sanford	3b	65	217	33	36	6	1	1	54	16	18	.166

Other teams played for: Greensboro (B), Danville (B), Reidsville (B)

Walker, Verlon Lee "Rube"

Year	Club	POS	G	AB	R	H	2B	3B	HR	BB	SB	RBI	BA
1948	Lumberton	c	60	195	21	50	4	3	0	14	4	24	.256

Other teams played for: Topeka (C), Nashville (AA), Sioux Falls (C), Macon (A), Des Moines (A), Paris (D), Pueblo (A), San Antonio (AA), Wenatchee (B)

Wall, Charles Dwight

Year	Club	POS	G	AB	R	H	2B	3B	HR	BB	SB	RBI	BA
1946	Dunn-Erwin	of	26	74	10	22	6	0	1	—	2	8	.297

Other teams played for: Snow Hill (D), Greenville, NC (D)

Wallace, John B.

Year	Club	POS	G	AB	R	H	2B	3B	HR	BB	SB	RBI	BA
1949	Fayetteville	p	17	24	4	3	1	0	0	7	0	3	.125

Year	Club	G	CG	W	L	IP	H	R	BB	SO	ERA
1949	Fayetteville	14	1	0	4	54	54	40	51	18	5.50

Other teams played for: None

Walters, Artis W.

Year	Club	POS	G	AB	R	H	2B	3B	HR	BB	SB	RBI	BA
1948	Warsaw	util	12	38	12	11	1	0	0	10	1	5	.289

Other teams played for: Hammond (D), Lafayette (D), Anderson (B)

Walther, Harold E. "Hal"

Year	Club	POS	G	AB	R	H	2B	3B	HR	BB	SB	RBI	BA
1949	Lumberton	of	65	269	46	86	22	3	6	12	11	70	.320

Other teams played for: York (B), Salisbury, NC (D), Geneva (D), Anderson (B), Alexandia (C), Monroe (C), Natchez (C)

Walther, John Charles Jr.

Year	Club	POS	G	AB	R	H	2B	3B	HR	BB	SB	RBI	BA
1948	Clinton	ss	139	535	115	132	15	1	1	132	11	66	.247
1949	Clinton	3b	137	519	79	124	17	7	2	65	14	54	.239

Other teams played for: Hornell (D), Uniontown (C), Watertown (C), Kingston (B), Augusta (A), Alexandria (C)

12. Player Register—Walther

Walther, William Leonard "Buddy"

Year	Club	POS	G	AB	R	H	2B	3B	HR	BB	SB	RBI	BA
1948	Dunn-Erwin	c	64	171	20	35	4	0	0	25	0	6	.205

Other teams played for: None

Ward, William David

Year	Club	POS	G	AB	R	H	2B	3B	HR	BB	SB	RBI	BA
1947	Clinton	c	59	182	32	53	3	1	0	22	3	31	.291

Other teams played for: Lawrenceville (D)

Warfield, Donald Mansfield "Tex"

Year	Club	POS	G	AB	R	H	2B	3B	HR	BB	SB	RBI	BA
1949	Red Springs	1b	36	132	24	46	11	7	6	14	4	40	.348

Other teams played for: Oil City (C), Thomasville (D), Johnstown (C), Salisbury (D), Kingston (D), Federalsburg (D), Tarboro (D), Sunbury (B), Hopewell (D), Elizabeth City (D), Durham (B)

Warren, Carl E. "Smokey"

Year	Club	POS	G	AB	R	H	2B	3B	HR	BB	SB	RBI	BA
1948	Smith.-Selma	of	112	401	72	92	17	5	0	57	12	45	.229
1949	Smith.-Selma	of	122	490	94	128	15	4	2	55	15	58	.261
1950	Smith.-Selma	of	109	420	66	113	19	3	2	70	8	51	.269

Other teams played for: Lakeland (C), Wilson (D)

Warren, Jefferson Eugene Jr. (Shot Gun)

Year	Club	POS	G	AB	R	H	2B	3B	HR	BB	SB	RBI	BA
1947	Red Springs	p	23	52	8	13	1	0	0	7	0	5	.250

Year	Club	G	CG	W	L	IP	H	R	BB	SO	ERA
1947	Red Springs	21	12	9	7	143	144	88	85	76	4.09

Other teams played for: Moultrie (D), Savannah (A), West Palm Beach (B), Brunswick (D)

Waters, Norman Brant

Year	Club	POS	G	AB	R	H	2B	3B	HR	BB	SB	RBI	BA
1946	Clinton	3b	1										
	Dunn-Erwin	3b	23										
	totals:	3b	24	94	14	26	3	1	0	—	0	11	.277
1947	Smith.-Selma	3b	13	40	5	10	0	0	1	8	0	6	.250

Other teams played for: None

12. Player Register—Wesley

Watson, Guthrie M.

Year	Club	POS	G	AB	R	H	2B	3B	HR	BB	SB	RBI	BA
1947	Sanford	of	49	128	29	35	3	2	1	21	3	15	.273
1948	Sanford	3b	127	479	76	144	23	6	3	55	6	72	.301

Other teams played for: Durham (C)

Weaver, Claude William "Buck"

Year	Club	POS	G	AB	R	H	2B	3B	HR	BB	SB	RBI	BA
1948	Smith.-Selma	p	12	18	3	6	0	0	0	3	0	4	.333
1949	Smith.-Selma	p	21	45	2	4	1	0	0	1	0	3	.089

Year	Club	G	CG	W	L	IP	H	R	BB	SO	ERA
1948	Smith.-Selma	11	4	6	0	46	49	14	4	21	1.57
1949	Smith.-Selma	20	8	5	8	107	137	65	20	57	3.45

Other teams played for: Mayodan (D), Leaksville (D), Burlington (D), Lynchburg (B), Durham (B), Montreal (AA), St. Paul (AA), Portsmouth (B), Newport News (B), Chattanooga (AA), Milwaukee (AAA), Vicksburg (B), Shreveport (AA), Lawrenceville (D), Suffolk (D), Reidsville (B)

Weaver, Harold

Year	Club	POS	G	AB	R	H	2B	3B	HR	BB	SB	RBI	BA
1947	Red Springs	util	15	48	8	5	0	0	0	8	0	1	.104

Other teams played for: None

Weeks, James

Year	Club	G	CG	W	L	IP	H	R	BB	SO	ERA
1946	Clinton	2	—	0	0	9	—	—	—	—	—

Other teams played for: None

Welch, Cleo Z.

Year	Club	POS	G	AB	R	H	2B	3B	HR	BB	SB	RBI	BA
1950	Rockingham	c	41	131	9	34	4	0	0	12	0	30	.260

Other teams played for: None

Wesley, Francis E.

Year	Club	POS	G	AB	R	H	2B	3B	HR	BB	SB	RBI	BA
1948	Wilmington	ss	25	64	8	11	1	0	0	5	1	1	.172

Other teams played for: Lawrenceville (D)

12. Player Register—White

White, Walter Samuel "Sam"

Year	Club	POS	G	AB	R	H	2B	3B	HR	BB	SB	RBI	BA
1948	Lumberton	c	58	195	14	31	4	3	3	10	0	14	.159

Other teams played for: None

Whitmire, Richard B.

Year	Club	POS	G	AB	R	H	2B	3B	HR	BB	SB	RBI	BA
1947	Warsaw	p	31	70	9	15	3	1	0	12	1	10	.214
1948	Sanford	p	26	56	13	17	4	0	1	9	1	14	.304

Year	Club	G	CG	W	L	IP	H	R	BB	SO	ERA
1947	Warsaw	21	13	9	6	144	175	104	68	98	4.37
1948	Sanford	21	9	9	9	126	137	88	55	64	4.64

Other teams played for: None

Whitney, James F.

Year	Club	POS	G	AB	R	H	2B	3B	HR	BB	SB	RBI	BA
1948	Warsaw	c	26	81	11	16	0	1	1	14	1	11	.198

Other teams played for: Newnan (D)

Wicker, Robert L.

Year	Club	POS	G	AB	R	H	2B	3B	HR	BB	SB	RBI	BA
1946	Sanford	util	12	28	5	13	2	1	1	—	0	6	.464

Other teams played for: None

Wiggins, Bradford

Year	Club	POS	G	AB	R	H	2B	3B	HR	BB	SB	RBI	BA
1950	Whiteville	p	18	30	1	7	1	2	0	8	0	10	.233

Year	Club	G	CG	W	L	IP	H	R	BB	SO	ERA
1950	Whiteville	10	—	—	—	—	—	—	—	—	—

Other teams played for: None

Wiggs, Charles W.

Year	Club	POS	G	AB	R	H	2B	3B	HR	BB	SB	RBI	BA
1947	Smith.-Selma	of	19	72	6	13	3	1	0	5	3	5	.181
1948	Smith.-Selma	of	42										
	Wilmington	of	2										
	totals:	of	44	109	15	26	3	0	0	9	0	11	.239

Other teams played for: None

Wilbourne, John E.

Year	Club	POS	G	AB	R	H	2B	3B	HR	BB	SB	RBI	BA
1946	Wilmington	p	20	41	5	6	0	0	0	—	0	4	.146

Year	Club	G	CG	W	L	IP	H	R	BB	SO	ERA
1946	Wilmington	12	9	7	3	93	71	43	45	54	—

Other teams played for: Sanford (D), Rocky Mount (D), Montgomery (B)

Wilcox, Lloyd Stanley

Year	Club	POS	G	AB	R	H	2B	3B	HR	BB	SB	RBI	BA
1950	Whiteville	of	16	56	9	11	0	1	0	10	1	1	.196

Other teams played for: Radford (D), North Wilkesboro (D), Morganton (D), New Iberia (C)

Wilder,

Year	Club	POS	G	AB	R	H	2B	3B	HR	BB	SB	RBI	BA
1946	Smith.-Selma	—	<10	—	—	—	—	—	—	—	—	—	—

Other teams played for: Unknown

Wiles, Robert Lee "Lefty"

Year	Club	G	CG	W	L	IP	H	R	BB	SO	ERA
1948	Lumberton	—	—	—	—	<45	—	—	—	—	—

Other teams played for: Bradford (D), St, Augustine (D), Augusta (A)

Williams, Claude Emmett

Year	Club	POS	G	AB	R	H	2B	3B	HR	BB	SB	RBI	BA
1947	Dunn-Erwin	p	36	95	19	33	9	2	0	11	0	16	.347
1948	Dunn-Erwin	p	31	69	2	8	0	1	0	3	1	8	.116

Year	Club	G	CG	W	L	IP	H	R	BB	SO	ERA
1947	Dunn-Erwin	15	8	8	4	115	127	96	87	99	5.63
1948	Dunn-Erwin	27	7	3	9	131	192	128	55	42	6.66

Other teams played for: None

Williams, James Harold

Year	Club	POS	G	AB	R	H	2B	3B	HR	BB	SB	RBI	BA
1948	Clinton	of	83	283	44	107	18	4	1	33	2	55	.378

Other teams played for: Rome (D), Montgomery (B), West Palm Beach (B)

12. Player Register—Williams

Williams, Kenneth E.

Year	Club	POS	G	AB	R	H	2B	3B	HR	BB	SB	RBI	BA
1949	Lumberton	of	17	78	8	18	1	0	0	0	1	8	.231

Other teams played for: None

Williamson, Robert H.

Year	Club	POS	G	AB	R	H	2B	3B	HR	BB	SB	RBI	BA
1950	Rockingham	3b	16	47	7	8	0	0	0	14	2	0	.170

Other teams played for: None

Wilmer, Garland Graydon "Grady"

Year	Club	POS	G	AB	R	H	2B	3B	HR	BB	SB	RBI	BA
1946	Angier-Fuquay	util	18	44	6	11	2	0	0	—	0	8	.250
1947	Warsaw	2b	45	189	26	48	6	0	1	7	3	28	.254
1948	Smith.-Selma	2b	17	67	8	12	0	0	0	4	0	7	.179

Other teams played for: Johnson City (D)

Wilson, James Alvin "Jimmy"

Year	Club	POS	G	AB	R	H	2B	3B	HR	BB	SB	RBI	BA
1947	Sanford	of	122	532	133	205	39	10	3	43	66	116	.385
1948	Sanford	of	135	605	145	212	32	14	0	38	49	67	.350

Other teams played for: None

Wisecup, John Herbert

Year	Club	G	CG	W	L	IP	H	R	BB	SO	ERA
1946	Angier-Fuquay	3									
	Clinton	2									
	totals:	5	1	2	2	20	37	27	17	9	—

Other teams played for: Leaksville (C)

Wisniewski, John J.

Year	Club	POS	G	AB	R	H	2B	3B	HR	BB	SB	RBI	BA
1948	Red Springs	of	111	342	68	98	13	8	2	53	14	54	.287
1949	Red Springs	of	105	419	78	114	14	4	3	56	11	53	.272

Other teams played for: Tarboro (D), Youngstown (C), Fayetteville (B), Lincoln (A), Drummondville (C)

Wobbleton, Albert Virgil

Year	Club	POS	G	AB	R	H	2B	3B	HR	BB	SB	RBI	BA
1948	Clinton	util	13	32	3	9	1	3	0	8	0	4	.281

Other teams played for: None

12. Player Register—Woods

Wolfe, Robert P.

Year	Club	POS	G	AB	R	H	2B	3B	HR	BB	SB	RBI	BA
1947	Red Springs	3b	118	468	60	120	22	5	2	26	17	66	.258
1948	Red Springs	3b	136	506	115	138	22	10	5	106	12	61	.273

Other teams played for: None

Wood, George Harold

Year	Club	POS	G	AB	R	H	2B	3B	HR	BB	SB	RBI	BA
1947	Red Springs	2b	69	225	34	51	6	1	3	20	3	34	.227
1948	Red Springs	p	40	104	10	27	3	0	0	7	0	18	.260

Year	Club	G	CG	W	L	IP	H	R	BB	SO	ERA
1948	Red Springs	31	20	17	9	217	185	94	99	114	3.24

Other teams played for: Lexington (D), Buffalo (AAA), Fayetteville (B), Savannah (A), San Antonio (AA)

Wood, James Billie

Year	Club	POS	G	AB	R	H	2B	3B	HR	BB	SB	RBI	BA
1949	Red Springs	of	68	239	44	62	8	3	1	47	8	38	.259

Other teams played for: Lexington (D), Martinsville (C), Morganton (D), Mooresville (D),

Wood, William Francis "Billy"

Year	Club	POS	G	AB	R	H	2B	3B	HR	BB	SB	RBI	BA
1947	Lumberton	ss	47	180	33	56	5	3	4	20	0	23	.311
1949	Sanford	3b	59	219	47	67	10	0	1	23	11	31	.306

Other teams played for: Greenville (D), Sioux Falls (C), Raleigh (B), Greensboro (B)

Woodard, Richard

Year	Club	POS	G	AB	R	H	2B	3B	HR	BB	SB	RBI	BA
1946	Smith.-Selma	of	104	422	78	142	19	11	7	—	4	98	.336
1947	Smith.-Selma	of	69	270	41	103	13	4	2	19	2	49	.381
1948	Smith.-Selma	of	36	138	32	55	11	2	2	14	0	33	.399
1949	Smith.-Selma	of	119	450	106	180	35	2	13	89	0	113	.400
1950	Smith.-Selma	of	106	359	76	126	33	8	9	104	1	79	.351

Other teams played for: Burlington (C), Raleigh (B)

Woods, Richard M. "Dickie"

Year	Club	POS	G	AB	R	H	2B	3B	HR	BB	SB	RBI	BA
1950	Lumberton	p	11	27	4	7	0	0	0	2	1	0	.259

12. Player Register—Worthington

Year	Club	G	CG	W	L	IP	H	R	BB	SO	ERA
1950	Lumberton	11	1	1	3	55	75	53	29	23	7.63

Other teams played for: Kinston (D), Mooresville (D)

Worthington, Carl

Year	Club	POS	G	AB	R	H	2B	3B	HR	BB	SB	RBI	BA
1949	Lumberton	ss	14	46	11	9	0	0	0	7	0	6	.196

Other teams played for: None

Wright, George Robert

Year	Club	POS	G	AB	R	H	2B	3B	HR	BB	SB	RBI	BA
1950	Clinton	3b	49	162	25	36	8	1	0	33	3	9	.222

Other teams played for: High Point-Thomasville (D), Kingsport (D), Rock Hill (B), Richmond (B)

Wright, Survern Edward

Year	Club	POS	G	AB	R	H	2B	3B	HR	BB	SB	RBI	BA
1947	Clinton	p	36	82	15	25	6	1	2	14	0	20	.305

Year	Club	G	CG	W	L	IP	H	R	BB	SO	ERA
1947	Clinton	25	17	14	9	176	168	105	82	160	4.03

Other teams played for: Kannapolis (D), Lexington (D), Saginaw (D), Spartanburg (B), Rock Hill (B), Chattanooga (AA), Charlotte (B)

Yednak, William Jr.

Year	Club	POS	G	AB	R	H	2B	3B	HR	BB	SB	RBI	BA
1950	Wilmington	p	1										
	Whiteville	p	6										
	Clinton	p	5										
	Rockingham	p	9										
	totals:	p	21	32	1	4	1	0	0	3	0	0	.125

Year	Club	G	CG	W	L	IP	H	R	BB	SO	ERA
1950	Wilmington	1									
	Whiteville	6									
	Clinton	5									
	Rockingham	9									
	totals:	21	2	4	4	76	84	63	50	30	6.28

Other teams played for: Harlan (D), Morristown (D), Lafayette (C), Pauls Valley (D), Seminole (D)

12. Player Register—Zupnick

Yeider, Marshall James "Jimmy"

Year	Club	G	CG	W	L	IP	H	R	BB	SO	ERA
1950	Wilmington	9	2	0	6	45	50	44	42	43	5.60

Other teams played for: New River (D), Greenville (D), Rocky Mount (D), Vidalia (D), New Bern (D)

Young, William Harmon

Year	Club	POS	G	AB	R	H	2B	3B	HR	BB	SB	RBI	BA
1947	Dunn-Erwin	3b	14	46	15	15	3	0	0	8	3	10	.326

Other teams played for: Suffolk (D), Elizabeth City (D), Jacksonville Beach (D), Jesup (D)

Zakoski, Bernard J.

Year	Club	POS	G	AB	R	H	2B	3B	HR	BB	SB	RBI	BA
1947	Smith.-Selma	p	37	66	5	10	0	0	0	3	1	5	.152

Year	Club	G	CG	W	L	IP	H	R	BB	SO	ERA
1947	Smith.-Selma	34	7	4	8	156	197	121	56	81	5.02

Other teams played for: None

Zazzaro, Daniel J. "Nonny"

Year	Club	POS	G	AB	R	H	2B	3B	HR	BB	SB	RBI	BA
1946	Wilmington	3b	22	66	9	11	3	1	0	—	3	10	.159

Other teams played for: None

Zmijewski, John S.

Year	Club	POS	G	AB	R	H	2B	3B	HR	BB	SB	RBI	BA
1947	Lumberton	p	21	39	1	6	0	1	0	2	0	5	.154

Year	Club	G	CG	W	L	IP	H	R	BB	SO	ERA
1947	Lumberton	22	3	5	6	96	116	89	39	65	5.34

Other teams played for: None

Zupnick, William R. "Bill"

Year	Club	G	CG	W	L	IP	H	R	BB	SO	ERA
1950	Lumberton	—	—	—	—	<45	—	—	—	—	—

Other teams played for: Bristol (B), New Iberia (C)

Bibliography

Books

Gaunt, Robert. *We Would Have Played Forever: The Story of the Coastal Plain Baseball League.* Durham, NC: Baseball America, 1997.
Holaday, J. Chris. *Professional Baseball in North Carolina.* Jefferson, NC: McFarland, 1998.
Holaday, Chris, ed. *Baseball in the Carolinas.* Jefferson, NC: McFarland, 2002.
Johnson, Lloyd, and Miles Wolff, eds. *Encyclopedia of Minor League Baseball,* 2d ed. Durham NC: Baseball America, 1997.
Lupton, Webster. *A Place to Play: Glory Days of Baseball in Angier, NC,* Cornelius, NC: Warren, 2007.

Newspapers and Websites

Baseball-Reference (www.baseball-reference.com).
The Duplin Times (Kenansville, NC).
Durham Morning Herald (Durham, NC).
The Fayetteville Observer (Fayetteville, NC).
News and Observer (Raleigh, NC).
Richmond County Journal (Rockingham, NC).
The Robesonian (Lumberton, NC).
Wilmington Morning Star (Wilmington, NC).

Index

Abernathy, Talmadge Lafayette "Tal" 72, 74, 143
Aiken 143
Akens, James M. "Jim" 143
Alexander, (Theodore?) 143
Allegue, Manuel 143
Allen, Oliver "Snag" 144
Allen, Sam 15
Allen, William "Bill" 144
Alsenauer, William E. "Bill" 143
Ammons, Wallace 144
Andrews, Clayton C. "Jack" 55, 67, 144
Andrews, Nathan Hardy "Nate" 25, 33, 94, 95, 112, 145
Andrews, Winfred "Wink" 145
Arakelian, Zaven Joseph 145
Armbruster, Eugene R. "Gene" 145
Askew 145
Askew, Charles F. 37, 145
Atlanta Braves 10
Auman, Howard Claude 3, 21, 110, 138, 146
Ayden Aces 11, 91, 92, 100, 230, 248

Backner, Thomas A. 146
Baham, Carl Alton 55, 146
Balikes, Nicholas "Nicky" 146
Balla, Michael "Mickey" 20, 22, 92, 96, 110, 112, 113, 115, 146
Ballerini, John Frank 147
Ballinger, William H. 147
Balogh, James E. "Jimmy" 147
Baltimore Colt 141
Baltimore Orioles 49, 57, 104, 127, 135
Bangs, Lester Meredith, Jr. 147
Bankhead, Walter 147
Barbee, Walter "Bud" 147

Bare, Frank Burman 147
Barnes, Jack J. 148
Barnett, Gilmus 148
Barneycastle, Michael "Mike" 148
Barnham, Ovie C. 148
Barr, James "Jim" 148
Barrett, William Joseph "Billy" 148
Basile, Peter 149
Bass, Earl C. 149
Bass, Edward Oliver 25, 26, 80, 110, 113, 149
Bassler, Robert E. 149
Bauder, Raymond Thomas "Ray" 52, 149
Becker, Henry C. 149
Beeson, Harry Leon 150
Belcher, Neil Edwin 150
Bell, Earl Jackson "Jack" 71, 73, 95, 106, 150
Bell, Luby Francis 150
Bennett, John Wilber "Jack" 150
Benson, Archie 150
Benton, Clint D. 151
Benton, Rube 10
Benton, William E. "Billy" 33, 40, 115, 151
Berger, Eugene W. "Gene" 151
Bernardini, Ralph Frank 151
Bernier, William Joseph 66, 116, 151
Bernstein (Burnstein), Leonard "Lenny" 37, 151
Bidwell, Alonzo William 152
Bird, Alton G. Sr. 22, 152
Bi-State League 10, 18, 39, 160
Blackwell, Vernon C. 41, 42, 98, 152
Blair, Robert Burns 152–53
Blake, Dean P. 153
Bland, Edward Bernard 152

Index

Bodney, Al 11
Bohannon, Elmer Leroy "Bo" 153
Bohlender, William Lee 54, 115, 153
Bohonko, John J. 153
Bold, Bernard 153
Bollinger, William 154
Bomar, Raymond E. 24, 154
Bonds, Kenneth Lee 143
Boos, Minor Herschel 143
Border Belt League 77, 86
Borneman, Henry D. 154
Bortz, George W. 30, 113, 154
Bosley, Arthur Roland 155
Bosser, Melvin Edward "Mel"
Bost, Edwin "Babe" 10, 46, 100, 122
Boston Braves 70, 94, 101, 106, 173
Boston Red Sox 17, 33, 102, 138
Bowen, Warren J. 155
Bowman 155
Boyco 155
Brady, Richard T. 155
Bramham, William G. 26, 27
Breece, Oscar 48
Brenner, John Andrew "Jack" 155
Brewer, Orbie Lee 156
Brickner, Arthur J. 156
Bridges, Harry 33, 156
Bridgman, Newton Boyce 44, 156
Brisson, Virgil Evans 156
Britt, John W. 156
Brittain, August Schuster "Gus" 25, 26, 90, 104, 156
Brooklyn Dodgers 33, 36, 43, 93, 94, 96, 136, 137, 236
Brockman, Irwin Ernest "Ernie" 40, 157
Brooks, George J. 110, 157
Brooks, Kenneth C. 157
Broseker, Gordon H. 157
Brown 157
Brown, Lawrence R. 157
Brown, Richard I. 158
Brown, Wade Andrew "Weenie" 158
Bryant 158
Budzin, Joe? 158
Bullock, Frank N. 158
Burch, Alfred D. 40, 158
Burda, William J. 159
Burgess, Lewis 159
Burk, Ronald Edward 159
Burnham, John Edward 159
Burns 159
Burris, Carl Jackson 159
Burrows, John 22, 159
Butcher, Edward "Ned" 30, 160
Butler, Lester 160
Byrd, Carl L. 160
Byrne, Tommy 11, 12, 14

Cabaniss, Proctor Eugene "Jerry" 32, 112, 160
Calo, Antonio 160
Campau, William J. 110, 113, 160
Campbell, Thomas Carl "Bud" 115, 160
Campbell University 11, 49, 138, 139
Cape Fear Crocs 87
Cape Fear League 30, 83 85
Carabba, David 161
Cardillo, Joseph 161
Carolina League 5, 13, 36, 37, 41, 52, 54, 56, 59, 62, 70, 71, 74, 78, 79, 80, 81, 85, 86, 87, 103, 105, 138, 140, 169
Carpenter, Wallace Reid 51, 52, 161
Carrabus, Rudolph 161
Carroll, Preston Welch 37, 41, 161
Carter, Donald James "Don" 141, 161
Castagna, Vincent 161
Castleberry, Hoyt Gold 162
Catapano, Joseph Anthony 162
Causey, Richard Douglas "Rick" 67, 162
Chafin, Loran 162
Chambers, George 162
Cheshire, John Lewis 33, 34, 40, 59, 63, 113, 128, 130, 162
Chicago Cubs 22, 28, 54, 135, 138, 140, 159
Childers, John G. 163
Childs, William Brown 163
Chinnis, Warner M. 163
Chorbora, Michael 163
Chute, William Elwin "Charlie," Jr. 163
Ciani, Nicholas Joseph "Nick" 163
Cieply, Walter 163
Cieslinski (aka Cecil), Henry E. 164
Cincinnati Reds 10, 14, 25, 76, 84, 90, 91, 94, 101, 104, 135, 142, 145, 155, 156
Clayton, John E. 164
Clayton, Thomas Hill 115, 164
Clegg, Hoyt 30, 39, 55, 67, 116, 164
Clemmer 164
Cleveland Indians 66, 94, 139, 145
Clinard, Cloris H. 164

Index

Coakley, John B. 165
Coastal Plain League 4, 5, 11, 17, 20, 37, 41, 42, 43, 46, 48, 49, 52, 56, 62, 77, 79, 82, 85, 87, 108, 283
Colclough, John C. "Julius" 165
Collins, Fleet Marion 165
Collins, Leonard Thomas 165
Collins, Stephen C. "Steve" 76, 108, 165
Colones, John 165
Condit, Clarence L. "Clancy," Jr. 51, 78, 115, 166
Conn, Hampton T. 166
Conn, James C. 166
Connelly, William F. 166
Conte, Mike 49, 128, 130
Cooper, Kenneth Wilson 166
Cope, Tom 63, 84, 125, 127, 128, 129
Corbett, Charles Sprunt "Charlie," Jr. 43, 167
Costinette, Robert H. 167
Costler 167
Cotten, Cecil H. 167
Covahay, William "Billy" 168
Cowan, James H. 168
Coward, Clarence Wesley "Dink" 168
Craddock, William W. "Bill" 168
Crawford, Paul Louis 21, 110, 168, 169
Crocker, Thomas G. 168
Cronin, Francis Michael 169
Cropcho, John 169
Cross, Jack R. 169
Crouch, George 170
Crummie, Arthur T. 170
Crummie, William E. "Willie" 32, 170
Cudemo, Michael N. 170
Cullen, Andrew A. "Andy," Jr. 25, 110, 113, 170
Cummings, Joseph 170
Curry 179

Dalton, William M. 32, 170
Damon, Robert 171
Daniels, Alexander D. "Alex" 110, 171
Daniels, William "Bill" 171
Dardes, Nicholas 171
Davis, Hargrove Bellamy "Hoggie" 1, 33, 40, 47, 59, 71, 104, 115, 139, 171
Davis, Jesse O. 171–72
Davis, Lawrence "Crash" 13, 14
Davis, Walter 172
DeLapp, Royal Stokes "Mike," Jr. 172

Dellinger, Francis William 172
Del Piano, Ronald J.? 172
Dendy, Robert Gerald "Bobby" 172
Denning, Elmer Parker "Mickey Mouse" 172
Denning, Granville Morrison "Shamrock" 25, 26, 34, 46, 51, 61, 77, 79, 110, 112, 116, 173
DePriest, Fay E. 173
Detroit Lions 57
Detroit Tigers 42, 43, 98, 139, 189, 218
Detweiler, Robert Sterling "Ducky" 3, 70, 105, 106, 116, 173
Dexheimer, Bob 11
Diaz, Amado Quintana 57, 173
Dichara, Walter DiChiara? 173
Dicola, Charles G. "Chick" 173
Diehl, Leonard E., Jr. 174
Diem, Arthur A. 174
Dietrich, Raymond Allen 52, 174
Dillard, Rudolph W. "Rudy" 174
Dillinger, Francis 174
DiOrio, Lawrence "Larry" 174
Dissinger, Roy 62, 65, 66, 82, 84, 129
Dixon, Ralph William 32, 175
Dixon, Robert M. 175
Doak, Chick 9, 139
Doak, Robert Renfrow "Peanut" 51, 139, 175
Dobias, John E. 175
Dominic, Raymond 175
Dopkin, John P. "Lefty" 43, 175
Dornbusch, John William 175
Dosch, Dean Anthony 176
Drew, John A. 176
Duffy, William I. "Bill" 71, 83, 176
Dugan, James J. 176
Duke, Willie Eleanor 20, 21, 39, 71, 93, 110, 113, 139, 176
Duke University 10, 13, 14, 100, 140
Dulworth, Randall "Randy" 54, 176
Duncan, Romas Hicks, Jr. 176
Dunkleburger, Charles H. 177
Dunlap, Joseph Paul 20, 24, 91, 177
Dunmore, John G. 177
Durham Bulls 4, 5, 10 11, 13, 21, 66, 78, 93, 102, 103, 105, 106, 107, 108, 137, 139, 148, 153, 163, 168, 169, 176, 181, 187, 213, 216, 218, 222, 245, 246, 247, 254, 260, 263, 264, 267, 270, 272, 274, 275
Duvall, Benjamin 177

Index

Dykema, Jack 177
Dziengielewski, Eugene L. 177

Eager, Jack 177
Eames, Paul Edward 178
Earich, Jerome Roderic "Rod" 178
Earl, Leslie Leroy "Les" 178
East Carolina University 10, 59
Eastern Carolina League 85
Edens, John Alton "Johnie" 1, 33, 59, 76, 85, 104, 140, 178
Edwards, James Robert 178
Edwards, Presley James 179
Ehrhardt, Willard H. "Billy" 32, 179
Einsel, William C. 179
Ellington, Paul W. 179
Ellis 179
Ellis, James N., Jr. 179
Elon College 21, 74, 91, 94, 97, 101, 105
Enogh 180
Eonta, Joseph Francis "Joe" 23, 31, 41, 97, 170, 180
Eraca, Francis Joseph "Frank" 180
Erath, George Snider 3, 141, 180
Erwin Cotton Mill 10, 16–17
Estes, John Leo "Jack" 180
Estevez, J. Ernesto 181
Estill, Anthony "Tony" 181
Ethier, Andre 138
Ethier, Pierre Leo "Pete" 66, 77, 138, 181
Eubanks, Ruie Arizona, Jr. 181
Eury, Fred Lee 181
Evans, Theron Odell 35, 181
Everette 182

Faircloth, James Sykes 34, 182
Fasano, Benjamin "Benny" 182
Fassler, Leonard 182
Fauci, Vincent F. 182
Fayetteville Generals 87
Fayetteville Hilanders 86
Fernandez, Frank 183
Fernandez, (possibly Frank) 182
Fish, Walter Pate "Archie" 183
Fister, James Peter "Jim" 75, 83, 142, 183
Flaim, Raymond S. 112, 183
Fleming, Eugene E., Jr. 183
Flint 183
Foote, Ambrose Clifton "Amby" 55, 85, 138, 183

Forbess, James H. "Jim" 184
Ford, Donald Thomas "Don" 184
Fortuna, Justin James 184
Fortune, Harry T. 24, 184
Foster, Arthur 184
Fowler 185
Fowler, Bill 86
Fox, James L. "Jimmie" 185
Francoline, James J. "Jim" 63, 65, 116, 129, 185
Franz, William P. "Bill" 185
Frazier 185
Frazier, Elton "Buddy" 3, 32, 123, 125, 126
Frazier, William C. 186
Freiberger, Arthur Lewis 186
Futrelle, Duncan Lacy, Jr. 3, 59, 141, 186

Gailes, Elwood Lonnie 186
Gales, James 186
Gallo, Anthony 186
Gallo, Ernest 186
Gallo, Joseph "Joe" 187
Gamache, Ray John 187
Garcia, Manuel R. 32, 187
Gardner 187
Gardner, Ava 17
Garrett, Edward Franklin 187
Garris, Reid 188
Gay, Frederick Leonard "Fred" 22, 188
Gentry, Roscoe 24, 188
Gerace, John J. 188
Geresy, Donald S. 188
Gettings, Matt 62, 63, 73, 129
Ghant, Roland Thomas 188
Gibson, Samuel Braxton 42, 55, 98, 188
Gibson, Samuel Clay "Gabby," Jr. 189
Gingerella, James L., Jr. 189
Giordanengo, Irvin R. "Beans" 189
Giuliano, Thomas "Tom" 189
Glose, Gordan N. 189
Gloser, Francis Joseph 189
Godfrey, Philip Lee "Phil" 190
Godwin, W. Troy 190
Golding, Fred James 190
Goldsboro Goldbugs 4, 42, 43, 49, 79, 92, 96, 98, 101, 102, 103, 140, 146, 150, 152, 153, 162, 163, 171, 173, 175, 178, 181, 182, 189, 197, 204, 206, 207, 208, 209, 210, 211, 214, 215,

Index

217, 227, 233, 239, 240, 243, 247, 251, 253, 254, 259, 266
Gonzales, Rigoberto 190
Gonzalez, Rogelio "Chango" 190
Good, William L. "Bill" 190
Goodwin, Harold 190
Goodwin, William Frederick 191
Graham, Walter Odell 191
Green, Andrew H. 191
Greene, Leonard Word "Doc" 54, 191
Greenfield Tigers 86
Gregory, Joseph 191
Griffy, James Norton 192
Grimm, Robert Eugene 192
Grubb, James Kenneth "Jim" 192
Grubbs, Frank 192
Guidice, Michael Joseph "Joe" 192
Guinn, James K. "Jimmy" 18, 25, 30, 32, 40, 89, 101, 110, 113, 115, 192

Hager, Richard "Dick" 193
Haidet, Wilford Lawrence 193
Haithcock, Claude 61, 193
Haley, Jack 48
Halkard, Robert Nicholas "Bob" 193
Ham, Charles L. 193
Hamson 193
Hardee, George Dewey, Jr. "Buck" 139, 193
Hardee, Raymond E. "Ray" 24, 85, 110, 194
Hardisky, Edward Joseph 115, 194
Hardy 194
Harrell, Boney 194
Harrington, Thomas Hayes 194
Harrington, William Womble "Bill" 52, 112, 136, 137, 194
Harrington, Zeb Strickland 21, 30, 31, 40, 63, 67, 91, 94, 97, 101, 105, 110, 113, 116, 121, 129, 195
Harris, James Emmet "Jimmy" 195
Harrison, William J. 195
Harvey, William E. 195
Hash, Joseph C. 195
Haswell, Jesse Lee 196
Hatsfield, William 196
Haynes, Barney Smith, Jr. 196
Hayward, Richard C. 196
Healey, John D. "Jack" 196
Heath, Norman Wade "Bud"? 196
Hedrick, Bruce B. 30, 110, 115, 196
Heffner, Arthur S. "Art" 197

Heitner, Bernard W. 197
Helms, John R. 103, 197
Helton, William "Bill" 197
Henson 197
Hepler, Claude L. 125, 197
Hergert, Walter 198
Hermann, Fred A. G. 198
Herrick, Wayne T. 198
Herring 198
Hester, Ben 59, 198
Hewlett, Emory Lee "Lefty" 198
Hines, Joseph 199
Hinton 199
Hlava, Julius P. 199
Hocke, Robert L. 199
Hockenbury, Thomas J. "Tom" 199
Holder, Hugh T. 52, 199
Holland, Bill 10
Holland, M. (probably R. McKinley) 200
Holland, Robert F. "Bob" 200
Holland, Rufus McKinley "Mack" 55, 200
Holliday, Andrew J. "Zero" 110, 200
Hollis, Nesbit Odell 200
Holmes, William O. 201
Holster 201
Holt, Carlton "Buddy" 201
Honeycutt 201
Hooks, David 201
Hooks, Gene 50
Hopper, James McDaniel "Jim" 72, 73, 74, 201
Hornsby, Leonard George "Lenny" 201
Horton, Harold 202
Horvath, Joseph F. 202
House, James F. "Jim" 24, 26, 30, 110, 202
House of David team 49
Howard, St. Pierre "Pete," Jr. 3, 23, 31, 37, 112, 114, 133, 142, 169, 202
Hudson, James Terrence 202
Hughes, Edward R. 203
Hunt, Paul V. 24, 110, 203
Hutchins, Charles Ben "Charlie" 43, 203

Ingle, Randolph M. 203
Ingram, Ralph 203
Isenhour, Lewis 14, 120, 123, 124, 126, 128, 129
Israel 203

289

Index

Jackson, Edward H. 204
Jackson, Elton Stanley 204
Jackson, Kenneth B. 24, 110, 112, 204
Jacobson, Irving S. "Rabbit" 204
Jacoby, Warren W. 204
Jamin, Charles Frances "Charlie" 32, 33, 34, 99, 204
Janik, Edmund 205
Jenkins, John Thayer 205
John, Angelo Patsy 205
Johnson, Carl "Cyclone" 34, 205
Johnson, Charles "Charlie" 205
Johnson, Harry T. 205
Johnson, Henry L. 205
Johnson, Rivers Dunn, Jr. 206
Jones, "Buck" 206 206
Jones, John Purcell 206
Jones, Raymond D. 206
Jones, Theodore Debonchard "T.D.," Jr. 34
Jones, Thomas J. "Tom" 206
Jones, William Clifton "Bill" 207
Jordan, Ford 3, 34, 207
Jordan, John Bill James, Jr. 52, 207
Jordan, Robert A. 207
Junker 207
Jurisich, Al 11

Kaires, William Robert 207
Kallas, William Thomas "Bill," Jr. 208
Kansas City Chiefs 141
Katkaveck, Leo Frank 43, 140, 208
Katkaveck, Stanley P. "Mickey" 20, 25, 90, 208
Katz, Harry 208
Kavek 208
Kay, William M. "Bill" 76, 116, 208
Keane, Robert Thomas "Bobby" 22, 40, 110, 113, 115, 209
Kelly 209
King, Claude, Jr. 43, 209
King, Culmer Lawrence 40, 209
Kinston Eagles 4, 25, 49, 77, 95, 97, 108, 154, 162, 165, 169, 173, 176, 178, 179, 180, 188, 196, 197, 199, 200, 205, 206, 208, 222, 230, 236, 241, 250, 265, 276, 269, 280
Kittrell, Julian U. "Kit" 57, 209
Kivett, Charles E. 209
Kivett, William Everett "Bill" 32, 112, 209
Kluk, Paul Peter 55, 102, 210

Kluttz, Alvin Clifton 76, 107, 210
Knight, Charles A. 210
Knisely, Gordon Louis 210
Koch, Henry F. 37, 210
Kohut, Joseph, Jr. 210
Komar, John 34, 211
Konkol, Robert 211
Kotchli, John 211
Kucharski, Louis A. 211
Kukulka, Edmund F. 112, 113, 211
Kunkle, Gerald David "Jerry" 211
Kurplewski, Edward John 212

Lacey, Jesse 212
Lagan, John Edwin "Lefty"
Lail, Robert Earl 212
LaMantia, Benedict 212
Lamb, John LeRoy "Roy" 33, 110, 212, 213
Lambeth, Harold Adams "Red" 213
Lance, Robert Merritt 213
Lancester, Clarence W. "Tex" 213
Landay, Harry W. 213
Lane, Wilmer Pitman "Red" 213, 214
Langston, James D. "Buck" 213
LaPorta, John J. 214
Larrieu, John D. 110, 214
Latta, William 214
Lauffer, Robert G. "Bob" 214
Leach, Riley T. 214
LeBlanc, Robert Joseph 215
Lee, Stanley Soott 215
Lefler, Neil Graham 215
Lehman, George F. 215
Lento, Alfred A. 215
Linder, Raymond R. 216
Lindsey, Haskell 216
Liner, Henry "Buck" 216
Litinski, Stanley A. 216
Lloyd, William H. "Bill" 41, 216
Lorenz, Marvin Peter 21, 43, 57, 81, 92, 99, 104, 107, 109, 110, 115, 116, 138, 217
Lorman, Douglas George 32, 33, 217
Los Angeles Dodgers 138
Lowenstein, Donald 217
Lowry, Curtis Grayson 115, 217
Lucas, Charles "Red" 32, 94, 101, 112, 115
Luchetta, Frank A. 217
Lynch, Charles Wright "Charley" 218
Lynch, Robert "Bob" 218

290

Index

Maas, Duane Frederick "Duke" 52, 137, 218
Mack, Connie 11, 121, 123, 124, 125, 126, 127, 129
MacLean, Donald Hector 43, 218
Magliolo, John A. 218
Malloy, John Thomas "Jack" 219
Maloney, Lloyd T. 219
Manara, Thomas 219
Mangini, Joseph Louis "Joe" 36, 40, 115, 219
Mann, Robert H. "Bob" 117, 219
Marino, Emil John 219
Marko, Stephen J. 51, 115, 219
Marsh, Frederick Dallas 220
Martin, Odell W. 220
Marx, Elzer Ino "Slats" 32, 33, 113, 220
Masinick, Julius "Bud" 220
Mason, Charles G. 220
Mason, Herman Buel 220
Matthews, Roy Lee 221
Matthews, Wesley Norton 221
May, Herbert A. 67, 221
Mazzei, Amerigo E. "Mego" 221
McBane, George L. 221
McBride, Stanley 222
McBryde, Myron Homer 222
McCarty, Edward Joseph 222
McClintock, James H. 222
McCormick, Lenwood 222
McCrary, James Ernest 222
McDonald, Gordon C. 54, 115, 223
McDuffie, Glenn 223
McElroy, Royce E. 223
McFadden, John A. 30, 32, 39, 115, 223
McGhee, Thomas Fred "Tommy" 43, 223
McIntosh, Joseph Pitt "Joe" 224
McIntosh, "Tootsie" 224
McKeithen, Ernest Harlan 224
McLaughlin, James T. "Jim" 224
McQuillen, Joseph Carl 33, 34
McVicker, Frank Blair 42, 224
McWhorter, Guy L. 225
Meador 225
Mehlhorn, Robert C. "Bob" 225
Mejido, Juan 225
Melvin, Donald M. 225
Merica, Frank Edward 226
Merrion, Donald J. 226
Mesmer, Edward James 226

Meyer, James F. 226
Micham, Jerry Marcus 226
Miller, Eddie 17
Miller, Gail Malcolm "Mick" 226
Miller, Henry Loftin "Hoggie" 79, 80, 115, 227
Miller, James W. "Jim" 227
Miller, Ronald Keith 71, 227
Mills, Joseph Doughton 227
Milner, James Richard ("Jim"; "Punch") 34, 35, 95, 112, 227
Milo 228
Milosevich, Michael "Mike" 66, 116, 228
Milwood, Grady Lee 228
Mitchell, Andrew 117
Mitchell, Robert Ernest 228
Mitchell, Robert Lincoln 229
Mitchell, Thomas E. 229
Moir, Charles Robert "Charlie" 76, 139, 229
Monterose, Dominick 118, 119, 229
Montgomery, Robert W. 229
Montsinger, R. M. 229
Mooney, James W. 230
Moore, A. 230
Moore, Arthur T. 30, 48, 63, 84, 112, 121, 124, 126, 128
Moore, John Jack 230
Morris, Noah C. 230
Morris, Phil 230
Moser, Floyd Pierce, Sr. 70, 230
Mossor, Earl Dalton 22, 110, 137, 230
Mottler, Ernest H. 231
Mueger, George H. 231
Mullarky, Armand J. 231
Mungo, Van Lingle 22, 25, 26, 34, 93, 34, 93, 94, 96, 136, 231
Murray, Harlan 231
Murray, John 232
Muscovitch, John J. "Ducky," Jr 232
Mustian, Vernon Martin "Preacher" 141, 232
Musumeci, Fred 33, 232
Musumeci, John 232

Nagle, Thomas J. 232
Napier, Richard Payne 233
Narleski, William Edward, Jr. 138, 233
Narron, Samuel Woody "Sam" 37, 41, 98, 138, 233
Nesselrode, Orville Burlin "Hank" 19,

Index

20, 21, 30, 32, 40, 54, 63, 110, 113, 115, 233
Nessing, Joseph Charles 21, 30, 110, 233
New Bern Bears 4, 49, 91, 92, 95, 100, 108, 148, 163, 172, 175, 186, 193, 197, 213, 215, 217, 219, 220, 232, 236, 245, 248, 263, 264, 266, 267, 268, 281
New Hanover High School 130, 135, 140
New York Giants 10, 25, 94, 96, 99, 101, 145, 189
New York Yankees 11, 12, 22, 43, 52, 66, 98, 137, 218, 228
Niezgoda, Leo 22, 110, 233
Niven, William Edward 234
Norman, Rown 234
Norris, Manuel C. "Red" 35, 40, 63, 96, 100, 112, 115, 127
North Carolina State League 5, 35, 59, 73
North Carolina State University 9, 43, 95
Northrop, Robert 234
Novack, Ernest W. "Ernie" 234
Novak, Walter 234

O'Brien 234
O'Coine, Marshall Joseph 235
Odom, David Everett "Dave" 235
Odom, Jim 117, 118, 119
Oehler, Edward 235
Olbert, Zigmond Stanley "Ziggy" 235
Olsen, Norman 236
O'Quinn, Mickey 10
Osgood, Charles Benjamin "Charlie" 32, 236
O'Shields, Garland Lee 236
Osofsky, Aaron M. 41, 236
Owens, Edward M. "Peg" 236

Pacific Coast League 4, 10, 11, 22, 54, 98, 138
Padgett, Dean Edward "Spec"
Palmer, Dennis A. 237
Papa, Alfonso P. 237
Parise, Joseph M. 55, 237
Parker, Eugene R. 237
Parker, Lloyd Benjamin 237
Parnell, Albert 70, 238
Parness, Leon S. 238

Parrish, Clyde 238
Parrish, Dennis 238
Pascal, Robert Michael 238
Pasteris, Emile John 238
Patkin, Max 66
Payne, Banks A. 239
Payne, Horace Virgil 41, 55, 63, 81, 85, 98, 101, 115, 239
Payne, James Cecil "Zip" 56, 102, 103, 239
Payonk, Andrew J., Jr. 32, 239
Paz, Louis Raymond 239
Peach Belt League 8
Peacock, Johnny 17
Pearce, Jacob A. "Jake" 239
Pearsall, Wallace A. "Wally" 32, 33, 240
Pellegrino, Michael 240
Penegar, Heath 62, 129
Pepio, Nicholas J. "Nick" 240
Perini, Edward Paul "Eddie" 240
Perry, Benjamin Franklin, Jr. 240
Perry, DeWitt 10
Perry, Edward, Jr. 240
Perry, Robert H. 240
Peterson, Lee Crandall 22, 241
Petti, Michael Anthony 241
Pettit, James Ray "Jim" 241
Pfeiffer, Allen W. 51, 52, 241
Philadelphia Athletics 12, 13, 14, 22, 28, 35, 52, 70, 72, 74, 106, 127, 135, 143, 159
Philadelphia Phillies 11, 77, 249, 270
Phillips, Buck 241
Piccin, Frank J. 214
Piccone, John 242
Pickard, George Armand 242
Piedmont League 4, 10, 11, 17, 25, 27, 33, 34, 42, 91, 102, 117, 119
Pierce, David Donald 242
Pierre, Robert "Bob" 242
Pilkington, Lewis "Bingo" 242
Pipak, Joseph R. 242
Pittsburgh Pirates 72, 91, 94, 101, 138, 201
Plantz, Stephen Edward 242
Plosica, Robert R. "Bob" 243
Poklemba, Andrew E. 110, 243
Pollock, Terry G. 243
Pontbriand, Roger "Chip" 243
Poole, James Ralph, Jr. 40, 243
Popelsky, Anthony 243
Port City Roosters 87

Index

Posevac, John 244
Poteat, Parks H. 244
Powell, Carl M. 244
Powell, Richard 244
Powers, Elmer 244
Praley, Albert Frank 244
Price, Eldridge C. 244
Price, Glenn 14
Price, Leslie Beecham "Billy" 57, 99, 112, 245
Pritchard, Thomas Marion
Privette, John B. 245
Prowell, Dean G. 245
Pryor, John Paul 245
Pugh, Robert Thomas "Bob" 30, 71, 110, 245
Purchia, Nicholas 57, 76, 107, 116, 246

Quigley, Albert 246

Rapp (Rzepczynski), Walter M. 246
Ratteree, William L. "Bill" 24, 113, 246
Ray, Daniel C. "Dan" 246
Reardon, John 246
Reaves 246
Reese, Kenneth E. "Kenny" 57, 247
Reges, James Clinton "Jim" 247
Reidsville Luckies 13, 74, 99, 135, 143, 145, 147, 184, 186, 189, 194, 210, 225, 229, 230, 232, 233, 244, 251, 267, 273, 265
Reiter, James Edward 247
Reside, Neal M. 247
Reynolds, Robert Arthur 247
Rhabe, Nicholas James 93, 103, 107, 247
Richards, Donald L. 248
Richards, John Edward 51, 61, 115, 248
Richards, Robert W. 248
Rickard, Charles Robert 248
Ridings, Brannon W. 248
Riley, Gaither William 3, 19, 20, 46, 91, 92, 100, 110, 248
Riley, Raymond D. 249
Ripple, Charles Dawson "Charlie" 77, 249
Ritter, Robert J. 249
Roberson, Aaron 249
Roberts, David 249
Roberts, Donald Vance 76, 249
Robertson, William M. 249
Robinson, Hearn James 22, 110, 249
Rodriguez, Virgil 250

Roebuck, Garland Lee 250
Roedel, Robert L. 250
Rogers, Angus W. "Gus" 24, 36, 250
Rogers, Marion Eugene "Tinky" 250
Rose, James Harold 250
Roseberry, Joseph Carl "Joe" 56, 103, 251
Rosenwinkel, Raymond L. 251
Rossi, Marion G. B. 251
Rothermel, William "Bill" 66, 251
Rowan, Linwood C. 251
Rowland, Charles H. "Buddy" 251
Rudden, Matthew 252
Russell, Eugene C. 252
Russell, Norman L. 252
Ryan, Connie 10
Ryan, Terence Aloysius "Terry" 10, 252

Sack, James Edward 252
Sailor, Rowland 252
St. Louis Cardinals 17, 20, 22, 37, 56, 62, 65, 94, 98, 145, 233
Saladino, James "Jim" 252
SALLY League 43, 65
Salmon, Homer 253
Salter, Clarence W. 39, 253
Salyer, Curtis William 253
Samson, Forrest LaVerne "Shine" 253
Sanders, Carol Victor "Pete" 253
Sanders, Paul David "Red" 253
Sanders, Vernon 253
Santomauro, Joseph L. 254
Saunders, Dennis R. 254
Scalli, Arthur R. "Art" 254
Scarborough, Ray 12, 14
Schroeder, Warren Frederick "Wally" 43, 254
Schubach, Frederick 141, 254
Schultz 254
Schumann, George R. 244
Schumann, Henry H. "Hank" 255
Scott, Edward Gregg 255
Scrobola, Andrew N. "Andy" 24, 34, 43, 57, 59, 115, 255
Seagate Gators 86
Sebastian, Sherman 255
Sellers, Samuel "Sam" 24, 255
Shelton, Baldwin Edwin 256
Shimko, Robert A. "Bob" 256
Shoffner, Phalti Moody 30, 110, 113, 256
Shokes, Eddie 14

293

Index

Short, George A. 256
Shrewsbury, Eugene Robert "Gene" 256
Shubeck, Charles B. 256
Sidoruk, Walter P. 257
Sikorski, Alfred "Fred" 257
Siler, Calvin Kenneth "C.K." 257
Silvers, Lewis D. 257
Simmons, Charles Roland 257
Simmons, Gerald 258
Simmons, Raymond C. 258
Singleton, Lee E. 258
Skinner, Robert "Bob" 110, 258
Sklodowski, Sigmund "Ziggy" 258
Slater, Walter 258
Smith, Alfred E. 259
Smith, Edwin F., Jr. 52, 259
Smith, Evert Weston Hjalmar 259
Smith, Herbert "Doc" 8, 92
Smith, James W. 259
Smith, Lonnie Harold 259
Smith, Milton R. 259
Smith, Norman B. 259
Smith, Paul R. 260
Smithey, Henry 62, 129
Somers, George William 80, 260
Southerland, Douglas 260
Spaine, Harry R. 260
Spicer, Robert Oberton "Bob" 32, 33, 112, 115, 136, 137, 260
Sprinker 260
Stamper, Clarence Watson "Snook" 261
Stanley, Shelton S. 32, 261
Staples, Griffin Lee, Jr. 110, 261
Staton, James Clifford 51, 63, 77, 97, 100, 108, 261
Steck, James T. "Jim," Jr. 261
Steckel, Robert K. "Bob" 261
Steele 261
Stephens, Otis Haley "Lobo" 3, 24, 34, 142, 262
Stephenson, Harry 262
Stephenson, James L. 110, 262
Stephenson, Louis Alton, Sr. 25, 89, 262
Stern, Joseph Michael "Joe" 59, 262
Stevens, George 262
Stevens, Malcolm Julius 263
Stewart, Frank 263
Stewart, Sherman Eugene 263
Stewart, Wayne J. 263

Stolte, William J. 263
Stone, Boyce Henry 263
Stone, William D. 21, 32, 112, 264
Storch, Harry P. 264
Streza, John 65, 66, 105, 138, 264
Strickland, Sherrill Alonza 264
Strickland, W.B. "Elliott" 264
Stringfellow, Charles Sidney 264
Subbiondo, Joseph "Joe" 265
Summerlin, Eugene A. "Gene" 265

Tate, John Loy 265
Taylor 265
Taylor, James Leon "Jim" 265
Taylor, Roscoe E. 266
Teague, Charlie 50
Teague, Dwight Eugene "Red" 76, 108, 266
Teater, Roland Dean "Rollie" 266
Teer, Harold A. 266
Texas League 8, 40, 54, 138
Texas Rangers 10
Thomas, Roland 266
Thomason, Curtis 267
Thompson, Marvin Hubert "Tommy" 267
Thrush, John Orrin "Jack" 267
Tiedemann, Albert F. "Ab" 57, 59, 104, 267
Timm, Charles A. 267
Toenes, James 267
Townsend, Thomas F. "Freddy" 86, 268
Trabucco, Peter Ralph
Trautman, George 80, 122
Trent, Walter Edgar 268
Trentalange, Joseph T. 268
Tri-State League 18, 48, 56, 62, 105
Trombetta, John Joseph, Jr. 268
Turnage, James Elmon 25, 269
Turner, John Wesley "Jack" 269
Turowicz, Nicholas Francis "Nick" 269
Turowski, Andrew 269
Tutterrow, Gerald M. 269
Twin State League 46
Tyson, Cecil Washington "Turkey" 3, 51, 54, 71, 75, 106, 269

Uhls, William Joseph 270
University of Alabama 57
University of Florida 54

Index

University of Georgia 55
University of North Carolina 20, 34, 91, 95, 139
University of Richmond 12
Upchurch, Woody 11, 12

Van Nordheim, Edward L. 270
Varlotta, Anthony M. "Tony" or "Rabbits" 270
Vaughan, Porter 12, 14
Vaughn, Raymond Morris 270
Vaughn, Robert R. 271
Vazquez, Ralph 270
Vendetta, Joseph P. 271
Vereault, George H. "Lefty" 116, 271
Verespy, George J. 271
Viera (Vierira), August A. "Gus" 54, 271
Vinajeras, Efrain J. 272
Vojcsik, James Emerick ("Jim"; "Snake Eyes") 52, 272
Vorell, Robert F. "Bob" 36, 272
Voss, Charles William 272

Wade, J.E.L. "Jimmy" 18, 120
Wagner, Bruce C. 272
Wake Forest University 11, 12, 14, 49, 50, 77, 90
Walker, Stephen Edward 273
Walker, Verlon Lee "Rube" 45, 138, 273
Wall, Charles Dwight 25, 89, 273
Wallace, John B. 273
Walters, Artis W. 273
Walther, Harold E. "Hal" 273
Walther, John Charles, Jr. 273
Walther, William Leonard "Buddy" 274
Ward, William David 274
Warfield, Donald Mansfield "Tex" 52, 274
Warren, Carl E. "Smokey" 55, 274
Warren, Jefferson Eugene, Jr. (Shot Gun) 274
Washington Capitols 43, 140, 141
Washington Senators 10, 54
Waters, Norman Brant 274
Watson, Guthrie M. 30, 275
Weaver, Claude William "Buck" 55, 101, 275
Weaver, Harold 275
Weeks, James 275

Welch, Cleo Z. 275
Wesley, Francis E. 275
White, Walter Samuel "Sam" 276
Whiteville Red Comets 77
Whitmire, Richard B. 40, 112, 276
Whitney, James F. 276
Wicker, Robert L. 276
Wiggins, Bradford 276
Wiggs, Charles W. 276
Wilbourne, John E. 90, 277
Wilcox, Lloyd Stanley 277
Wilder 277
Wiles, Robert Lee "Lefty" 277
Williams, Claude Emmett 45, 142, 277
Williams, James Harold 43, 277
Williams, Kenneth E. 278
Williamson, Paul 77, 130
Williamson, Robert H. 278
Wilmer, Garland Graydon "Grady" 278
Wilmington Sharks 87
Wilmington Waves 87
Wilson, James Alvin "Jimmy" 30, 32, 39, 115, 278
Wilson Tobs 4, 37, 41, 49, 87, 91, 92, 100, 1455, 147, 148, 149, 151, 153, 156, 162, 173, 192, 195, 196, 200, 208, 215, 216, 229, 230, 247, 248, 251, 264, 265, 267, 274
Wisecup, John Herbert 278
Wisniewski, John J. 278
Wobbleton, Albert Virgil 278
Wolfe, Robert P. 279
Wood, George Harold 40, 279
Wood, James Billie 279
Wood, William Francis "Billy" 32, 279
Woodard, Richard 22, 37, 41, 55, 81, 110, 279
Woods, Richard M. "Dickie" 279–80
Worthington, Carl 280
Wright, George Robert 280
Wright, Survern Edward 35, 96, 112, 280

Yednak, William, Jr. 280
Yeider, Marshall James "Jimmy" 281
Young, William Harmon 281

Zakoski, Bernard J. 281
Zazzaro, Daniel J. "Nonny" 281
Zmijewski, John S. 32, 281
Zupnick, William R. "Bill" 281

www.ingramcontent.com/pod-product-compliance
Ingram Content Group UK Ltd.
Pitfield, Milton Keynes, MK11 3LW, UK
UKHW021844140426
5217IPUK00022B/1578